ORATORY IN NATIVE NORTH AMERICA

Oratory in Native North America

William M. Clements

The University of Arizona Press

Tucson

The University of Arizona Press
© 2002 Arizona Board of Regents
All rights reserved
♾ This book is printed on acid-free, archival-quality paper.
Manufactured in the United States of America
First Printing

07   06   05   04   03   02   6   5   4   3   2   1

Library of Congress Cataloging-in-Publication Data
Clements, William M., 1945–
    Oratory in Native North America / William M. Clements.
        p. cm.
Includes bibliographical references and index.
    ISBN 0-8165-2182-4
1. Speeches, addresses, etc., Indian—North America.
2. Oratory—North America. I. Title.
E98.O7 C54 2002
808.5′1′08997—dc21   2002000559

British Library Cataloguing-in-Publication Data
A catalogue record for this book is available from the British Library.

Publication of this book is made possible in part by the proceeds of a permanent
endowment created with the assistance of a Challenge Grant from the National
Endowment for the Humanities, a federal agency.

For John T. Clements III (1941–1998)

CONTENTS

Preface   ix
Acknowledgments   xvii

1. The Attraction of Eloquence: Why Oratory?   3
2. Sources and Resources for Native American Oratory   23
3. The Play of Tropes in Native American Oratory   79
4. From Performance through Dialogism to Efficacy   103
   Epilogue: Whither Oratory?   124

Appendix   131
Notes   159
References   163
Index   179

PREFACE

During the conversations that were published in 1989 as *Ancestral Voice,* Charles L. Woodard asked N. Scott Momaday, the author whose Pulitzer Prize–winning *House Made of Dawn* might be said to have initiated the late twentieth-century renaissance in Native American verbal art, to list some of the "most powerful statements you know." Without hesitation Momaday responded, "Many things in the Bible and in Shakespeare and in great orations by Indian chiefs." Becoming more specific, he cited "[o]ne of the greatest orations ever . . . delivered": a speech by the Kiowa Satethieday (Satanta) in October 1867 on Medicine Lodge Creek in Kansas. "It would be hard," Momaday told Woodard, "to find language more direct or simple than the language in that statement" (Woodard 1989, 94).

Momaday had probably read a text of Satethieday's speech in James Mooney's "Calendar History of the Kiowa Indians," a publication by the Bureau of American Ethnology that Momaday had used in his historical-autobiographical work, *The Way to Rainy Mountain.* In this government-sponsored survey of Kiowa history and ethnology, Mooney had written that

> Set-t'ainte, whose name among the Kiowa is still one to conjure by, first acquired his title of "Orator of the Plains" in connection with the events which led to the treaty of Medicine Lodge, in 1867. He was already sufficiently distinguished among his own people as a leader on the warpath. In May preceding the treaty he visited Fort Larned, and, confronting General Hancock, he denounced agent Leavenworth and complained of the aggression of the white men in a fiery speech, which is described as a masterly effort, from its opening, when he called the

sun to witness that he would "talk straight," to the close, when looking around over the prairie, he said that it was large and good, and declared that he did not want it stained with blood. (Mooney 1898, 207)

Then follows the text of Satethieday's speech, which had originally been published in the *New York Times* on 20 November 1867, as well as some other textual examples of Kiowa oratory.

Momaday, of course, takes considerable pride in his Kiowa identity, but to rank an oration even by one of the heroes of Kiowa history with two of the most respected and time-tested repositories of Western literary expression seems extreme even for a cultural partisan. For someone who perceives a Kiowa—and perhaps everyman—as a "man made of words," though, perhaps his immediate selection of Satethieday's oration as a "powerful statement" is not so strange. For American Indians, if we are to believe relatively "scientific" observers like Mooney or more impressionistic commentators like the scads of explorers, travelers, missionaries, soldiers, and government officials who wrote of Native Americans in their travelogues, memoirs, and reports, oratory was an important way of establishing self-worth. No matter what attributes of Western civilization might be found lacking in Indian cultures, excellence in oratory remained a constant in the writings of virtually everyone from the seventeenth through the nineteenth centuries except for the most extreme Indian haters. For Momaday, a product of formal education in comparative Western literature at Stanford University and of an education in the traditional culture of his father's Kiowa heritage, the choices he made to illustrate "powerful statements" should not seem all that far-fetched. A knowledge of the written literary heritage of the West would probably cause many of us to think immediately of the Bible and of Shakespeare. Were we as committed to another literary tradition as Momaday grew to be in regard to Kiowa, we would likely also cite something from that tradition. Following the lead of many commentators on Native American verbal expression, Momaday chose oratory.

One purpose of this project is to consider why this might be so. Why did not only N. Scott Momaday, ardent believer in the power of oral tradition and himself an American Indian, perceive oratory as the paradigmatic literary expression of his people, but why also did oratory receive the attention that it customarily did in treatment after treatment of Indian cultures prepared by Europeans and then Euro-Americans whose contact with those cultures emerged from a variety of impetuses?

But the question why is only the beginning if we are to hope to understand how oratory figured in actual Indian lifeways and the exoteric images of those lifeways that continue to color our view of them. Another purpose of this project, then, is to sample critically the materials available on Native North American oratory from the earliest records in the seventeenth century through the emergence of scientific ethnography in the early twentieth century. Though central to the images of Native Americans that began to emerge at least as early as the seventeenth century in what is now Canada and the United States, much of this material is regarded today as having only minimal value, particularly by those who are interested in oratory and other forms of verbal expression for their artistic qualities, not just as information to supplement the conventional historical record. And with good reason. Early attempts to document the oral expressions of American Indians faced several obstacles: the mechanics of recording what was said without the aid of tape recorders, the linguistic inadequacies of most of the people who did the recording, and the intellectual baggage that shaped what they said and heard, to name only a few. To accept blindly the reliability of documents treating oratory—or, in fact, any feature of Native American life—would be foolish.

John Wesley Powell tells an illustrative anecdote in his prefatory matter for the first *Annual Report* of the Bureau of (later, American) Ethnology. An art historian,, Grant Allen, had taken an incident from one of George Catlin's letters as evidence that Native Americans were unable to understand the concept of the profile, an assertion that, of course, is incorrect. Powell wrote, "It should never be forgotten that accounts of travelers and other persons who write for the sake of making good stories must be used with the utmost caution. Catlin is only one of a thousand such who can be used with safety only by persons so thoroughly acquainted with the subject that they are able to divide facts actually observed from creations of fancy. But Mr. Catlin must not be held responsible for illogical deductions even from his facts" (Powell 1881b, 85).

However, if we take an extremist position and dismiss all early sources as inevitably flawed beyond redemption, how can we know anything about American Indian oratory before the ethnopoetically aware, ethnographically sensitive reports of the late twentieth century? And if we don't know anything about Native American oratory of a century or more ago, we will lose the opportunity to share such powerful expressions as that of Satethieday which came so readily to Momaday's consciousness. My position—one already developed for records of Indian verbal art in general (Clements 1996)—is that while concerns about the reliability of the published record are indeed valid, they should not deter us from attempting to learn what we can from that record.

An initial issue in a project of this sort should involve terminology. "Oratory" is a Western term that came to be applied glibly and hegemonically to certain kinds of verbal performances that, from the perspective of contemporary European commentators, resembled what they would call "oratory" back home. Each Indian society, of course, would have its own term or set of terms for these performances. The Tlingit term *kaan kik' eetx' yoo x'atánk,* for example, means "speaking in public" (Dauenhauer and Dauenhauer 1990, 146) and like most such indigenous generic designations can be translated as well as any abstraction can into English—with "oratory" providing the most suitable match.

Often, though, indigenous terminology might not correspond so exactly, particularly when several generic names might represent what Europeans would blend together as "oratory." Anthony Seeger reports that among the Suyá of Brazil, the term "oratory" can apparently be equated with several indigenous discourse genres: *kapérni kahr ído* ("the exhortative speech of any older adult man addressing the entire village from the village plaza"), *mê mbari hwa kapérni* ("highly structured public speech, with long phrases and cadences. . . . spoken by political and ceremonial leaders, . . . [exhorting] the community to behave 'correctly' "), and *huru iarén, ngatu iarén,* and *gaiyi iarén* ("recitative-like addresses in ceremonies in which certain members of the village are publicly instructed to take certain ritual steps") (Seeger 1986, 61–62). Ideally, the student of "oratory" should approach performances in such culture-specific terms, but that would restrict him or her to one society or group of related societies. So I am going to stick with the term "oratory" while heeding Joel Sherzer's reminder that the "nature and role of speaking are not universal, not everywhere the same" (Sherzer 1983, 8).

Fortunately, precedent exists among anthropologists for using this etic term in cross-cultural situations. A couple of collections of essays which sample the public-speaking traditions of societies around the world have appeared during the last generation (Bloch 1975b, Paine 1981b), and while the individual authors working with particular societies opt for indigenous terminology, their collective efforts are subsumed under the general rubric "oratory" (or the related term "rhetoric") without significant loss in understanding. But I should not stop here and blithely use the term without some consideration of what it means.

The most comprehensive attempt at defining oratory in a Native American context that I know of is Donald M. Bahr's article on the subject in the *Dictionary of Native American Literature* (Bahr 1994). Therein Bahr defines oratory as speech "by a mortal person to mortal people" that "argues a position on what is good for the community." Oratory, Bahr suggests, is "an engine of persuasion" tied to "the practice of contentious . . . communal argument: politics" (107–108). As persuasive discourse intended to work for the good of the community, Native American oratory was encountered most directly by commentators in the context of the westward expansion of Euroamerica, when speakers representing sovereign nations addressed representatives of the colonial (and later state and federal) governments on behalf of their societies' interests. While Bahr assumes that oratory occurred in intrasocietal settings as well, he correctly notes that our knowledge of those settings is limited.

The strength of Bahr's definition is its highlighting the culture-specific implications of the term "oratory." From this perspective, the term should be applied only to those Native American verbal expressions that resemble what Europeans conceived oratory to be. To use "oratory" for other speech forms would, in this light, be inappropriate, misleading, perhaps even ethnocentric. Thus, Bahr and a number of other commentators (e.g., Miller 1996) exclude many publicly delivered discourse forms from the rubric of oratory: sermons and prayers, for example. At the same time, though, some way of approaching a larger variety of verbal art forms than may be encompassed by using "oratory" only in the Western sense has some merit. Sermons, oratory proper, and even prayers and other ritual discourse indeed share many features, and a too exclusive definition may result in distinctions that are not apparent either to the outsider or to the verbal artist and his or her audience.

If I am to err, I would prefer to do so in the direction of inclusiveness. Hence, I have turned to anthropology and have adapted an operational definition of "oratory" from Alessandro Duranti, whose field researches in Oceania provide him a cross-cultural perspective and who has quite handily defined the term from an ethnographic perspective for the *International Encyclopedia of Communications* (1989). Based on Duranti's definition and amplified by the perspectives of some other ethnographers of oratorical performances, I think of oratory in these defining terms: that oratory is verbal art that evinces many of the esthetic qualities of other verbal art; that oratory emerges from and generates particular kinds of situations (political and otherwise), culturally specific but often quite similar cross-culturally; that oratory requires the immediate presence of both a performer and an audience (though sometimes the mortal audience may be ostensible observers rather than direct addressees); and that oratory has a practical efficacy that more explicitly involves persuasion than some other verbal art forms.

The first chapter of this project deals with an issue that has puzzled me since I began examining the early records of Native North American verbal art a quarter of a century ago: why oratory received so much favorable attention from European and Euro-American commentators while other verbal art forms such as storytelling and singing were treated dismissively. Answering this question requires some consideration of the motives of those who have written of oratory, matters that I deem crucial to understanding what they have recorded. This chapter is followed by the longest section of the project, an overview of the kinds of sources that are available for a consideration of early oratorical performances. It looks in some detail at several examples that represent both different kinds of source material and, to some degree, the range of culture areas in Native North America that were treated in the early sources. Chapters 3 and 4 use examples from records of Native American verbal performance to deconstruct the definition of oratory that informs the work—that derived from Duranti. Synthesizing from the available materials, Chapter 3 treats the verbal artistry of oratory with special consideration of how that artistry responds to and shapes the particular discourse situations in which oratory has been reported to occur. Chapter 4 then examines the nonverbal performance dynamics of oratory and their role—along with that of the words—in making oratory efficacious speech, the very components, as we will see, that early representations of oratory tended to emphasize. An epilogue considers some of the recent work on Native American oratory and offers some suggestions for further study.

Acknowledgments

There are many institutions and individuals whose assistance and encouragement have played a role in developing this project. I am especially grateful to Charles Carr, chair of the Department of English and Philosophy at Arkansas State University, and Richard McGhee, dean of the College of Arts and Sciences during the period when most of the work was done, for their assisting me in finding the time to devote to it. I also appreciate the efforts of my colleagues Norman E. Stafford and Steven L. Mayes for their help in easing some of the editorial duties for *Arkansas Review* to which I am assigned. Graduate assistants Rhonda Curbo, Guy Lancaster, Anna Hayes, Paige Morgan, Kimberley Opper, Karen Powers, Kevin Saunders, and Virginia Sturgeon also relieved me of some responsibilities. The interlibrary loan department of the Dean B. Ellis Library at Arkansas State University has been an invaluable source of material. Some of the work for the project was also done at libraries at the University of Arizona, Ohio State University, and West Virginia University. I appreciate the help provided by their staffs. I am also grateful to Brian Swann and Arnold Krupat, who encouraged early work on the project, and to Donald Bahr and Keith Cunningham, who offered advice at its later stages. Needless to say, they bear no blame for its shortcomings. I am also indebted to the staff of the University of Arizona Press, especially Patti Hartmann and Richard von Kleinsmid, for shepherding the project into its final form. My most extensive and intensive debt is to Frances M. Malpezzi for support of almost every sort.

ORATORY IN NATIVE NORTH AMERICA

CHAPTER 1

THE ATTRACTION OF ELOQUENCE

WHY ORATORY?

The image of the Native North American has gone through many vicissitudes during the almost five centuries that Europeans and Euro-Americans have been articulating it: from noble to bestial, from honest to deceptive, from attuned to nature to lazy, from honorable to scheming. The ways in which this image has changed through various eras and in various media have received considerable academic attention (e.g., Berkhofer 1978, Stedman 1982). One feature though—eloquence—seems to be more or less consistent, despite those occasional manifestations that reduce the Indian to little more than a grunting mute, as someone "expressively handicapped" (Camp 1978, 816).[1] One proponent of this view, Lewis Cass, governor of Michigan Territory during the 1820s, secretary of war during the administration of Andrew Jackson, and someone who had specific and extensive political dealings with Native Americans, frequently and inevitably pounced upon any evidence he could find to support his negative view of Indian humanity. Even though he had grudgingly to admit the existence of "Indian eloquence," Cass wrote of one notable American Indian politician whose oratory undoubtedly played a role in his success in forging intertribal opposition to Euro-American encroachments: "Tecumthé was not an able composer of speeches. We understand he was particularly deficient in those powers of the imagination, to which we have been indebted for the boldest flights of Indian eloquence. He was sometimes confused, and generally tedious and circumlocutory" (Cass 1826, 99n).

There have in fact existed two contrasting stereotypes of the American

Indian speaker. One depicts a "Calibanesque speaker of gibberish," and the other portrays a "speaker of a language that is fully transparent and universally acceptable" (Gustafson 2000, 90). But most often the Indian of imagery evinces a natural eloquence that manifests itself in oratory. From Pierre Biard's characterization of the Montagnais whom he encountered in 1616 as "the greatest speech-makers on earth" (Thwaites 1959a, 3:225) to the writer for the *Knickerbocker* in 1836 who held that Native American public speakers demonstrated a "sublimity of style which rivals the highest productions of their more cultivated enemies" (in Clements 1986, 11), one who examines what was (and is still) written about Native Americans finds that it frequently praises their oratorical agility and ability. This interest in oratory has persisted, if the continuing publication of "texts" of Indian speeches during the last few decades is any indication. From scholarly works focusing on a particular tribal heritage (e.g., Dauenhauer and Dauenhauer 1990) to anthologies that purport to reprint speeches in order to represent a Native view of American history (e.g., Armstrong 1971) to popular presentations for young readers of the ecological oratory attributed to Sealth (Chief Seattle) (e.g., Jeffers 1991),[2] American Indian speech making continues to capture our interest.

The earliest references to this skill appeared in some of the first written documents to come out of the northern reaches of the western hemisphere, and throughout the history of Native American contact with Europeans and their American descendants, oratory almost "never failed to excite admiration" (Aumann 1965, 251). Explorers, missionaries, soldiers, even occasionally captives—as well as more "scientifically" oriented observers such as pioneering linguists and ethnographers—usually had something to say in a positive way about Indian oratory. By far oratory is the genre of verbal art that has received the most attention, especially from early commentators.

The reasons for this interest are complex and manifold. They differ from era to era and often from commentator to commentator. We can offer some generalized speculations, though, to account for why oratory rather than mythology or lyric poetry (songs without the music) especially appealed to the literary sensibilities of writers schooled in a European verbal esthetic. One obvious reason that the image of the American Indian as skilled orator appears so often is because it is accurate. Even though observers and commentators may have misinterpreted what was being said and

misunderstood why it was said, they were usually on the mark in stressing the importance of oratory in Native American public life. Surveying
the political systems of Native North America, Robert H. Lowie has cited
three features that consistently characterized what he calls "titular chiefs"
throughout the continent: their role as arbiters or peacemakers, their gener-
osity, and their oratorical skills (Lowie 1967, 73–76). He writes, "[T]he
most typical American chief is not a lawgiver, executive, or judge, but a
pacifier, a benefactor of the poor, and a prolix Polonius" (76). Despite the
negativism implied by his Shakespearean allusion, Lowie's generalization
represents a commonplace when anthropologists consider power acquisi-
tion and retention in those societies politically structured as "bands" or
"tribes": Leaders are not formally chosen to fill formal offices; instead they
"emerge" as ad hoc "firsts among equals" based on their skills, including the
ability to persuade others through rhetoric. Effective oratory was one route
to success and prestige in the kinds of political systems that traditionally
characterized the societies of most pre-Columbian North Americans and
their descendants for several centuries following European contact.

One survey, based on case studies of one hundred Native American political leaders and drawing upon data recorded in eighteenth- and
nineteenth-century sources—the same kinds of sources that are being used
here—ranks the ability to speak effectively in public as the fifth most frequently occurring trait in effective leaders, following intellect, general
good-naturedness, dignity, and moral courage (Bernard 1928, 304). One-
third of the figures included in the sampling were reported to have possessed
oratorical skills, which though perhaps not the basis for their attaining
leadership positions, were important for retaining their status. Characterized as "the most effective single tool of an Indian leader," oratory might
involve a number of verbal devices, including sarcasm, flattery, and threat
(Bernard 1928, 313). The reason for the importance of oratory lay "in the
prevailingly direct, face-to-face, and personal type of leadership. Indians
could scarcely have achieved indirect, abstract, and impersonal leadership
because of the lack of abstract communication. All influencing of followers had to be through the use of direct techniques" (314).[3] In sum, oratory among these hundred "chiefs" was the "almost indispensable technical
method" of exerting political control once it had been achieved (315). Or as
Jesse P. Williamson, an observer of Dakota culture early in the twentieth

century, claimed, "Many chiefs held their positions by virtue of their oratorical ability" (quoted in Buswell 1935, 323).

But accuracy surely is not enough to account for the persistent appeal of oratory to European and Euro-American characterizers of Indian life. After all, every Native American society also possessed a rich heritage of story and song, neither of which, early on at least, received quite the adulation or even attention that attached to oratory. Songs, both in performance and in their verbal texts, were, in fact, targets of considerable distaste. Paul Le Jeune, superior of the Jesuit mission in New France during the mid-seventeenth century and often favorably disposed toward those evidences of Indian humanity (including oratory) that marked the "savages" as susceptible to the appeal of Christianity, found little to attract him in Native American singing. His *Relation* for 1632 contains the following comment about music that he had encountered at Tadoussac: "Their singing seemed to me very disagreeable; their cadence always ended with reiterated aspirations, 'oh! oh! oh! ah! ah! ah! hem! hem! hem!' *etc.*" (Thwaites 1959a, 5:27). John Bradbury, whose memoirs of his travels in the "Interior of America" came out in a second edition in 1819, remarked on the singing of a party of Arikaras, Mandans, and Gros Ventres, "The song is very rude, and it does not appear that they combine the expression of ideas and music, the whole of their singing consisting in the repetition of the word *ha* six or seven times in one tone, after which they rise or fall a third, fourth, or fifth, and the same in quick time" (Thwaites 1966, 5:116). Even Henry Rowe Schoolcraft, who had achieved some celebrity by mid-nineteenth century for his publications of Anishinaabe verbal art, came to an appreciation of Indian singing only with reluctance. In what is apparently his earliest reference to this art (a journal entry from 1820), he noted, "It [Anishinaabe dance and music] is perhaps all we could expect from untutored savages, but there is nothing about it which has ever struck me as either interesting or amusing, and after having seen these performances once or twice, they become particularly tedious" (Schoolcraft 1953, 128).

Storytelling did not come in for as much opprobrium as singing received, but neither did it generate the effusive praise usually enjoyed by oratory. A characteristic attitude was struck by the surveyor John Lawson, who traveled among Native Americans in Carolina during the first decade of the eighteenth century. He devotes a few lines to summarizing "a long Tale of a great Rattle-Snake" (apparently of Tuscarora provenience) before apologizing to his readers: "I have been something tedious upon this subject, on purpose to shew what strange ridiculous Stories these Wretches are inclinable to believe. I suppose, these Doctors [i.e., shamans such as his source for the story] understand a little better themselves, than to give Credit to any such Fooleries; for I reckon them the cunningnest Knaves in all the Pack" (Lawson 1709, 213). As we will see, Lawson was much more favorably disposed toward oratory.

The problem with American Indian singing for most European and Euro-American commentators lay in its unfamiliarity. Native American musical scales were different, performance strategies were different, the purposes of singing were different from what the commentators knew. To appreciate non-Western music required an esthetic relativism that remains difficult to attain even today. Moreover, songs did often rely extensively upon vocables, which missionaries, travelers, and even pioneer ethnologists commonly dismissed as "cabalistic choruses" of "traditionary monosyllables" (Schoolcraft 1851, 368–369; 1853, 326). If lack of esthetic relativism explained the commentators' problem regarding songs, their difficulties with storytelling lay much deeper, for many narratives summarized (though seldom fully transcribed) by early commentators were origin myths that explicitly contradicted their own treasured cosmogonic scheme recorded in the Book of Genesis. Louis Hennepin demonstrated unusual sympathy for the differing views of essential truths of existence that Europeans and Native Americans might espouse when he recorded how one of his Indian interlocutors reacted to European responses to Native American mythology:

When we related to them the history of our Creation, and the mysteries of the Christian religion, they tell su [sic] that we are right, and then they relate their fables, and when we reply that what they say, is not true, they retort, that they agreed to what we said, and that it is not showing sense to interrupt a man when he is speaking and to tell him that he lies. "This is all very well," they say, "for your countryman; for them it is as you say, but not for us who belong to another nation." (Hennepin 1880, 335–36)

While Hennepin's tone is one of bemusement, others were more likely to brush aside American Indian narratives, especially but not exclusively myths, as superstitious nonsense.

Oratory, on the other hand, was much more accessible to European ears and minds than singing. Nor did it necessarily reveal intellects benighted by superstition. Instead, it could reveal what Europeans regarded as the best of Native virtues: directness, courage, and spiritual grandeur, to name only a few that early observers were likely to appreciate. Even when Native orators were using the skills in the struggle against European empire building, their speeches were intelligible.

Oratory was also accessible in the sense that Europeans were much more likely to encounter speech making by Native Americans than they were to hear singing or storytelling. The nature of the contact situation, which often involved diplomatic councils, lent itself to oratorical performance. In fact, from the perspectives of many American Indian groups, speeches were essential components of the diplomatic process, though that may not have been the case in the cloistered, clandestine diplomatic negotiations of Europe (cf. Bahr 1994, 108–109). Certainly an obvious reason that European commentators paid more attention to oratory than to other forms of verbal art was that it was part of their routine experience in dealing with Native Americans. Even the most casual traveler might hear an oration, and even if—as the soldier Richard Irving Dodge suggested (Dodge 1882, 51)—the circumstances did not allow it to manifest the highest qualities of this verbal art form, an oration was more likely to be performed for a European or Euro-American audience than a song or a story would be.

But there was more to the appeal of oratory than just its accessibility and the negative quality of not necessarily being tied to an alien cosmology. The Indian-as-orator idea must have touched some responsive chords in European perceptions of mankind in the "uncivilized" state for it to be so popular. Probably the most important of those chords—actually a combination of two inharmonious tones—arose from attitudes toward artful discourse that have appeared in Western thought concurrently and successively from time to time. On one hand was the Aristotelian perspective, which held that oratory and its sister, rhetoric, represented the height of human achievement, that the pursuit of eloquence was one of the chief aims of mankind. On the other was the Cartesian viewpoint, which held that rhetoric was a device by which the sly concealed the truth, that the pursuit of eloquence was antirational, that plain speaking and action were what men and women should aspire to (Paine 1981b, 3). American Indian oratory, as reported by early commentators, could provide support for either perspective, and therein lay at least some of its appeal.

As public speakers, Indian orators were practicing "primary rhetoric"—the art of persuasion (in the broadest sense) within the context of civil life. Such persuasion was an "act of enunciation on a specific occasion" based on no text (though Euro-Americans might subsequently treat the enunciation as a text) (Kennedy 1980, 4). The view of Renaissance humanists toward such primary rhetoric as artful discourse held that "[t]rue eloquence . . . could arise only out of a harmonious union between wisdom and style; its aim was to guide men toward virtue and worthwhile goals, not to mislead them for vicious or trivial purposes" (Gray 1963, 498). The skilled speaker was using one of humanity's distinctive gifts, an ability shared with a deity who had *spoken* creation into existence: "Man was made in the image of God, his mind dimly reflecting the divine mind, his word retaining a vestige of the power of God's creating Word" (Mulder 1969, 20–21). Ben Jonson's comment voiced a Renaissance commonplace: "Speech is the only benefit man hath to express his excellency of mind above other creatures" (quoted in Sherry 1975, 247). John Donne reiterated the necessary association between humans and language in a sermon preached to the king in 1629:

> Man is but a voice, but a sound, but a noise, he begins the noise himselfe, when he comes crying into the world; and when he goes out, perchance friends celebrate, perhaps enemies calumniate him, with a diverse voice, a diverse noise. A melancholique man, is but a groaning; a sportfull man, but a song; an active man, but a Trumpet; a mighty man, but a thunderclap: Every man but *Ish,* but a sound, but a noyse. (Donne 1953–62, 9:61–62)

To speak well was to be human, and even the most degraded of humans could be expected to retain some vestiges of this human trait. Native Americans, whether regarded as just beginning their climb toward civilization or as having fallen from a previous state of high culture, held on to the divinely granted humanness that manifested itself in their speaking ability. Eons of life in the savage state had perhaps even refined their eloquence according to many early commentators, especially missionaries who wanted to convince possible financial supporters that the Indians were indeed potentially receptive to the Christian message. Consider the comments of Jesuit missionary Joseph Jouvency in the early 1610s:

> No one among them [the Indians of Acadia] is stupid or sluggish, a fact which is evident in their inborn foresight in deliberation and their fluency in speaking. Indeed, they have often been heard to make a peroration so well calculated for persuasion, and that off-hand, that they would excite the admiration of the most experienced in the arena of eloquence. (Thwaites 1959a, 1:277–79)

Or attend to the rhapsodies of a writer for the *North American Review* two centuries later, who noted that the American Indian

> sometimes gives utterance to a brilliant thought, which would be applauded, coming from a cultivated mind. Living in the midst of primeval forests, gazing upon the stars of heaven, witnessing the succession and touching phenomena of the passing seasons, his mind is sometimes filled with emotions of the beautiful and sublime, to which he gives utterance in bold and figurative language. A sentiment imbued with natural feeling, an image borrowed from external objects, a comparison snatched from the tree, the bird, the mountain, the waterfall, occasionally impart to his discourse the air of poetry, and fill the mind of the hearer with delight. (*Review of History* 1838, 139–40)

Early commentators, even those who did not understand the languages in which they heard Native American orations, frequently recognized the rhythmic regularity of this public speech. Critics of Milton's *Paradise Lost* have noted that the epic poet carefully contrasted the "measured rhythms and steady grace" of divine articulations with the "irregular" and "restless rhythms" of "infernal speech" (Sherry 1975, 253–54). The careful listener could detect in what Dell Hymes would later call the "measured verse" of some Native American verbal art (Hymes 1981, 175–78) at least glimmerings of the Indians' essential and divinely granted humanness even before they heard the interpreters' renderings of the sense of their messages.

The ability to speak well allied Indians with classical antiquity, a point that received considerable emphasis from those who, influenced by Renaissance humanism, saw the roots of their own cultural heritage as extending into the soil of Athens, especially to the verbal artists it had nurtured. In fact, the only synthetic and theoretical overview by a Jesuit of the Native American cultures of New France on which his missionary colleagues had reported from their specific field experiences was an attempt to show parallels between those cultures and classical civilization. Joseph François Lafitau's *Moeurs des sauvages ameriquains comparées aux moeurs des premiers temps* (Lafitau 1974–1977; first published in 1724) tried to demonstrate a continuity between western and eastern hemispheres attributable to a universal revelation in prehistory. That Native Americans could speak with Attic eloquence was an important exhibit in support of his thesis.

Artful discourse in oratory might also confirm a favorite hypothesis about the origin of the Indians. Those who were interested in advancing the connection between Native Americans and the Ten Lost Tribes of Israel, an idea that had enjoyed currency since at least the sixteenth century, could suggest that the eloquence Indian orators employed established their connection with biblical forebears. The Hebrew-Indian hypothesis particularly informed the work of James Adair, who wrote,

> They often change the sense of words into a different signification from the natural, exactly after the manner also of the orientalists. Even, their common speech is full of it; like the prophetic writings, and the book of Job, their orations are concise, strong, and full of fire; which sufficiently confutes the wild notion which some have espoused of the North American Indians being Prae-Adamites, or a separate race of men, created for that continent. What stronger circumstantial proofs can be expected, than that they, being disjoined from the rest of the world, time immemorial, and destitute also of the use of letters, should have, and still retain the ancient standard of speech, conveyed down by oral tradition from father to son, to the present generation? (Williams 1930, 12)

The positive view of rhetoric and eloquence, the foundations of oratory, persisted through the Revolutionary period of American history,
when the man of action and the man of words were compatible and often
identical (Baskerville 1979, 9–10). Effectiveness in speaking remained the
"mark of a well-educated and thoughtful citizen," and rhetoric was identified as the "art that contributed the most toward the proper workings of the
political process, the disposition of justice, and the maintenance of public
welfare and social conscience" (Johnson 1993, 139). *Littel's Living Age* magazine asserted in 1851 that "eloquence . . . is beyond all question the greatest
exertion of the human mind" (quoted in Baskerville 1979, 1–2), and oratory stood as perhaps the principal evidence that a national literary culture
was flourishing in the United States. Indian orators provided evidence that
such expression was endemic to being human and that it could not be stifled
by even the most degraded forms of savagery.

Perhaps the most famous example of the use of "oratory" (I think the
term perhaps misapplied in this case)[4] by the use of an apologist for the
Indians' essential humanity and for their classical parallels occurs in Thomas
Jefferson's *Notes on the State of Virginia*. This is an account of a "speech"
(again, probably not the best term) supposedly delivered by the Mingo
Tahgahjute, or James Logan, in conjunction with a treaty-making parley to
end what was known as Lord Dunmore's War (Jefferson 1982, 63). Jefferson
includes the information on Tahgahjute's speech in a chapter entitled "Productions Mineral, Vegetable and Animal," the purpose of which was in part
to defend the western hemisphere from the invidious comments of the
Comte de Buffon. In particular, Jefferson used Tahgahjute's eloquence to
refute Buffon's claim that the American aborigine was inferior in every way
to European mankind. Jefferson responded directly to the charge that the
Indian "has no vivacity, no activity of mind" (58) with an offer to "challenge
the whole orations of Demosthenes and Cicero, and of any more eminent
orator, if Europe has produced any more eminent, to produce a single
passage superior to" Tahgahjute's words (62). Not only does he offer this
exhibit as empirical evidence *contra* Buffon, but he neatly places the Indian
within the tradition of classical literary expression. Moreover, he notes the
lack of "letters" among the Indians—a condition that may serve to elevate
Tahgahjute's accomplishment even higher, since he instanced the high art of
oratory without the aid of writing (63).

Meanwhile, though, the Cartesian perspective, rooted in criticism of the "sophistic" strand of rhetoric, which emerged in fifth-century Greece and elevated the role of the speaker above the ideas presented, perceived verbal artistry with suspicion. In its most extreme form, seventeenth-century manifestations of this view contrasted the geometrical logic of Descartes and Pascal to the "deception" inherent in artful speech (Kennedy 1980, 222). The eloquent speaker, so this viewpoint suggested, "is a sophist . . . who stoops to deceit and half-truth and employs sleight of tongue" (Bailey 1981, 25). John Locke apparently defined eloquence as "the Art of deceiving agreeably" (Lawson 1972, 126). He wrote that when "we would speak of things as they are, we must allow that all the art of rhetoric, besides order and clearness; all the artificial and figurative application of words eloquence has invented, are for nothing else but to insinuate wrong ideas, move the passions, and thereby mislead the judgment; and so indeed are perfect cheats" (quoted in Soskice 1985, 13). In the series of lectures on the art of oratory that he delivered at Harvard between 1806 and 1809, John Quincy Adams identified three major critical charges leveled at oratorical eloquence and rhetoric, its sister science:

> First, that rhetoric is a pedantic science, overcharged with scholarly subtleties, and innumerable divisions and subdivisions, burdensome to the memory, oppressive to genius, and never applicable to any valuable purpose in the business of the world. Second, that it is a frivolous science, substituting childish declamation instead of manly sense, and adapted rather to the pageantry of a public festival, than to the sober concerns of real life. And third, that it is a pernicious science; the purpose of which is to mislead the judgment by fascinating the imagination. (Adams 1962, 1:54)

Though they might be able to apply any of these criticisms to Native American oratory, those who used the verbal abilities of Indians to indict rather than exalt them would most likely focus on the last. After all, the most silver-tongued orator in biblical history is Satan, "a virtuoso" who "sways his legions in heaven and hell, deceives Eve into reaching for the forbidden fruit, and still attracts the readers of *Paradise Lost* to his party" (Mulder 1969, 36). Mankind's special gift of speech, introduced with Adam, had become corrupted with his fall, induced by satanic rhetoric. Plain speaking like that of the prelapsarian Adam had vanished with his sin against his Creator. Though humanity had recovered some of that gift, it now existed only in corrupt form. Moreover, true eloquence could only speak the truth (i.e., Christian Truth). Otherwise the devices of rhetoric served the ends of sophistry (Sherry 1975, 248–52). Like Satan, who had suborned the Adamic corruption of plain speaking, the Indian orator perverted his divinely granted power of speech for the diabolic ends to which the arch-deceiver had inspired him. Instead of speaking plainly and thus being understood for what he really intended, the Indian orator used rhetorical flourishes to conceal and mislead. At best, rhetorical flourishes, according to the Cartesian perspective, represented "a luxurious linguistic dress or cosmetic, an embellishment of bare meaning, a verbal ornament that destabilizes and distracts" (Gustafson 2000, 26–27). Susan Gustafson quotes a contemporary critic of the Federalist orator Fisher Ames, who dismissed his adversary's oratory as being filled with rhetorical devices that had "less meaning" and "as little purpose" as similar devices used by American Indian public speakers (239–40).

Thus even the New England Puritans, no sympathizers with the state of savagery, might comment upon Indian eloquence. But their facility with words, according to this perspective, meant that the savage orators were sly and cunning, eloquent demons who could bend the ignorant, benighted multitudes to their diabolical ends. Puritans, even Roger Williams, who was less dismissive of Native New Englanders than were many of his contemporaries, believed that glib orators produced superstitious followers "held captive within their own communities through the persuasive force of eloquence" (Gustafson 2000, 33). A case in point appears in Benjamin Tompson's epic poem *New Englands Crisis,* first published in 1676. Treating King Philip's War, the poem begins with an account of how Metacom, the "greazy *Lout* / With all his pagan slaves coil'd round about," used oratory to convince his audience to join him in striking militarily at the English. Though delivered in "American Indian Pidgin English" (Goddard 1977), the speech reflects some of the very features that more sympathetic commentators attributed positively to the discourse of Native American public speakers. After listing reasons for going to war, particularly the double standard in the application of English law to colonists and colonized, Metacom is made to portray the spoils that will come to the victors in concrete, synecdochic language that also presents an image of the reversal of the status quo:

> Now if you'le fight Ile get you english coats,
> And wine to drink out of their Captains throats.
> The richest merchants houses shall be ours,
> Wee'l ly no more on matts or dwell in bowers
> Wee'l have their silken wives take they our Squaws,
> They shall be whipt by virtue of our laws.

Metacom's artful speech had an immediate effect. "This counsel lightning like their tribes invade," writes Tompson (White 1980, 86–87).

Such negative views of the oral artistry reflected in oratory persisted even into the twentieth century, though usually without the satanic associations noticed by some Puritans. For some observers the very term "oratory" held opprobrious connotations suggesting speech marked by "labored periods, gaudy verbal embellishments, and ostentatious histrionic display" (Baskerville 1979, 5). There were plenty of Americans, including some who made note of Native American speech making, to agree with Thomas Carlyle, who in 1850 held that "Skill in speaking is a sign of intellectual shallowness; one talks because he is incapable of thinking" (quoted in Baskerville 1979, 116).

In fact, the same features of oratory that received praise on one hand might also serve as evidence of the weakness of Native American intellects, especially as they revealed their poverty of language. A recurrent idea regarding "primitive" people has held that they are incapable of thinking abstractly, that they must deal with phenomena that lie beyond the physical senses in terms of immediate sensory experience. Native Americans' reliance in oratory on metaphor and other figures of speech, hailed by some commentators as suggestive of an innate proclivity for verbal artistry, derived from their languages' poverty. Those languages, reflecting the intellects of those who spoke them, were incapable of dealing with the higher truths, and even some of the lower ones, except by cloaking them in the concrete designs of figurative dress. An alliance with another group had to be described as a "chain," while the abstractions of "domesticity" and "home" could only be expressed by such concrete images as "fire" in the "overtroped" diction of American Indian eloquence (cf. Becker and Mannheim 1996, 238).[5] Ignoring the facts that even the deepest of European thinkers might use similar images to present their philosophical and theological points and that virtually all discourse relies to some extent upon figurative speech (Lakoff and Johnson 1980), commentators pointed to the metaphorical, imagistic diction of Native American oratory as proof of the weaknesses of their languages and of their minds.

So evidence from oratory could support diametrically opposing views of the Native American character and intellect. While on one hand their minds might be "above the ordinary stamp" (Parker 1838, 68) and their use of language a reminder of their place in the brotherhood of speech-endowed humanity, on the other their facility with words revealed the satanic principle at work within them as well as their inability to address abstract issues in any but concrete terms.

Another source of the usually positive attention paid to Native American oratory was its orality. That Native American orators did not speak from prepared, written texts also contributed—at least for some commentators—to a positive view of their oratory. Speaking extemporaneously suggested sincerity and inspiration, though some might contend that a text-based speech reflected more stability of thought. But for many who wrote out of the perspective of the Enlightenment or of Romanticism, the orator who performed without recourse to prepared text, notes, or outline manifested "greater authenticity than textbound white orators" (Gustafson 2000, xxii).

A vogue for the oral surfaced in English belles lettres in the 1760s and carried over to the American colonies. At the beginning of the decade, James Macpherson had published the first of several volumes of poetry that he claimed had survived in Scots oral tradition for centuries since their composition by the bard Ossian. Subsequent collections came out in 1762, 1763, and 1765, stimulating what one literary historian has called an "Ossianic rage" (Friedman 1961, 174). Translated into several European languages, Macpherson's Ossian poems probably influenced the publication of *Reliques of Ancient English Poetry* by Thomas Percy in 1765. While many readers came to doubt the authenticity of the Ossianic materials, during the last third of the eighteenth century Percy's three-volume anthology nevertheless helped to initiate a "ballad revival" (Friedman 1961), which resulted in the publication of a number of anthologies of oral poetry by the likes of Walter Scott.

As Arnold Krupat has noted, "[I]n the second half of the nineteenth [eighteenth?] century, the meaning of *literature* shifted away from an emphasis on the form of presentation (writing) toward an emphasis on the content of the presentation (imaginative and affective material)" (Krupat 1992, 174). The efforts by William Wordsworth and Samuel Taylor Coleridge to replicate oral forms in the poems in *Lyrical Ballads* (1798) and the former's famous advocacy of spontaneity as the source of poetic genius further entrenched the valuation of orality in literary circles. When the Romantic perception of literary genius was applied to people such as Native Americans, they were perceived to be "far-off 'primitive' peoples" thought "to represent the essence of the natural and instinctive poetic expression" (Finnegan 1977, 32). Oral expression was thought to allow the verbal artist spontaneously to articulate the passion that "bubbles up through him in the form of a poem" (Finnegan 1977, 31). American Indian orators who relied only on oral "inspiration" exemplified the ideal verbal artist.

Critics and students of religious oratory also advocated orality as the ideal for presenting straightforward spiritual truths, unmitigated by the interpretive commentaries that might burden carefully written out sermons. In the 1740s the Puritan divine Solomon Stoddard argued the case for orality in sermonizing: "Sermons that are read are not delivered with Authority" (quoted in Gustafson 2000, 45). His use of the upper case for "Authority" may reflect contemporary orthographic practice, but it also seems to connect oral effectiveness with spiritual inspiration. A particular premium was attached to extemporaneous sermonizing during the Second Awakening of the early nineteenth century. Along the Ohio Valley Frontier, where the camp meeting afforded situations where text-based preaching would be ineffective, the most celebrated preachers were those who relied upon oral composition techniques (cf. Rosenberg 1988). Peter Cartwright, a Methodist preacher who worked at many camp meetings in Kentucky, Illinois, and Indiana during the first third of the nineteenth century, expressed special contempt for those of his formally educated counterparts who read their sermons. For example, he described his association with a Presbyterian minister, "a very well educated man" who "had regularly studied theology in some of the Eastern states." When the Presbyterian settled in Springfield, Illinois, in the 1820s, he found his learned techniques served little purpose. Cartwright gave him some advice: "I told him he must quit reading his old manuscript sermons, and learn to speak extemporaneously; that the Western people were born and reared in hard times, and were an outspoken and off-hand people; that if he did not adopt this manner of preaching, the Methodists would set the whole Western world on fire before he would light his match." The minister apparently tried to follow Cartwright's suggestions, but "became discouraged, and left for parts unknown" (Cartwright 1956, 204).

Oratory founded on oral spontaneity was thus valued in both secular and spiritual circles during the time when many commentators were writing about American Indians. Though he would undoubtedly have rejected a suggestion of parallelism between Native American oratory and his own extemporaneous, divinely inspired sermonizing, Cartwright nevertheless recognized the role of speech making as a political tool in Indian life (Cartwright 1956, 188). Moreover, such speech making served as a model for the effectiveness of oratory that emerged directly out of oral performance. The popularity of accounts of public speaking by Native Americans owed something to the valuation of oral expression as being particularly "authentic" and "genuine."

Another probable reason that oratory appealed to Euro-American commentators, if not to their European progenitors and counterparts, lay in the desire to forge a distinctly *American* identity on the level of expressive culture as well as of politics. Throughout the nineteenth century and well into the twentieth, many American literati were declaring their cultural independence from Britain and other European centers of civilization. To do so, though, required a national literature that, while it had to be in the same language as English literature, should in some way manifest the distinctively American. Critics often turned to Native Americans for a foundation upon which to base that distinctiveness. An early such statement appeared in an essay by Walter Channing in the inaugural volume of the *North American Review.* After bemoaning the lack of a distinctive American cultural identity, partially due to the shared language with Britain, Channing suggested that the possibility of a uniquely indigenous literary heritage for the United States might lie with the "oral literature of the aborigines":

With him [the Indian] as with all other beings, language is but the expression of manner. It was made to express his emotions during his observance of nature, and these emotions were taught him at a school, in which the master was nature, and a most unsophisticated heart the scholar. Hence it is as bold as its own unshackled conceptions, and as rapid as his own step. It is now as rich as the soil on which he was nurtured, and ornamented with every blossom that blows in his path. It is now elevated and soaring, for his image is the eagle, and now precipitous and hoarse as the cataract among whose mists he is descanting. (Channing 1815, 313)

Meanwhile, some saw oratory as the particular foundation of a national literary culture. Writing near the end of the nineteenth century, Lorenzo Sears noted that oratory may predate all other forms of literature "as speech precedes writing, and prose poetry in ordinary composition" (Sears 1896, 22). Drawing on the contemporary anthropological vogue for unilinear cultural evolution, he continued,

For if the latest conclusion of evolutionists be accepted, supported as it is by ethnic examples, it will appear that the germ of oratory is found in the primitive laudation of a conqueror returning with the spoils of war, a brief and simple proclamation of victory at first, developed later into eulogistic speech. However this may be, it is evident that the orator left his mark upon primeval literatures along with the poet and the historian, the philosopher and the dramatist. (22)

The poet Alice Corbin Henderson made the connection between pre-Homeric literary expression and Native American verbal art clear. To discover what preceded Homer, she wrote, "one need merely project oneself physically on a two- or three-days' journey from any of the principal cities of the United States, and witness a dance drama of the south-western Indians, in order to discover at first hand what primitive poetry is like" (Henderson 1919, 330). Indeed, as noted above, Euro-Americans of a generation or so earlier than Henderson might find an indigenous Demosthenes in the likes of Sagoyewatha (Red Jacket), Thayendanégea (Joseph

Brant), Pondiac, or Tajgahjute, whose "speech" was like "something in the chorus of an old Greek tragedy" (Aumann 1965, 252). Though supporters of American literary independence could cite Euro-American exemplars of the art of oratory (Daniel Webster or Edward Everett, for example), they could also suggest that Indian speech making would provide some of the basis for a distinctive American heritage of letters (cf. Wroth 1975).

Oratory indeed came to be a sort of "national literature" for Americans during the nineteenth century, when anthologists "gleaned purple passages for preservation and admiration" and literary critics were devoting the same attention to the texts of public speeches that other literary genres received (Baskerville 1979, 83–85). And while most of this attention was directed at speeches by Euro-American luminaries, examples of Indian oratory received a fair amount of consideration. The frequent reprinting of Tahgahjute's speech in reading textbooks and anthologies of "world famous speeches" following its endorsement by Jefferson is a good example (Sutton 1966, 500; Sutton and Mitchell 1972, 144).

Several recent commentators have suggested still another source for the enduring popularity of the Indian-as-orator image. Since Native American speech makers often employed what Wolfgang Hochbruck calls a "traditional rhetoric of humility" (Hochbruck 1992, 159), nineteenth-century appreciations of Indian eloquence identified the typical message of that eloquence, particularly that of the previous century, to be one of "decline and death" (Hochbruck 1992, 157). Some orators were perceived to be projecting the "vanishing American" stereotype that has pervaded United States official policy and mainstream culture since the 1700s (Dippie 1982). As one twentieth-century writer has suggested, "On every frontier Indian oratory was dominated by one prevailing characteristic. . . . [T]here was the refrain of grievous wrongs long suffered and the pathos of a passing race. Here a word, there a gesture, all pointing to the realization of nothing left in life for the individual or the group" (Aumann 1965, 251–52). This "plaintive, melancholy note" (Aumann 1965, 254) held considerable attraction for Euro-Americans since it both appealed to romantic melancholia and reaffirmed the Indians' acceptance of the inevitability of their displacement by the superior Western civilization which, though, could cite the Indian orators as evidence of an indigenous literary tradition distinct from any in the "Old World" (Hochbruck 1992, 155). In fact, such "elegiac Indian oratory" had become "a staple of the salons" even before the War for Independence (Stegner 1992, 256). It revealed Indians as facing their fated and appropriate displacement by Euro-American civilization with a sense of noble doom (Murray 1991, 35). Even in speeches wherein the orators explicitly regretted what was facing them—examples being the oft-reprinted words of Tahgahjute and, to cite a later instance, Sealth's purported address to Governor Isaac Stevens—the fact that they were doing so as self-identified "vanishing Americans" allowed Euro-Americans some relief from any guilt about displacing their predecessors upon the American landscape. If the victims of imperialism noted—and sometimes accepted—their fate with such eloquent nobility, that fate must certainly be part of some cosmic design (cf. Murray 1991, 36; Furtwangler 1997, 44–45).

I do not suppose that I have addressed all of the reasons that the Indian as orator has continued to grasp the imagination. These suggestions, though, may be indicative of what is probably an obvious observation: that most of the time the image has responded to the needs of the commentators and that we learn as much—undoubtedly more, in many cases—about them as we do about orators and their art from reading their accounts. Nevertheless, we can learn something about Native American oratory even from those whose own intellectual agendas may have obscured as much as illuminated what they encountered. Different kinds of commentators brought different preconceptions to their descriptions and attempts to textualize American Indian speech making. Among the most important categories of sources have been published proceedings of treaty negotiations between Native and colonial (later, state and federal) governments; accounts by secular explorers and travelers such as that of John Lawson, who surveyed the Carolinas in the 1710s; missionary reports such as those produced more or less annually by the Jesuits beginning with their mission in New France in the early seventeenth century and continuing through the late nineteenth century with the work of such figures as Pierre De Smet; captivity narratives, an example being that of the controversial John Dunn Hunter; the memoirs of soldiers, the recollections of Henry Timberlake and of John Gregory Bourke being cases in point; newspaper reports such as those in three New York City publications documenting Red Cloud's speech before the Cooper Institute in 1870; and early ethnographic and linguistic surveys, including the work of the Smithsonian researcher Frank Russell among the Pima. A look at each of these sources offers an overview of what the investigator of early American Indian oratory has to work with.

But if such sources are so infused with preconceptions and prejudicial intellectual constructs, why bother with them except as additional evidence that Europeans and Euro-Americans often inaccurately characterized the Native cultures they encountered? How can these sources serve us if our interest is in reconstructing the Native American oratorical traditions of the past? Perhaps amidst the useless and misleading material we will be able to glean from these records something that points toward a cross-cultural perspective on Native American oratory as it existed through the end of the nineteenth century, when many American Indian societies were still relatively intact or were trying to maintain their traditional identities in one of the only ways they could: through eloquence. By using more recent work on oratory done under the influences of such movements as the ethnography of speaking and ethnopoetics, we may be able to reinforce or amplify the older records. I do not pretend that these older records can be trusted implicitly, but I do not believe that they are utterly worthless. And whatever gold glimmers in the offal should be dredged out.

CHAPTER 2

SOURCES AND RESOURCES FOR NATIVE
AMERICAN ORATORY

W hatever their reasons for doing so, European and Euro-American commentators of various stripes have recorded a substantial body of information about North American Indian speech making from at least as early as the seventeenth century. This trove of data includes texts of speeches (usually in translation), descriptions of situations when and where speeches were delivered, and accounts of how orators executed their deliveries. Writers whose contacts with Indians emerged from a variety of causes produced material relevant to oratory. The purpose of this chapter is to survey and sample some of these disparate sources.

What the sources present are "texts," a term critical to Boasian anthropology, anthropological linguistics, folklore studies, and literary criticism. In recent scholarship, what constitutes a text has expanded in at least some of those disciplines. Traditionally, texts have been equated with the written or printed record of the verbal component of discourse in an indigenous language: "material dictated or recorded by a native speaker and member of the culture in the native language," according to the Boasian view (Codere 1966, xiv). The broader approach to text that has emerged recently sees texts in terms of "textualization"—defined by James Clifford as the process "through which unwritten behavior, speech, beliefs, oral tradition, and ritual come to be marked as a corpus, a potentially meaningful ensemble separated out from an immediate discursive or performative situation." He adds, "In the moment of textualization this meaningful corpus assumes a more or less stable relation to a context" (Clifford 1988, 38). In other words, textualization is the transmutation of dynamic action into static text. When the behavior is verbal, textualization becomes what Richard Bauman and Charles Briggs call "entextualization." They define their neologism as "the process of rendering discourse extractable, of making a stretch of linguistic production into a unit—a *text*—that can be lifted out of its interactional setting" (Bauman and Briggs 1990, 73). Viewed thus, *textualization* and its more precisely conceived kin *entextualization* represent more than the transcription of speech into written words. They are, in fact, an attempt to represent an event as holistically as possible. In the cases that we will be considering, the kind of event will be delivery of an oration, and the products of the ethnographic treatment of such an event might be better denominated "textualizations" or "entextualizations" than "texts" to emphasize that they should be more than simply transcription of the spoken words.

Though I incline toward salvaging what is usable from the sources instead of automatically dismissing them for their evident shortcomings, I hold—perhaps paradoxically—a rather stringent and idealistic view of what a record of oral expression should include (Clements 1996, 6–14). This view comes in large part from three sources: the ethnography of speaking, performance folkloristics, and ethnopoetics. None of the examples I will consider measures up to my rigorous expectations. These expectations are probably, in fact, unrealistic, especially given the inevitable ethnocentrism of the textualizers and the state of technology available to them. Yet that does not necessarily mean that they can contribute nothing toward our understanding of oral performances as they have occurred even as long ago as almost four centuries.

The ethnography of speaking (or communication) emerged as an approach to the study of discourse during the 1960s.[1] Its essential argument holds that an understanding of communication involves more than simply examining the message, what was said or written. Instead, a full appreciation of a speech "event" requires that one take into account all of its components. These might include, according to an analytical framework provided by Dell Hymes, one of the founders of the approach (Hymes 1974, 9–16), the participants in the event (in oratory, for example, the principal and secondary speakers and their audience), available channels of communication (primarily the verbal in oratory, but amplified by paralinguistic and kinesic devices as well perhaps as by accouterments from material culture such as mode of dress or badge of office), the codes the participants share (that is, the indigenous language and gestural system), the setting (the specific situation where and when the oration occurs such as intratribal council, treaty negotiation, or funeral), the genres used in the message (not comprehended by just the external term "oratory," but also by Native terminology for all the kinds of discourse that figure into the event), the subject matter (often the only feature of the event that survives recording, publishing, and reprinting), the context (by which I mean the cultural, intellectual, and emotional matrices that have influenced speaker[s] and audience), and the event as a holistic entity.[2]

Most important, then, the ethnography of speaking insists on a comprehensive approach to considering discourse, one that does not emphasize what is said at the expense of other components of the experience. This is a particularly important consideration in evaluating specific sources. Meanwhile, ethnographers of speaking appreciate the distinctiveness of each speech event. For example, recitations of the same ritual oration text by the same orator will be unique experiences no matter how punctiliously the speaker replicates what he says each time. Even in the unlikely case that the words are exactly the same, other components of the occasion will differ. The audience may not consist of the same individuals, the location may be changed, even such factors as the temperature of the surroundings will probably vary and consequently affect the nature of the experience.

An ethnographic approach to an oration treats it comprehensively and notes its distinctiveness. What one is recording when entextualizing an oration is an experience, and the textualizer's obligation is to represent that experience as completely and as vividly as possible. Moreover, some speech events will favor one of the components—not always the message, or subject matter (Hymes 1972, 37–38). A song performance may emphasize channel and code at the expense of message, for example. Cross-culturally, American Indian song is noted for its brevity, its repetitiveness, its use of vocables, and messages that translators often try to render almost as imagistic poetry. This explains the difficulty and, in fact, lack of success of most attempts to produce written ethnographies of singing. As some performances may emphasize something other than messages, representations of them may favor a component of the event other than the spoken words themselves. In singing, the "lyrics" represent only a small portion of the total experience, so the ethnographer may legitimately pay less attention to the singer's words than to other components of the event. Though message may be more central in oratory than in singing, a record of an oratorical event need not include an accurate rendition of *what* was said to have some ethnographic value.

Moreover, even an accurately rendered replication of the message does not by itself make for a fully adequate textualization. Representations of Native American verbal art by linguists, following a lead established by Franz Boas and his students, meticulously capture what the storyteller or orator said, but they often ignore or treat cursorily every other feature of the event when the saying occurred. Meanwhile, many earlier commentators on American Indian oratory—writers whose work is drawn upon here—have not been very successful at replicating the uttered words, but they may be able to provide descriptions of the performance situation, of audience responses, of cultural contexts, and of kinesic and paralinguistic dimensions of the orator's performance. If the textmaker provides such information about the participants in the event or about the event situation, the ethnographically oriented investigator of verbal expression should recognize the value of that information even if other data have not been satisfactorily preserved. Even when those elements are misunderstood, as was often the case with European and Euro-American attempts to document Native American oratory, thoroughly informed analysis can provide accurate appreciation as long as information to work with has been preserved.

Performance folkloristics developed from the ethnography of speaking in the late 1960s and early 1970s. Given its fullest synthesis by Richard Bauman (1984),[3] this approach to the study of verbal art begins from the ethnographic assumption that the unit of study is not the text but the performance, not the story but the "storytelling event" (Georges 1969). What is said is only a part of the artistic enactment. Though criteria for what constitutes "performance" must be culture-specific, generally the phenomenon occurs when a speaker assumes "responsibility to an audience for a display of communicative competence." Furthermore, the speaker holds him- or herself accountable to the audience "for the way in which the communication is carried out, above and beyond it referential content." Performance also occurs when participants in a verbal expressive event recognize it as "available for the enhancement of experience, through the present enjoyment of the intrinsic qualities of the act of expression itself" (Bauman 1984, 11). Every verbal expression does not constitute performance, and as Hymes has suggested, different degrees of performance can be identified according to the amount of esthetic commitment by the speaker (Hymes 1981, 80–86). In Bauman's terminology, performance is "emergent"; it is a product of unique combinations of resources at particular points in time (37–38).

This take on performance should remind ethnographers that not every telling of a story or delivery of a speech will manifest the full artistry of the relevant tradition and that, in fact, the artistry lies in the realization of the verbal expression at a particular time and place, not in any formal literary features that the verbalization may possess. Thinking in terms of performance leads to a "discourse approach" to verbal art (cf. Urban 1991). My position is that an ethnographer has an obligation to represent only what does occur in a specific situation, even if doing so may not represent the full artistic potential of which the expresser and his or her tradition are capable. This emphasizes what some might consider "surface poetry" at the expense of a "deep poetry" that endures through even the most truncated performance realizations (cf. Zolbrod 1995), but the ethnographic approach to entextualization (as opposed to or, better yet, complementary to a literary approach) holds that an accurate and comprehensive treatment of something less than a fully realized performance has more value than an ethnographer's speculations about what that fully realized performance should be, particularly if the ethnographer is an outsider to the tradition.

A probable example of the results of a textmaker's trying to create oratorical artistry where none may have existed in the original is the well-known, often-repeated "lament" attributed to the Mingo Tahgahjute (James Logan). Originally published in the *Virginia Gazette* and canonized by Thomas Jefferson in his argument against the dismissive treatment of western hemisphere phenomena by Comte de Buffon, this "speech" was apparently given privately by Tahgahjute to Colonel John Gibson to explain his refusal to sign the treaty ending Lord Dunmore's War. Though not performed publicly, Tahgahjute's words would not necessarily lack eloquence, but the presentation would have differed from a public address. In an analysis of the text, Thomas McElwain assumes that Tahgahjute would have spoken to Gibson in an Iroquoian language and that the English version that has survived would thus be a translation from that language (McElwain 2001, 113). Attempting to back-translate from that English, he finds that the diction cannot represent with any degree of reliability an Iroquois original. Hence, although Tahgahjute undoubtedly did deliver some sort of message to explain his position, the text that made its way into Jefferson's *Notes on Virginia* by way of the *Virginia Gazette* represents—as do so many other translations of Native American verbal art—little if any of what the speaker originally said.

But one need not assume that the source of the English text was misrepresenting Tahgahjute out of malignity—as McElwain does (116). It is just as likely that whoever was responsible for converting Tahgahjute's Iroquois message into the English that appeared in the *Gazette* was intent on providing it with an artistry that approximated his or her preconceptions about what such artistry should be. Making Indian speakers into verbal artists in a Euro-American mode provided justification in many editors' minds for liberties such as those that have apparently been taken with Tahgahjute's words (Clements 1996, 93–110). One might compare, for example, what has possibly happened to this "speech" to Henry Timberlake's rendering of a Cherokee war song in heroic couplets, the first "translation" of American Indian lyric poetry into English (Timberlake 1765, 56–58). The result is a text that many Europeans and Euro-Americans found attractive, but that does not necessarily represent what Tahgahjute said—except in very broad terms—and certainly nothing of how he might have said it. The proper role of the ethnographer of verbal art is to represent what was actually articulated, not to supply an esthetic that was not fully realized in the original rendering.

Ethnopoetics, the third major influence on the view of textmaking espoused here, focuses primarily on the message itself and sometimes on the channels through which it emerges and requires that the ethnographer try to capture the indigenous esthetic when verbal art is represented in print. As Hymes has put it, the ethnopoetically inclined entextualizer must first "work out a 'grammar' of the local world of discourse and work out the internal relations of a text in relation to that grammar" (Hymes 1985, 395). Joel Sherzer and Greg Urban have noted the typical features that help to identify Native South American discourse as "poetic": "the organization of discourse into lines and other units, the employment of forms of repetition, especially parallelism, to create verbal patterns, the use of such symbolic processes as metaphor, the dramatization of the voice, and the development of distinctive narrative styles" (Sherzer and Urban 1986, 3). Of course, specific groups may stress any of these features or select others as part of their oratorical esthetic, but this list suggests the kinds of matters that advocates of ethnopoetics must confront. Moreover, in American Indian contexts ethnopoetically oriented ethnographers often perceive their efforts as acts of multi-dimensional translation, for they not only have to render into English (or some other Indo-European language) something that was originally said in a Native American language, but also must transmute oral expression into printed text (cf. Fine 1984). Meanwhile, they should take into account the gulf of understanding that may separate the cultural assumptions that underlie the oral expression from those implicit in the consciousnesses of their potential readers. Attempts to ethnopoeticize have included the "total translation" of Jerome Rothenberg (1992), the "verse analysis" of Dell Hymes (1981), and Dennis Tedlock's representations of the tempo, dynamics, and timbres of speech through what has been called "pause phrasing" and typographic manipulation (1972)—to cite three of the more influential approaches. While not necessarily endorsing any of these particular ethnopoetic perspectives, I do recognize that the ideal representation should reflect the esthetic values of the verbal artist as fully as possible.

My ideal representation of a Native American oration, then, has these characteristics. First, it represents a particular verbal art event that occurred at a particular place and time. Before we can generalize an oratorical esthetic for a culture, we must understand and appreciate the importance of the components of specific enactments within that esthetic. While some of these components may figure into other (perhaps all) oratorical enactments in the culture, others likely will be unique and situation-specific.

Based on this initial requirement, I believe that this ideal representation of an oration should include the words of the message, rendered in a translation that favors the source language without ignoring the needs of readers of the target language. This translation should derive from a verbatim text in the original language, and its format should reflect the competence and indigenous artistry manifest in the particular enactment and only that enactment. This may yield a translation with false starts and hesitations that reflect the competence and confidence of the speaker on the particular occasion. It may also yield a translation filled with repetitions and other devices that stem from oral delivery. The orality of the original should also be reflected through signals that suggest the rhythm and pace of the speaker (probably through use of line breaks; cf. Sherzer 1990, 22–26); changes in tempo, pitch, and vocal timbre; and nonverbal components of the delivery. The more specifically this can be done, the more satisfactory the representation will be—as long as its reading accessibility is not irrevocably impaired. These are the features that Alan Dundes (1964) has characterized as "texture."

But the words of the speech are not the only (or necessarily the primary) feature of the ideal representation of verbal expression. I am also concerned that it include thorough description of the situation when and where the oration took place. This would encompass details about the nature of the audience (size and composition), their relationship to the speaker (psychologically, emotionally, and even spatially), a physical description of the venue (including visual, auditory, and olfactory features), and even such mundane details as the temperature and other conditions contributing to the ease and comfort of speaker and listeners.

Moreover, an ideal representation should be contextualized. By this I mean that it should be clearly placed within its cultural milieu. This would require providing background on the type of occasion when the oration occurred, on the relevant literary heritage (including generic identifications and definitions), on the socio-political milieu, and on the speaker (especially in terms of community reputation and position).

An ideal representation, then, would capture more than just the words spoken, no matter how "accurately" they were translated and how ethnopoetically their artistry was represented. An ideal act of entextualization is, of course, a kind of translation, but it involves a transfer of more than just linguistic content. It is a matter of representing in print an experience in a way that readers who were not a part of the experience can vicariously participate in it as fully as possible.

Even today few, if any published representations of Native American oratory measure up to my ideal. All entextualizations are "synecdochic" in relation to what they attempt to represent (Murray 1991, 44). But I believe that attempts that succeed in meeting some of my desiderata merit consideration. What this means is that value may lie in reports of oratory that do not present the words of the message effectively (or even at all) if they describe some of the other components of the ideal. This is why I believe that something useful can be found even in documentations of Native American verbal expression done in the less than optimum conditions for recording that have often characterized even the work of professional ethnographers. The following instances from the vast amount of potentially usable material on the subject produced during the "pre-ethnography-of-speaking, pre-performance-folkloristics, pre-ethnopoetics" era sample types of sources that students of American Indian public speaking might consider. They are intended to suggest what can be found even in less than ideal material and what must be known in order to identify what is valuable in it.

To do that requires a careful examination of each example with a view toward identifying those factors that may have influenced what and how the textmaker recorded what he or she did. Some features will be more or less constant: most examples involve Europeans or Euro-Americans whose command of the languages they heard was minimal or nonexistent, most did not have the observational skills that modern ethnographers acquire through training and experience, most did not have adequate methods for capturing what they heard on paper with much accuracy, and most were outsiders with little ability to overcome ethnocentric assessments of what they experienced. Some assumed adversarial stances toward the people whose oratory they were recording, and some had an eye toward exploiting those people. To such generalizations must be added, though, the specific intellectual constructs that shaped each record maker's view of oratory and of Indians.

In a previous work (Clements 1996) I have tried to demonstrate how this may be done in a range of Native American verbal art. Harry Robie has worked out a model for such investigation applied specifically to American Indian oratory. In an investigation of a speech attributed to the Seneca orator Sagoyewatha (Red Jacket), Robie has suggested four areas that the researcher interested in establishing the "authenticity" of a Native American oratorical text might examine: whether the orator was someone who might have had the skills to deliver the speech attributed to him or her, the credentials of the interpreter or translator, the publication history of the text, and whether the text conforms to the verbal art tradition of which it purports to be a part (Robie 1986, 100–101). Looking at the record of Sagoyewatha's speech from these four perspectives establishes its validity, and Robie has offered an excellent model to follow if one is concerned with oratorical message only. While I will adapt some of his procedures in the examples that follow, my interest in the totality of oratory as an event involving much more than message renders Robie's approach useful, but not comprehensive enough to address all the issues with which I am concerned.[4]

TREATIES

Europeans and Euro-Americans probably encountered formal oratory most frequently as a component of external diplomacy. Speech making almost invariably figured into treaty negotiations, for example. Native American diplomats assumed that they and their counterparts would be relying upon persuasive discourse to achieve the ends of treaties, since in many cases that is how their societies' internal political affairs as well as foreign relations were traditionally handled. While persuasion might occur most usually in clandestine circumstances in European diplomacy, at least some of it took place in public forums when Native Americans were involved. Few records of treaty negotiations fail at least to mention that speeches occurred. Many go further and preserve the gist, if not the translated text of the speeches, and very importantly they are likely to record the sense of an oration in relationship to the content of other speeches, thus enabling the student to see how a series of orations might operate in dialogic, dialectic response to one another.

Between 1736 and 1762 Benjamin Franklin printed thirteen folio versions of treaty proceedings involving representatives of the Commonwealth of Pennsylvania and delegates from the region's Native inhabitants, mostly members of the Six Nations of the Iroquois.[5] These represent, in Carl Van Doren's words, "diplomatic dramas in a form prescribed by Iroquois ritual" (Van Doren and Boyd 1938, x). Indeed, the protocols of the Condolence Ceremony seem to have been central to the shaping of treaty-making agendas, which often began with ritual cleansing of the spirits of all involved and declarations of mutual amnesty before the proceedings moved on to the specific matters at hand (Jones 1988, 186–87). The governor or commissioners of Pennsylvania would usually then open the negotiations with a speech consisting of several articles, each of which was presented with an accompanying wampum belt. The Indians would probably delay their response until the following day, the interim providing an opportunity to consider the issues and to determine who would answer the colonial spokesperson. The Native American orator would take up each article and offer the collective response, translated by an interpreter (Conrad Weiser, in most of the proceedings presented by Franklin) and recorded by the council's secretary. Van Doren suggests the degree of accuracy which these documents achieved: "Accuracy in such cases was art. Now and then the secretaries left out speeches or parts of speeches uttered by the hard tongues of the Indians, but there was not too much expurgation, and there was no literary self-consciousness" (Van Doren and Boyd 1938, xviii). Of course, we cannot know for sure how much secretaries might have omitted purposefully or by accident, but given Weiser's knowledge and reputation, we can assume that the translations were fairly close to what the Indian orators said. Weiser had learned the Mohawk dialect of the Iroquois language from extended contact with the Indians and served as the Commonwealth's principal interpreter throughout the mid–eighteenth century.

An example of Franklin's work that reveals the value of such documents for a consideration of Native American oratory is his rendering of "A Treaty Between the President and Council of the Province of Pennsylvania and the Indians of Ohio, Held at Philadelphia, Nov. 13, 1747" (Van Doren and Boyd 1938, 101–108).[6] The document begins by listing the individuals representing Pennsylvania who were present and notes that a delegation of ten Iroquois warriors from Ohio had appeared in the colony's capital rather unexpectedly. Anthony Palmer, president, summoned the delegation along with Weiser so that he and his councilors might hear what they had to "communicate." Franklin then presents a speech by someone identified by the secretary for the council, Richard Peters, only as the "principal Warrior," but whom we know to have been the Oneida leader Scarouady (Wallace 1945, 259–60), on "Behalf of ourselves, and the rest of the Warriors of the *Six Nations*."

The speaker begins by rehearsing the history of treaties of friendship between the English and the Six Nations and asserts that his people have "always preserv'd the Chain bright"—using a metaphor that had special resonance in diplomatic relations between the two groups going back to the previous century. He reminds the English that when hostilities had broken out between them and the French, they had urged the Indians to stay out of the conflict. The Six Nations had so acted because they believed the warfare would be confined to the sea. He continues,

> But some Time after this, Messengers were sent by all the *English* to *Onondago,* to tell us that the French had begun the War on the Land in the *Indian* Countries, and had done a great deal of Mischiefe to the *English,* and they now desired their Brethren, the *Indians,* would take up the Hatchet against the *French* [using another metaphorical commonplace], and likewise prevail with their Allies to do the same.

While the elders opposed Indian involvement in the conflict between the European colonial powers, the English had persuaded younger warriors to "lay their old People aside" and join the war on their side. But they had provided insufficient arms to those they desired for allies: "[W]e now come to tell you, that the *French* have hard Heads, and that we have nothing strong enough to break them. We have only little Sticks, and Hickeries, and such Things, that will do little or no service against the hard Heads of the *French*." The orator then presented a wampum belt to affirm the Indians' desire to receive the needed weapons from the English.

Next the speaker accuses the English of not pursuing their own cause with enough ardor and, in fact, expecting the Six Nations to carry out the war on their own:

> When once we, the young Warriors, engaged, we put a great deal of Fire under our Kettle, and the Kettle boil'd high, and so it does still *(meaning they carried the War on briskly)* that the *Frenchmens* Heads might soon be boil'd. But when we look'd about us, to see how it was with the *English* Kettle, we saw the Fire was almost out, and that it hardly boil'd at all; and that no *Frenchmens* Heads were like to be in it. This truly surprizes us, and we are come down on Purpose to know the Reason of it. How comes it to pass, that the *English,* who brought us into the War, will not fight themselves? This has not a good Appearance.

The speaker then offers another string of wampum "to hearten and encourage you, to desire you wou'd put more Fire under your Kettle."

A final point raised by the speakers seems something of an afterthought:

the situation of "old Scaiohady." Apparently, this refers to the Oneida leader Onkiswathetami (known as Skikellamy to the Pennsylvanians) who had been an important architect, along with Conrad Weiser and the important Pennsylvania official James Logan, of the 1736 treaty between the colony and the Six Nations (exclusive of the Mohawks). Skikellamy had received a wampum belt from Logan which guaranteed that his needs in old age would be supplied. The orator presented the belt so that the elder could receive his due.

The council adjourned following this speech to reconvene the next morning (14 November), but lack of a quorum prevented any action save giving instructions to Weiser to research the Indians' position more fully. Two days later Weiser presented his findings and urged the council at least to acknowledge the "Service done to the *English* by their seasonable Declaration in their Favour" and offer them presents valued at a minimum of a hundred pounds. At four o'clock that afternoon, the Six Nations delegation came to hear President Palmer respond to their demands. Palmer praised them for their activity against the French, explained the English hesitancy as arising from their delaying an invasion of Canada due to their prosecution of a maritime campaign against the French, promised that the English would be more active on land in the future, specified that presents would be offered to cultivate and improve relations, and guaranteed that Skikellamy would receive support in his old age. Palmer confirmed each point with wampum.

Richard Peters, the secretary who entered the document on 25 November 1747, concluded by noting the Native response to Palmer's remarks:

> The *Indian* Speaker having consulted with *Scaiohady,* took up the Belt and Strings of Wampum in the Order they were presented, and repeating the Substance of every Paragraph, express'd high Satisfaction at what the Council had said. . . . And in Testimony of their intire Satisfaction and Devotion to the *English* Interest, they gave the *Indian* Marks of Approbation, and danc'd the Warrior Dance.

The value of this document for the student of oratory is, I think, significant. Not only do we have as accurate a rendering of what the Native orator said as was possible at the time, but we have a clear idea of its intellectual and affective situation. We know precisely to whom he was speaking and what occasioned his words. We are also able to perceive the speaker's remarks—both those that are represented verbatim and those which Secretary Peters summarizes—as part of the series of events that made up this negotiation. While the influence of Conrad Weiser was certainly a factor in the outcome of the proceedings, which afforded the Indians what they wanted, we can see how a timely metaphor, the boiling kettle, played a role in the structure of the speaker's argument. That trope had ambiguous import in Iroquois oratory (Jennings et al. 1985, 119), but it seems generally to have represented warfare. For example, Cadwallader Colden reports the Iroquois orator Dekanisora having used it in that way (Colden 1958, 143). The resulting document reveals a dramatic dimension that has suggested to some commentators that treaty records were the first "national literature" of America (Wroth 1975).

Colden's *History of the Five Indian Nations* (originally published in 1727) provides another rich repository of examples of treaty negotiations with direct oratorical quotations that, in many cases, are unavailable elsewhere. His work focuses on negotiations between the League of the Iroquois and the colony of New York in the seventeenth century. Colden, who had been trained as a physician in Scotland before moving to Philadelphia in 1710, came to New York in 1718. Until his death in 1776, he was active in the colony's political affairs, serving as surveyor general, as adviser to Governors William Burnet and then George Clinton, and then as governor himself beginning in 1761. His history, which presents the Iroquois (still only Five Nations for the period he covered—roughly the last quarter of the seventeenth century) in a very favorable light (Jacobs 1973), carefully includes many examples of oratorical eloquence "[t]hat thereby the Genius of the Indians might better appear" (Colden 1958, x). He recognizes that much is lost from the record of that eloquence because of the nature of interpretation, which might have to go from the relevant Iroquois dialect first into Dutch and then into English. He characterizes the essence of the interpreter's problem—though also evoking the "poverty-of-language" conceit to which we will return in chapter 3:

> I suspect our Interpreters may not have done Justice to the Indian
> Eloquence. For, the Indians having but few words, and few complex
> Ideas, use many Metaphors in their Discourse, which interpreted by

an hesitating Tongue, may appear mean, and strike our Imagination faintly, but under the Pen of a skilful Interpreter may strongly move our Passions by their lively Images. I have heard an old Indian Sachem speak with much Vivacity and Elocution, so that the Speaker pleas'd and moved the Auditors with the manner of delivering his Discourse, which, however, as it came from the Interpreter, disappointed us in our Expectations. After the Speaker had employ'd a considerable time in Haranguing with much Elocution, the Interpreter often explained the whole by one single Sentence. (1958, xi)

Nevertheless, Colden offers the contemporary reader a wealth of examples of oratory—not only that of the Iroquois diplomats but of their British counterparts as well—within treaty-making settings.

One instance constitutes the eighth chapter of the second part of Colden's book, entitled "The Five Nations Treat with Captain Ingoldsby." Upon the death of Henry Sloughter, governor of New York, Richard Ingoldesby (rank apparently major), who headed the colonial infantry, assumed interim executive responsibility, a development that Colden views with disfavor. On 6 June 1692 Ingoldesby met with delegates of the Five Nations at Albany to ensure their continued support in the British struggles against the French, which have come to be known as King William's War. Most of the acting governor's introductory speech assumed a scolding tone as he chastised the Iroquois for not prosecuting the war against the French with enough enthusiasm and for being taken in by enemy proposals for peace. He stressed the perfidy of the French and emphasized that there could be no peace between British and French in North America as long as the two nations were at war in Europe.

Cheda, an Oneida *sachem,* offered an oratorical rejoinder immediately following the remarks by Ingoldesby, whom he addressed as "Corlear," the conventional title for the chief executive of New York. He began by asking that the governor not offer reproaches to his allies, who had also lost warriors to the French. Instead, he urged him to remember that British and Iroquois had "one Head, one Heart, one Interest, and are all ingaged in the same War." The Indians had no intention of accepting French terms of peace, Cheda averred, and he urged the British to carry out their military responsibilities as avidly as the Iroquois intended to do. He also noted a discrepancy: that the wealthy British, whose war they were fighting, had raised the price of powder for a nation so much smaller and poorer.

Moreover, Cheda wondered about the whereabouts of the British troops who would aid the Five Nations warriors in protecting the frontier from French incursions. He strongly asserted—reinforcing his words with a presentation of ten beavers—that the Five Nations intended to renew their covenant with the British and would preserve it "as long as the Sun shall shine in the Heavens." But he wondered again about the commitment of other colonists to war with the French and, in fact, expressed his fear that the British would be lured into a peace with their adversaries long before the Iroquois were. Nevertheless, despite the accusations that Cheda turned back upon Ingoldesby, he ended his oration by proclaiming unequivocally: "We now renew the old Chain, and here plant the Tree of Prosperity and Peace. May it grow and thrive, and spread its Roots even beyond Canada" (124–27).

Colden's book is essentially a political history, stressing the diplomatic relations between Indians and Europeans. He has little concern for the esthetics of oral presentation and consequently presents nothing in the way of performance description except for noting when Cheda reinforces a point by presenting beaver or otter hides or wampum belts. Nevertheless, he cannot escape from the artistry of Cheda's presentation. Metaphor figures prominently in the way in which the Oneida orator expresses himself, and he uses tropes that had become conventional in treaty negotiations: the covenant chain and the tree of peace. Something of the verbal artistry may have indeed survived the rigors of translation.

But in this case, that is not what is most valuable. In fact, Cheda's speech in and of itself must yield place—in a turn of analysis that recalls Lévi-Strauss on totemism—to its relationship to what precedes it. What we get regardless of the skill and sensitivity of the interpreter or the recorder is a picture of an adroit, politically astute oratorical mind at work. Whatever is rich and artful in Cheda's words becomes more so through our knowledge that he is manipulating the tropes of public speaking in a way that not only is defensively effective, but assumes the offensive when appropriate. Cheda shows that Ingoldesby's accusations lack merit and that the British have been acting with less than good faith in their treatment of the very people whom the governor of New York has chastised for not being loyal and ardent enough allies.

This point is, I think, of particular value to the student of the oratory of treaty negotiations, dauntingly dull though they sometimes may seem to be: it recalls that oratory is usually reactionary discourse, if not answering some action or inaction then responding directly to other oratory. Even when, as was often the case, the responsive speech may have come after a day's consultation with his peers, the orator represented in treaty documentation nevertheless revealed himself and his art within the context of diplomatic give-and-take. In treaty accounts, whose "official" status requires accuracy on the level of sense of the message if not on other levels, we get glimpses of the oratorical mind at work in its natural situation—responsively, sometimes spontaneously.

Accounts by Travelers and Explorers

Europeans traveled in North America and Euro-Americans traveled beyond their society's contact zone with what they regarded as "virgin land" for a variety of reasons. Some were simply in search of adventure, doing what corresponded more or less to the more effete and "civilized" Grand Tour of European centers of culture. Others traveled for commercial reasons, usually to generate trading partnerships with Native American communities. Even those who traveled ostensibly for the pursuit of knowledge, such as the Corps of Discovery led by Lewis and Clark, often had as one of their principal motives the exploration of potential routes for movement of commerce. Some travelers and explorers went to the "frontier" to prepare the way for immigrants by identifying and surveying "available" land for their settlement. Still others, with an eye on print and the lecture circuit, traveled in search of marketable topics to present to their readers or auditors.

Whatever their motives, travelers and explorers who had anything beyond the most cursory contact with Native Americans were likely to have something to say about oratory when they wrote up their comments. The journals of the Corps of Discovery, for example, contain numerous records of speech making by the orators whom Lewis, Clark, and their companions encountered (e.g., Thwaites 1959b, 1:131). Rufus P. Sage, who went west in the 1840s very literally in search of material for the lecture circuit, included several orations in the written account of his travels (Sage 1846, 57–60, 70–71, 100–101). The possibilities for sampling from the work of travelers and explorers are vast.

For an example we will turn to the travel narrative of John Lawson, whose ethnographic account of the southeastern Indians has drawn praise from recent historians (e.g., Diket 1966; Randolph 1973, 78, 88; Tate 1983, 300) and served as a source for ethnological overviews of Native southeasterners (Swanton 1946, Hudson 1976). Lawson came to North America sometime in 1700 and by the end of the year had joined a group of Europeans and Indians who set out from Charleston, South Carolina, heading north to the mouth of the Santee River. Turning inland, Lawson crossed what is now South Carolina and then traveled northeastward through North Carolina, completing a fifty-nine-day trek at the estuary of Pamlico Sound, near where he would later help found the communities of Bath and New Bern. During the next few years, Lawson served as deputy surveyor for the colony of North Carolina, work that took him into Indian country on several occasions. These experiences, together with what he had learned during his original travels, provided the material for *A New Voyage to Carolina,* which appeared in London in 1709. After a stint in England to see his book through to publication, Lawson returned to America as surveyor-general for North Carolina. He also assisted the organization of a Palatine settlement at New Bern and continued his explorations of the Carolina interior, encroachments that earned the hostility of the Tuscaroras. The Indians killed Lawson in 1711 while he was on a surveying expedition (Merrell 1989, 1–7; Randolph 1973, 78–79, 88).

Lawson's book consists of four parts: a journal of his 1701 travels; a general description of North Carolina, which presents data on the colony's topography, natural history, and contemporary economy; an overview of the colony's Native Americans, based on his thousand-mile journey in 1701 and his subsequent contacts as deputy-surveyor; and the text of the colony's second royal charter. For present purposes, the third section, which one modern commentator believes to be "the most complete and authoritative source" on the Indians of North Carolina (Savage 1979, 24), is of most interest, for Lawson devotes some seventy pages to accounts of various features of Native life, some generalized and some culture specific. Included is a lengthy description of an occasion for oratory.

"The Burial of their Dead," writes Lawson, "is perform'd with a great deal of Ceremony, in which one Nation differs, in some few Circumstances, from another, yet not so much but we may, by a general Relation, pretty nearly account for them all" (Lawson 1709, 179). He then proceeds to a generalized description of mortuary customs, apparently reflecting especially the practice of the Catawbas. After the deceased has been mourned by his near relations for a day or so, Lawson reports, the body is wrapped in cane or reed mats in anticipation of the public funeral. In attendance at this event are relations as well as everyone with whom the deceased had had some kind of association during his life. Our particular concern starts when "the Doctor or Conjurer" appears on the scene and silences the assembled mourners with "a sort of *O-yes.*" Then begins an "Indian *Funeral Sermon,*" which relates

> who the dead Person was, and how stout a Man he approv'd himself; how many Enemies and Captives he had kill'd and taken; how strong, tall, and nimble he was; that he was a great Hunter, a Lover of his Country, and possess'd of a great many beautiful Wives and Children, esteem'd the greatest of Blessings among these Savages, in which they have a true Notion.

The oration continues, "extolling the dead Man, for his Valour, Conduct, Strength, Riches, and Good-Humour; and enumerating his Guns, Slaves and almost every thing he was possess'd of." Following this panegyric, the funeral orator directs his discourse more specifically at the audience and urges them to emulate the departed so that they too will partake of the blessings of the afterlife with him: "the Enjoyment of handsome young Women, great Store of Deer to hunt, never [to] meet with Hunger, Cold or Fatigue, but every thing to answer his Expectation and Desire" (180).

Lawson refers to this part of the address as a "harangue" (a term frequently used for American Indian speech making and having some of the same opprobrious connotations that it has today). The speech continues as the orator "diverts the People with some of their Traditions, as when there was a violent hot Summer, or very hard Winter; when any notable Distempers rag'd amongst them; when they were at War with such and such Nations; how victorious they were; and what were the Names of their War-Captains." He confirms the historicity of his account by referring to a bunch of marked reeds, mnemonic devices to whose accuracy Lawson paid special attention (181). Other speakers follow the initial orator. Every "Doctor" present relates "one and the same thing." After the oratory, the ceremony continues with the interment of the body and subsequent mourning.

This account of funeral oratory does not present a "text"—that is, in the sense of a record that quotes directly a particular set of speeches delivered over the remains of a particular person at a specific time and place. Yet the essence of what an orator might say at what appears to be a generic funeral suggests how oratory may transcend situational specifics and its primarily persuasive function to reinforce foundational values. For the speech is not just an enumeration of the qualities of the deceased. It is also a rehearsal of tribal history (and probably myth) together with an admonition to the mourners concerning what they should do to attain eternal bliss. Clearly, they must adhere to the norms and subscribe to the values that permeate Catawba culture.

The orator whose performance Lawson describes is well placed to serve as a repository for cultural values. He is apparently someone who is attuned to the spiritual through mystical, shamanic experience, so he knows whereof he speaks. The past, which is not really the past, becomes present in ordinary reality, as it is always present in the nonordinary reality of what the historian of religions Mircea Eliade has called "sacred time" (Eliade 1959, 68-113). What Lawson has depicted is an instance of a "ritual oration," a term that has entered the lexicon of some commentators and anthologists (e.g., Bierhorst 1971).

Rituals were common occasions for oratory in the narrowest sense when a human speaker was addressing human listeners as well as for related forms of public speaking such as prayer or chant. European and Euro-American commentators were not as likely to report these latter forms probably because they encountered them less frequently. When they did report addresses made to spiritual beings, lack of understanding might color their descriptions. For example, the traveler H. M. Brackenridge evoked the satanic imagery characteristic of Puritan depictions of Native American culture when he described an Osage prayer he encountered in 1811:

> In the morning, before daylight, we were awakened by the most hideous howlings I ever heard. They proceeded from the Osages, among whom this is a prevailing custom. On inquiry, I found that they were unable to give any satisfactory reason for it; I could only learn, that it was partly devotional, and if it be true, as is supposed by some, that they offer worship only to the evil spirit, the orison was certainly not unworthy of him. I much doubt whether any more lugubrious and infernal wailings ever issued from Pandamonium itself. . . . I never had before, so good a conception of Virgil's fine description of that place of the infernal regions, set apart for the punishment of the wicked. (Thwaites 1966, 6:61–62)

While travelers such as Lawson might encounter oratory in ritual circumstances, they also discovered that situations that might not otherwise have been considered ceremonial at least by European and Euro-American outsiders could become ritualized through what an orator had to say. For example, the artist George Catlin, who traveled throughout the Missouri River Valley and the Plains during the 1830s, includes the translated text (restored "from partial notes and recollection") of an oration directed at him and his party after they had "been arrested by the Sioux" (Catlin 1841, 2:172). At issue was a proposed visit by the group of which Catlin was a part to the pipestone quarry in what is now Minnesota. Te-o-kun-hko ("The Swift Man")—characterized as one of the "copper-visaged advocates of their country's rights"—raised concerns about Euro-American interest in this important site. He believed Catlin's group had been sent by the federal government to survey the quarry for possible purchase. His objections to this impending deal involved an oratorical invocation of sacred time: "[T]his red pipe [fashioned from clay from the quarry] was given to the red men by the Great Spirit—it is a part of our flesh, and therefore is great *medicine*" (2:172). The reference to a past when a special relationship between Indians and spiritual beings had been forged reminds the audience that such a relationship remains valid, that what happened in sacred time continues to happen.

What we can learn from these examples is how ritual and oratory might come together in Native American life: sometimes oratory was a conventional component of ritual, sometimes oratory might be specifically directed at the spiritual forces to whom ritual was intended to appeal, sometimes oratory served to ritualize an event by contextualizing it within a group's foundational values. In these cases, oratory became "ritual oratory"—one means of accessing the timelessness of sacred time and thus restoring people to a sense of oneness with the cosmos and of supplying them with spiritual power that could be derived only from the past. Though the verbal texts are questionable (and, in the examples from Lawson and Brackenridge, nonexistent), these travelers' accounts afford an opportunity to consider the relationship between oratory and the sacred in Native American cultures, a relationship that continues to figure into accounts of oratorical discourse by ethnographers (e.g., Dauenhauer and Dauenhauer 1990; Foster 1974). Though travelers such as Lawson, Brackenridge, and Catlin may have lacked the cultural and linguistic sensitivity to represent fully and accurately what was said, their accounts provide timely (albeit ethnocentric) depictions of the general and particular situations that might call for oratory. Each account by traveler or explorer must be considered on its own terms, but at least Lawson's, and perhaps Catlin's, should receive high marks for their representations of situation and context.

MISSIONARIES' REPORTS

Without a doubt the most comprehensive ethnographic treatment of Native Americans and their cultures, including the verbal art of oratory, written by missionaries appears in the series of volumes known as the *Jesuit Relations*. Submitted more or less annually by the superior of the Society of Jesus' mission in New France, the *Relations* derive from the reports that came to him from his charges, who were spreading the Gospel to the Algonquians and Iroquoians primarily in what is now southern Canada and western New York state. The *Relations* contain plenty of information on oral expression, especially oratory, and the value of what the Jesuits recorded for ethnographic and literary purposes has received some attention (e.g., Clements 1996, 53–72). Moreover, ethnohistorians have used the Jesuit documents as bases for reconstructing the nature of treaty making, including the requisite speeches, between Europeans and Native Americans during the colonial period (e.g., Jennings et al. 1985). Because commentators have already examined and employed these Jesuit materials from New France so extensively, I will turn elsewhere for a missionary example.

Because the Jesuit perspective on missionary work lent itself particularly to the relatively sympathetic depiction of many aspects of Native American cultures, including some kinds of verbal art, I will consider the records of another member of the Society of Jesus, Pierre De Smet, who evangelized to groups in the Plateau and Northern Plains culture areas during the middle third of the nineteenth century.

De Smet, a native of Belgium, arrived in Saint Louis in 1823 as a novitiate. He took his vows the following year and was ordained to the priesthood in 1827. His work in the Missouri city included teaching and particularly serving as the order's treasurer. In 1834 he made the first of many fund-raising trips back to Europe but, because of ill health, asked to be released from the Jesuits the following year. However, his return to the laity was shortlived, for he went back to Missouri in 1837, again as a novitiate. His first foray into Indian Country came soon after he was readmitted to the Society of Jesus, and he then began a lifelong career of attempting to raise money to support Indian missions.

In 1840 De Smet was part of the first mission to visit the Flatheads (Killoren 1994, 46–69). The oration that I am going to discuss, one of many that he noted during extensive contacts with Plateau and Northern Plains tribes which lasted until his death in 1873, occurred on this visit.

The intellectual baggage De Smet carried with him into the wilderness included ideas about "savage" humanity that had characterized Jesuit missions in New France and especially in Paraguay. Essentially, their attitude held that non-Europeans need not totally abandon their indigenous cultures to become Christians. The spirit behind much Jesuit missionizing stressed that even non-Christians might be living rational lives in a "state of pure nature." Individuals existing in this condition were, like all humanity, sullied by original sin, consequently fallen, and as yet unredeemed by acceptance of Christianity. But they did possess reason, were capable of practicing a degree of virtue based on that faculty, and, most important for the Jesuit argument, had the potential for accepting their Gospel teachings.

Moreover, Jesuit anthropology held out the possibility of a worldwide, pre-Mosaic revelation, traces of which might still be found in the religious beliefs and practices of Native Americans and other non-European peoples. Also, Jesuit acceptance of probabilistic ethics allowed them to posit that some Indian behaviors, while distasteful to their own European sensibilities, might be regarded as moral from an indigenous cultural perspective (Clements 1996, 59–60). Finally, Jesuits and other Roman Catholic missionaries may have been more accepting of Native ceremonialism than their Protestant counterparts because their own liturgies had such a rich tradition of ceremony. In fact, one biographer of De Smet has attributed his success in establishing rapport with various Native American communities to his willingness to endure ritual protocols: "With a patience that was more than tolerance he accommodated himself to prolonged oratory and lengthy preliminary feasting" (Killoren 1994, 57).

Thus intellectually equipped and encumbered, De Smet set out on his first missionary adventure. The party of which he was a member left Westport, Missouri, on 30 April 1840. Numbering about forty and led by Andrew Drips, an American Fur Company agent, they followed the recently demarcated Oregon Trail to Fort Laramie. De Smet crossed the Rocky Mountains for the first time at South Pass in late June and spent a few days at the annual Green River Rendezvous. In early July, his party headed farther into the wilderness and arrived at Pierre's Hole, west of the Teton Mountains, where they came upon a considerable encampment of Flatheads and Pend d'Oreilles.

This first encounter between De Smet and the Indians among whom he would be establishing his first mission began auspiciously. In an epistle addressed to a former missionary who had retired to Ghent, De Smet noted that the encampment had anticipated his arrival. About sixteen hundred men, women, and children welcomed him, many of them eager to shake his hand: "The elders wept with joy, while the young men expressed their satisfaction by leaps and shouts of happiness" (Chittenden and Richardson 1905, 1:223). This multitude escorted the missionary to Big Face (also known as Bear Looking Up or Standing Grizzly Bear), a man of "truly patriarchal aspect" (1:223). This tribal elder, who apparently died soon after De Smet's arrival (Teit 1930, 377), received the Jesuit "in the midst of his whole council with the liveliest cordiality" (Chittenden and Richardson 1905, 1:223). Part of Big Face's welcome consisted of an oration, which De

Smet conveyed to his correspondent "word for word, to give you an idea of his eloquence and his character":

> Black-robe, you are welcome in my nation. Today Kyleeeyou (the Great Spirit) has fulfilled our wishes. Our hearts are big, for our great desire is gratified. You are in the midst of a poor and rude people, plunged in the darkness of ignorance. I have always exhorted my children to love Kyleeeyou. We know that everything belongs to him, and that our whole dependence is upon his liberal hand. From time to time good white men have given us good advice, and we have followed it; and in the eagerness of our hearts, to be taught everything that concerns our salvation, we have several times sent our people to the great Black-robe at St. Louis (the bishop) that he might send us a Father to speak with us. - Black-robe, we will follow the words of your mouth. (1:224)

In evaluating this text, for which De Smet offers no more commentary, we should note a couple of points that make it immediately suspect. On one hand, De Smet was hearing it through an interpreter, so his testimony that it is "word for word" must be taken with some skepticism. Meanwhile, much of the content reflects the sort of monotheistic consciousness that De Smet and others who were interested in promoting Indian missions and who accepted the Figurist position of a universal revelation would try to found upon even the slightest intimations.

The problem with the intermediation of an interpreter must color this document (as it does most other early reports of Native American discourse), but before dismissing the speech altogether for that reason, we should note that the Flatheads had, in fact, been exposed to Christianity long before De Smet's visit. The first contact may have come as early as the late eighteenth century, when Iroquois who had been trained by Jesuits at their Caughnawaga Mission came into Flathead country to trap for the Hudson's Bay Company (Frisch 1978). Early Euro-American explorers such as David Thompson and Jedediah Smith may have contributed to Flathead knowledge of Christianity as did Canadian trappers, one of whom, François Rivet, began living among the Flathead in 1809. "Because they generally regarded white men as brave, and because these men had been places and seen things the Flathead had not," according to one historian,

"the Indians probably felt the trappers were protected by powerful super-
natural guardians" (Fahey 1974, 67). Moreover, the Hudson's Bay Company had sent several Native American youths to study Christianity at Fort
Gary (now Winnipeg, Manitoba) in 1825. One of them, who came to be
called Spokane Gary, returned in 1829 and preached throughout the Plateau
(Walker and Sprague 1998, 144). In 1831 a party of Flatheads and Nez
Perces had tried to reach Saint Louis to request that missionaries be sent to
them. Though that attempt failed, the Flatheads had at least cursory contact
with Christian missionaries throughout the rest of the decade. Moreover,
they sent at least two other delegations to St. Louis (in 1835 and 1837), and
De Smet himself had received one such delegation in 1839 while he was at
St. Joseph Mission (Fahey 1974, 66–70; Teit 1930, 385–86).

Flathead oral tradition has identified another source of the group's pre-
Jesuit receptivity to Christian teachings, the prophecies of Shining Shirt, a
chief and shaman who had supposedly appeared among the Flathead or
perhaps the neighboring Kalispel prior to De Smet's arrival. According to
Harry Holbert Turney-High's informant, who was alleged to be over a
hundred years old when the anthropologist interviewed him in the 1930s,
Shining Shirt dated from "long before his grandfather's birth" (Turney-
High 1937, 41)—presumably, then, from the end of the eighteenth century.
While reiterating the traditional Flathead cosmogony, Shining Shirt had
indicated that their knowledge of the creator god was yet undeveloped.
They could expect further insight "when men with fair skins dressed in long
black skirts would come who would teach them the truth" (41). The Black-
robes would prescribe laws, rename the people, and convert them to a new
way of life. As a token of its validity, the "Power" that revealed this future to
Shining Shirt gave him "a talisman of terrific strength": an amulet inscribed
with a cross (41–42).

Most likely, of course, this account exemplifies what Jarold Ramsey has
called "retroactive prophecy" (Ramsey 1983, 152–65), since by the time
Turney-High collected his data the Flatheads had been hearing the Christian message directly from Jesuits and other missionaries for some three
generations. But it or similar prophecies were in circulation in the 1840s, or
it may represent folk memory of pre-missionary exposure to hints of Christianity heard from the trappers and traders mentioned above. Certainly it
suggests that a Flathead in the 1930s would not necessarily have questioned

the authenticity of the content of Big Face's speech to De Smet. There seems little doubt that by the time the Jesuit missionary reached them in 1840, the Flatheads had absorbed enough Christianity to enable Big Face to speak as he did.[7] It seems reasonable to accept the content of the speech as reported by De Smet as generally accurate (even if not "word for word"), not totally the result of the Blackrobe's wishful desire or manipulations to impress potential European supporters of his mission.

Moreover, the situation for the speech as described by De Smet is plausible. Traditions among many Native American groups, including the Flatheads, prescribed that visitors be welcomed with oratory. Alexander Ross, who helped to establish John Jacob Astor's Pacific Fur Company, described such an occasion involving Indians whom his party encountered at the mouth of the Walla Walla River:

> But in the midst of our perplexity we perceived a great body of men issuing from the camp, all armed and painted, and preceded by three chiefs. The whole array came moving on in solemn and regular order till within twenty yards of our tent. Here the three chiefs harangued us, each in his turn; all the rest giving, every now and then, a vociferous shout of approbation when the speaker happened to utter some emphatical expression. The purport of these harangues was friendly, and as soon as the chiefs had finished they all sat down on the grass in a large circle, when the great calumet of peace was produced, and the smoking began. (Ross 1849, 126)

Though he does not mention oratory as part of the occasion, Ross Cox reported that his group had been "quite charmed" with the "frank and hospitable reception" they had received from the Flatheads more than a decade before De Smet heard Big Face's welcoming speech (Cox 1832, 102). What Big Face's speech may show is the flexibility of this welcoming custom, its adaptability to the specific situation. Presumably, the references to the "Great Spirit" would more likely characterize a speech welcoming a Blackrobe than one greeting a trader or other commercial traveler.

Traditional forms with the flexibility to accommodate innovative ideas provide the basis for the ways in which many Native American cultures have incorporated Christianity into their systems of belief and behavior. A very relevant case of such syncretism among the Flathead was reported by Verne Dusenberry, who related a ghost story that a priest had heard from a Flathead apparently soon after the narrated incident occurred in 1912. The story, which Dusenberry labels "a curious blend of primitive and Christian belief" (Dusenberry 1959, 156), tells how an Indian on his way to a wake passed an abandoned dwelling. The soul of the former inhabitant, who had been dead for several years, accosted the passerby, begging him to take care of some unpaid debts so that the deceased might enjoy some peace. While the story could be the product of a purely Christian belief construct, Dusenberry argues that it also reflects pre-Christian notions about the soul extant among the Flatheads and neighboring Salish-speaking groups (157–59). Similarly, Big Face easily blended the traditional practice of welcoming oratory with the intimations of Christianity that had already entered the Flatheads' world view and with their decade-long interest in attracting missionary attention.

Even though its verbal component is available to us only through De Smet's recollection of what an interpreter translated for him, Big Face's speech does suggest the flexibility and adaptability of oratory as genre. While formulas certainly figured into probably all oratorical performances in every ethnic context (perhaps, for example, Big Face's opening statement of welcome), and while some oratorical occasions required relatively rigid structures and contents (for instance, the Iroquois Condolence Council [Foster 1974]), the skilled public speaker also had available a tradition on which he or she could draw to meet the particular needs of a variety of situations. No doubt, Big Face had welcomed delegations of Nez Perce allies against presumed Blackfeet hostilities with words much different from those used for the Blackrobe, but he was nevertheless working within a customary framework, which De Smet may have reported with as much accuracy as his linguistic deficiencies and lack of mechanical recording equipment made possible. The value of De Smet's report lies in its revelation of the potential malleability of traditional oratory in what might be considered nontraditional circumstances.

Captivity Narratives

One would think that that important genre of early American literature, the captivity narrative, would offer useful material on Native American oratory.

Published even into the twentieth century, these works—which might run to an article-length few pages or extend to book length—recounted the experiences of individuals who lived in enforced intimacy with Indians, sometimes, if their captivity lasted long enough, becoming virtual members of their communities. Since occasional writers of these stories had become captives while they were children, much of their enculturation had been on Native American terms. They had learned the languages and the protocols for their use very early in life. Undoubtedly even those who became captives as adults and whose experiences spanned only a few months had opportunities to encounter oratory in situations where no other Euro-Americans were likely to be present, and for captives whose time with Indian groups extended over long periods of their lives, familiarity with relevant cultural modalities could attune them to oratorical nuances that even the most sensitive ethnographer might misconstrue.

In fact, occasional oration texts and more frequent depictions of oratorical performances do appear in captivity narratives. For example, Mary Rowlandson, who spent some twelve weeks with the Narragansetts in 1676, wrote a brief description of how her captors responded to oratory that preceded their going to war: "[A]t the end of every sentence in his speaking, they all assented, humming or muttering with their mouthes, and striking upon the ground with their hands" (VanDerBeets 1973, 76). Peter Williamson, taken captive by either Shawnees or Lenapés in 1754, wrote of how orators incorporated accounts of their experiences when speaking at festive occasions: "[I]n all their festivals and dances, they relate what successes they have had, and what damages they have sustained in their expeditions; in which I now unhappily became a part of their theme" (VanDerBeets 1973, 223). Charles Johnston, captured in 1790 and remaining among the Indians for some five weeks, gave a more detailed account of the performance style of a Shawnee orator: "An old chief of that tribe took a position at one end of the line of fire, and harangued the party for ten or fifteen minutes. He frequently raised his eyes and pointed to the sun, sometimes to the earth, and then to me." Discomfited by the speaker's singling him out, Johnston found comfort when another Indian informed him that he was simply being claimed as his special prisoner by the "old chief" (VanDerBeets 1973, 257).

While these cursory references are valuable (perhaps as much so as those in other kinds of sources), one should nevertheless view with some circumspection any attempts in captivity narratives to reproduce the text of an oration. Though authors who had been captives may have had some advantages in their opportunity to observe and sometimes to participate in tribal cultures closely, they were almost invariably writing after the fact. Years might pass between when a captive heard a speech and the composition of his or her narrative. While one may encounter similar time spans between event and publication in the works of travelers and others, those authors may have availed themselves of the opportunity to keep journals and notebooks from which they were working as they composed for publication. Captives rarely had resources in either time or materials to keep journals of their imprisonment. It was a rare captive who, like Charles Johnston, managed to maintain a contemporary record of the experiences he or she was undergoing. Regarding his journal, Johnston recalled, "I was very imperfectly provided with the means of accomplishing my purpose. A copy of the Debates of the Convention of Virginia . . . was found in one of the boats taken on the Ohio. . . . [O]n the margins of its pages I determined to write my notes. The quill of a wild turkey was the best I could procure, of which I made a pen with a scalping knife. I furnished myself with ink by mixing water and coal dust together, and began my daily minutes of our progress and its incidents" (VanDerBeets 1973, 265–66). Few of those taken prisoner by Indians were as resourceful or as fortunate as Johnston.

Moreover, former captives seldom wrote approvingly of Indian behavior. Recalling their sufferings—which might include not only their own imprisonment but also the capture, torture, and death of family members and friends—captivity narrators often depicted Native Americans in terms that minimized their common humanity. With opinions shaped by such forces as a Puritan anthropology (in the case of Mary Rowlandson, for example) that identified Indians with the demonic forces that opposed the establishment of a "city set on a hill" in New England and perhaps shaped by a fear of succumbing to the temptations of savagery (Slotkin 1973), recounters of their own captivities had little trouble in dismissing oratory or other signs of Indian humanness as aberrations. If they recognized any artistry in American Indian speech making, most would definitely identify rhetorical flourishes with the glibness of a loquacious Satan.

Because the captivity narrative remained a particularly popular genre of literary expression well into the nineteenth century even after the threat of capture by Indians at least in the eastern states waned, some writers continued to capitalize on the market that still existed for tales of imprisonment among the Indians. But such tales had to be convincing. Among the marks of authenticity that a writer might employ were careful descriptions of "manners and customs" of the communities in which they were imprisoned.[8] Since other published accounts of Native American life—those of travelers and missionaries, for example—emphasized oratory as an important feature of Indian verbal culture, writers of captivity narratives may have been tempted to include descriptions and even texts of speeches for the purpose of fulfilling reader expectations and of establishing firmly their own claims to be taken seriously even when they themselves had scanty knowledge of instances of this verbal art.

A captivity narrative especially interesting to students of Native American oratory is that of John Dunn Hunter, first published in 1823. The author claimed to have been taken captive by the Osage as a very young child of two or three years. He had no memory of life on Euro-American terms and thus had received most of his early enculturation among the Indians. He knew their ways as if he were an Osage himself. When he returned to Euro-American society in 1816 as a young adult, he had essentially lived his whole life as an Indian. Certainly this perspective would be valuable to students of virtually any aspect of the cultures he had encountered on such an intimate basis. Another positive feature about his story, entitled in its third and most complete manifestation *Memoirs of a Captivity Among the Indians of North America, from Childhood to the Age of Nineteen,* is its essentially sober tone. It lacks the sensational portrayals of gory bloodletting that characterize many examples of the genre and probably accounted, in part at least, for their enduring appeal. Instead, Hunter relates his story in a matter-of-fact manner. Moreover, in a marked departure from the conventions of captivity narration, instead of demonizing his captors, he tends to portray them in very human terms. Apparently, he was motivated to publish by his desire to set the record straight about the Indians, and his London publisher was certainly attracted to the memoir's potential role in contrasting the inhumanity of United States Indian policy with the humanity of the victims of that policy. Like some missionary accounts of Indian life and unlike most captivity narratives, Hunter's story required him to depict the people among whom he claimed to have lived most of his life as positively as possible. As missionaries wanted to attract donors to their cause, Hunter wanted to appeal to his readers for support in schemes he was developing to ameliorate the condition of the Indians.

As captivity narratives go, then, Hunter's memoir seems to have real potential for the student of Indian culture, including oratory. The work's drawback, though, damns it, for the book's authenticity was challenged soon after it was published and continues to remain in doubt. Perhaps one can dismiss most of the contemporary charges leveled by Lewis Cass in a review of Hunter's book that appeared in the *North American Review* in 1826. Though recognized by his contemporaries for his knowledge of Native American life, Cass held extremely negative views of Indians. His role in formulating and implementing the federal policies that British readers were using Hunter's book to criticize ensured that his reading of that book would suffer from bias. Most contemporary critics of Hunter—including novelist John Neal and linguist P. S. Duponceau—were similarly suspect, as Richard Drinnon, Hunter's most vociferous advocate in recent years, has demonstrated (Drinnon 1972, 95–152).

But what continues to impugn the truth of Hunter's work is the lack of confirmation of details of his experience which do indeed challenge credulity. Perhaps the most difficult to accept for many readers is his account of a trip that he claims to have made in the company of his Osage companions (for they were not really captors from his perspective by this time) to the Pacific Ocean.[9] Another detail, more relevant to present concerns, also seems to undercut the book's reliability. Hunter presents a concretely specific account together with a complete text of an oration delivered by Tecumseh to the Osages apparently about 1812. On first consideration (assuming indeed that Hunter's work is not the fabrication that Cass and others claimed it to be), this appears to be a valuable resource for the student of Native American oratory. More careful examination, though, suggests that it may be suspect and that its doubtful status contributes evidence to the case against Hunter's memoirs.

According to Hunter, at a time when the Osage were receiving considerable encouragement even by some Euro-Americans to "take up the tomahawk against the traders," Tecumseh, accompanied by his brother Tenskatawa (The Prophet), paid them a visit. The Shawnee statesman's intent was to enlist the Osage in a confederation of American Indian groups that would pose a much more potent barrier to further Euro-American incursions than each group could do on its own. Noted for his oratory (a trait that virtually every commentator except Lewis Cass praised in Tecumseh), he used his rhetorical skills to work upon the Osages. Hunter's description is thorough. He sets the scene for the event, describes how the audience responded to Tecumseh's "harangue," and depicts in general terms the paralinguistic devices used by the Shawnee speaker: "[S]uch language, such gestures, and such feelings and fullness of soul contending for utterance, were exhibited by this untutored native in the central wilds of America, as no audience, I am persuaded, either in ancient or modern times ever before witnessed" (Hunter 1973, 28). Hunter even presents Tecumseh's words, indeed a rarity in captivity narratives. Though the "discourse made an impression on my mind, which, I think, will last as long as I live," he said, Hunter admitted that he could not repeat the Shawnee's words verbatim. Nonetheless, he includes an oratory text running for more than a dozen paragraphs, set in quotation marks, and characterized by such artistic devices as the parallelism and figurative language that admirers of American Indian speech making had conventionally lauded. The effect is not that of outline, summary, or paraphrase; it is that of the exact words that Tecumseh had spoken.

This seems to be an invaluable resource. Of course, a number of other presentations of Tecumseh's oratorical discourse are available, but none that I know of represents speeches that he made exclusively to other Indians. Invariably they recount the Shawnee's words in response to treaty or other negotiations with Euro-Americans, who were his principal audience. Though I do not believe that the speeches that Indians made in such circumstances had to be substantively different from those they made in situations involving only other Native American groups, we cannot really know without the sort of record that Hunter's account of Tecumseh's speech to the Osages purports to be.

Some authorities seem to have more or less accepted Hunter's report at face value, or at least they have not overtly challenged it. For example, Carl F. Klinck, whose purpose was to offer up documentary accounts of Tecumseh without speculating on their reliability, includes the Hunter material with only the slight disclaimer that the author "*claimed* . . . that he had been present" on the occasion of Tecumseh's speech to the Osages

(Klinck 1961, 104–107). The strongly partisan Richard Drinnon correctly dismisses Lewis Cass's objections to the authenticity of the speech, since the general's case arose out of his belief, seconded by few if any other sources, that Tecumseh was not oratorically equipped to deliver a speech of this quality (Drinnon 1972, 70–72). But that Cass had criticized it for the wrong reason impugns Cass; it does not necessarily substantiate the speech. I believe there are several good reasons to doubt the authenticity of Hunter's entextualization.

The most obvious point against it is the very thoroughness of the account. Klinck dates the speech in 1811 or 1812. Hunter at the time was perhaps ten or so years old. He did not re-emerge into Euro-American society until 1816, five or six years later—at which time only did he begin to learn the English language. His memoir was published in 1823. Though one grants that Hunter recognizes the lack of feasibility in his having remembered the exact words of the speech after more than ten years, during which he had undergone intense culture shock and an amazingly rapid and complete assimilation into Euro-American culture, the reader has to note the effect of the quotation marks and of the stylistic mannerisms—what had become the stereotypical "Indianness" of the words. I would suggest that those features of the speech more likely came from written works praising Indian eloquence than from what Tecumseh might actually have said. I would be much more comfortable about Hunter's account if he had presented a summary, the essence of what he recalled, rather than passing off— despite protestations to the contrary—what he intends the reader to take as Tecumseh's words. Though similar charges could be leveled against other writers who have presented what they intend their readers to accept as the exact words of Indian orators, at least the possibility exists that they were working from notes made by themselves or by interpreters. No such possibility exists for Hunter's text.

Another difficulty I have in accepting the reliability of what Hunter reports lies in the historical record. Hunter's account seems to be the only basis for Tecumseh's visit to the Osages. Though a number of the Shawnee leader's biographers have mentioned the Osage visit, their sole authority is John Dunn Hunter. R. David Edmunds dismisses the Osage visit as "unsubstantiated" and characterizes Hunter's report of it as "spurious." In fact, Edmunds asserts, at the time the visit is supposed to have occurred, the

Osages were at war with two of Tecumseh's strongest allies, the Pota-watomis and the Kickapoos (Edmunds 1984, 218–19). Though another recent Tecumseh biographer (Sugden 1998) accepts the account as valid, Hunter's portrayal of the reception the Osages gave to the friend of their enemies remains questionable. Even though Hunter reports that the Osages turned down Tecumseh's request that they join his alliance against Euro-American incursions, he has them receiving the Shawnee more favorably than would probably have been the case given the enmity between them and his current allies, even if one factors in the obligations of hospitality.

However, the factor that most seriously calls into question the authen-ticity of Hunter's account arises from less substantive causes. In many ways, this captivity narrative breaks with the genre's conventions. Its relative lack of gory violence and the favorable attitude toward the Indians depart from the expectations of readers who had come to expect both titillation and confirmation of their ethnic presuppositions. In fact, captivity narratives most likely emphasized material that met conventional expectations. Some may have even invented material from whole cloth. It is clear that Hunter did not feel the need to do this, but he was preparing something other than a conventional captivity narrative. His work is much more in the tradition of those works that cast Indians—or at least some of them—as Noble Savages who were not only the victims of European expansionism but also represen-tatives of a common humanity shared by all. That Hunter had been influ-enced by Enlightenment and Romantic literature is evident. In fact, Drin-non has shown how one passage in the work most likely draws upon Charles Brockden Brown's novel *Edgar Huntly* (Drinnon 1972, 107).

When treating Native Americans as Noble Savages, writers frequently had recourse to their oratorical prowess. As noted in chapter 1, "natural eloquence" could be a mark of essential humanity, especially that which could be found uncorrupted by institutional existence. If Hunter's intended audience were those who had read *Edgar Huntly* and who would read James Fenimore Cooper's Leatherstocking novels, they would expect the Indians to be eloquent. Thomas Jefferson himself had established the speech-making facility of Native American orators as clear evidence of their com-parability with the best in European culture.

Hunter obliged with the requisite oratorical material. He could wax as effusive as anyone about the unstudied rhetorical powers of his captors:

"They resort much to figures, which are generally poetic, bold, and appropriate: in fact, if I am a competent judge, their eloquence is more persuasive, lofty, and commanding, and their orators far more numerous, in proportion to numbers, than is common among any class of people on the globe" (97). And Tecumseh is not the only specific verbal artist of whom he makes note. Hunter refers to the "sage counsels, inspiring narratives, and traditionary tales" that he and other boys heard from Tshut-che-nau (15), for example, and to the experience of Tare-heem, who entered the rank of orators after achieving a reputation for leadership in the field (51).

The burden of demonstrating Native American natural eloquence in specific terms fell upon the Tecumseh material, however, and that material was particularly well suited to make Hunter's point. After all, most readers would not know Tshut-che-nau or Tare-heem, nor would they necessarily accept Hunter's rhapsodies about the general nature of Indian verbal art as authoritative, particularly given his recent and precipitous immersion in European and Euro-American culture. But Tecumseh was well known, and part of his reputation had come from his oratorical abilities. For example, an unsigned essay published in *The Knickerbocker* in 1836 cited Tecumseh's speech answering William Henry Harrison at negotiations at Vincennes, Indiana Territory, in 1810 as evincing the "characteristics of true eloquence." "No where," the writer believed, "can be found a poetic thought clothed in more captivating simplicity of expression" than in Tecumseh's oratory (quoted in Clements 1986, 5).

In sum, I believe that it is probable that Hunter introduced the Tecumseh speech to meet the expectations of the enlightened audience to whom he was addressing his captivity narrative just as he used a passage inspired by an early American novel to satisfy readers familiar with this burgeoning literary genre. Drinnon makes a good case for the authenticity of Hunter's book, much better than Cass's case against it. Ethnologists have drawn upon the work for information without doubting the validity of his data. I believe, though, that one would do well not to trust the reliability of the Tecumseh speech. There is so much to impugn it that the possibility of any aspect of it being a useful account of this Native American leader's oratory seems too remote for it to be trusted, even if one believes, like Drinnon, that most of Hunter's narrative is accurate and authentic.

My general sense is that captivity narratives are poor sources for records of any kind of Native American verbal art. The fundamental antipathy that the writers had for their captors and their way of life and the demands of an audience that required its dose of gore worked against any but the most cursory treatment of any artistic discourse that the captives might have encountered during their ordeals and had the ability to remember. Most of the early examples, particularly those published after the War for Independence and the beginnings of land speculation (which required the extermination of those who might block real estate development), served as anti-Indian propaganda, and later captivity narratives "were shaped by publishers exploiting a mass market that thrived on sensationalism" (Derounian-Stodola and Levernier 1993, 31). Though Hunter's narrative is notable for its sympathetic portrayal of people who became more family than captors for him and for its lack of sensationalistic touches, one probably should not place too much stock in anything he writes about verbal art except in its most general terms. The missionary, the explorer, even the military adventurer—writers about Indians from these categories were more likely to produce useful data on verbal art, though, of course, each particular source must be evaluated specifically.

SOLDIERS' MEMOIRS

The reminiscences of military men, often written at the end of a career, represent contact with Native Americans under highly adversarial conditions, ones that usually evoke unmitigatedly ethnocentric judgments. Nevertheless, some of these documents deal with the oratorical skills of Indians appreciatively. For instance, General Oliver O. Howard, notable in military history for his treating with the Apache Cochise and for his pursuit of Hinmah-too-yah-laht-ket (Chief Joseph) and the retreating Nez Perce, spent some fourteen years on the Indian frontier. His memoir of those experiences includes several oration texts: by Red Iron and Lion Bear, both Dakota (Howard 1907, 105–109), and Anahootz, probably Tlingit (307–308). He also generalized, "Our Indians are without exception natural orators" (561), and quoted approvingly the opinion of President Rutherford B. Hayes, whom he conducted on a tour of Oregon and Washington Territory in 1880: " 'What remarkable oratory! There is no hesitation. Their gestures are always natural and graceful, and not one of them has failed to make a good speech. . . . Their figures of speech are choice and well carried out. Indeed, they seemed to have been born orators'" (561–62).

Though less effusive than Howard and even more prone to evaluate Indians' lifeways by his own Euro-American standards, Captain Richard Irving Dodge could still find their oratory praiseworthy. "Almost every warrior speaks well," he wrote, "some few of them eloquently" (Dodge 1882, 51). John G. Bourke, adjutant to General George Crook and a future president of the American Folklore Society, found space in his memoir of his time with Crook to include the verbal texts of several Indian orations (e.g., Bourke 1891, 436–37). His records of speeches by the scouts Alchise and "Pedro" may be the only documentation of these figures' verbalization.

In 1882 Crook, who had already worked to mitigate the hostilities between various Apache groups and Euro-American intruders in their traditional homelands, returned to Arizona Territory to deal with conditions that had worsened since his departure several years previously. Before setting out on a campaign that would eventually take him into the Sierra Madre of Mexico, he interviewed some of the Apaches who remained friendly to the military and who had served as scouts and in other capacities. Bourke recorded what Alchise and "Pedro" had to say in his journal and reproduced their interactions with Crook in his memoir of his service with the general "as giving the way of thinking and the manner of expression of the Apaches" (Bourke 1891, 435). Both speakers heaped praise on Crook and blamed current problems on the policies and character of his successors. Though they may have been employing an oratorical trope in their effusive praise of Crook, the Apaches were more or less correct in attributing worsening relations between some of their people and the Euro-American establishment to the insensitivity of the latter. Speeches by more famous Apache leaders—Mangas Coloradas, Victorio, Cochise, and Geronimo, for example—appear in the memoirs of various soldiers and civilians who participated in the Apache wars of the late nineteenth century as well as in official documents, but Bourke's memoir is one of the few sources for lesser known figures such as Alchise and "Pedro." One value of soldiers' accounts is that they may preserve records of speakers and speeches that are not elsewhere available.

From an array of such military memoirs that extend back into colonial times, the student of American Indian oratory can find particular use for a volume written by one of the most sensitive soldiers to describe his experiences with Native Americans. Henry Timberlake's memoir of several months spent with the Overhills band of Cherokees was published posthumously in London in 1765. Well known today for presenting what is regarded as the first English translation of the words of a Native American song (Clements 1996, 73–92), which he rendered in the heroic couplets customary for English-language poetry at the time, Timberlake's memoir also includes oration texts with some description of their situations of delivery.

Timberlake had participated in the attempt to suppress the 1761 Cherokee Rebellion by the Second Virginia Regiment. Though the Virginians saw no combat, their presence in southwestern Virginia some two hundred miles from the scene of armed conflict made them a potential threat to the Overhills Cherokees in what is now eastern Tennessee. Pressing their advantage, Colonel Adam Stephen advanced his troops down the Holston River drawing ever closer to the Overhills communities. The Cherokees responded by sending a delegation led by Connetarke (Standing Turkey) to treat with the Virginians. Negotiations concluded the war for all practical purposes at least in the eyes of the Cherokees and the Virginians, but previous dealings between Cherokee and British diplomats had not always ended happily for the Indians. Connetarke requested that a delegation from the Second Virginia Regiment accompany him home to "convince the nation of the intentions and sincerity of the English toward them" (Timberlake 1765, 39). Accompanied by Sergeant Thomas Sumpter, the interpreter John McCormack (who may have been Cherokee himself), and a servant, Henry Timberlake undertook this diplomatic mission.

The Virginians reached the Overhills community in mid-December of 1761 and remained there until the following March. During that time Timberlake was able to observe enough of Cherokee lifeways to prepare one of the better colonial ethnographic descriptions of an Indian group. Though not exhaustive, his account of Cherokee culture covers a range of subjects from agriculture to weaponry. He also includes two translated texts of Cherokee oratory, both delivered by the well-known figure Ostenaco. Timberlake's accounts were not the first attempts at such for Cherokee oratory. He had been preceded in this endeavor, for example, by Alexander Long, who had traded with the Cherokees for more than a decade when he wrote of them in 1725 (Long 1969, 14–16), by explorer Alexander Cuming, who visited the Cherokee towns in the 1730s (Cuming 1928, 142–43), and by Ludovick Grant, whose memories from the 1720s appeared in the Charleston, South Carolina, probate records some thirty years later (Grant 1909, 62–63). But Timberlake seems to have had a bit more literary sensitivity—suggested by his translation of the Cherokee war song in his memoirs—than these earlier reporters. Moreover, the knowledge we have of Ostenaco from other sources adds considerably to Timberlake's data.

Apparently born in the first decade of the century, Ostenaco already had plenty of experience with Euro-Americans by the time of Timberlake's visit. In the 1750s, for example, he had defended the presence of English traders among the Overhills communities when an anti-English faction was suggesting they should be expelled. In 1753 he had visited the colonial governor in Charleston with a Cherokee delegation that won trade concessions from him. In 1756 he appeared in Williamsburg. Though generally an advocate of the English among his people, Ostenaco nevertheless was active in some military ventures against the colonials and at one time held the honorific "Second Warrior of the Cherokees" (Evans 1976, 42–45).

When Timberlake arrived at the Overhills community of Timothly, he enjoyed the special hospitality of Ostenaco, whom he called "the commander in chief" (Timberlake 1765, 30) and who became an important advocate for treating with the British. The historian David H. Corkran, in fact, characterizes him as one of the "stalwarts of the pro-English faction" among the Cherokees (Corkran 1962, 30). Timberlake records the text of a speech that the Cherokee leader gave to encourage acceptance of British terms. This oration reminds us of the importance of persuasion, since even a so-called "commander in chief" among the Cherokees could not arbitrarily exert his will upon others (Gearing 1962, 49–50). Ostenaco spoke immediately after the articles of peace had been read at the "town-house" at the Cherokee community of Chota:

> The bloody tommahawke, so long lifted against our brethren the English, must now be buried deep, deep in the ground, never to be raised again [in a note here Timberlake added a gloss explaining this widely used trope]; and whoever shall act contrary to any of these articles, must expect a punishment equal to his offence [here again Timberlake added a note: that the traditional lack of power to punish by Cherokee politi-

cal leaders was being abrogated by the treaty]. Should a strict observance of them be neglected, a war must necessarily follow, and a second peace may not be so easily obtained. I therefor once recommend to you, to take particular care of your behaviour towards the English, whom we must now look upon as ourselves; they have the French and Spaniards to fight, and we enough of our own colour, without medling with either nation. I desire likewise, that the white warrior, who has ventured himself here with us [i.e., Timberlake], may be well used and respected by all, wherever he goes amongst us. (33–34)

This is not the only account of Ostenaco's oratory that has come down to us. Timberlake recorded one other instance when Ostenaco had to respond to rumors of Cherokee deaths perpetrated by Shawnees who were reputed to have had British support (85). Moreover, other sources include accounts of his speech making: the official documents of South Carolina (quoted in Evans 1976, 43, 45), for instance. We even have a comment from Thomas Jefferson, champion of Indian eloquence as manifested in the "speech" of Tahgahjute, about Ostenaco's oratorical skills. Ostenaco had accompanied Timberlake back to Williamsburg after the Virginian had completed his diplomatic mission and in May 1762 was a member of a Cherokee delegation that Timberlake escorted to London. The young Jefferson was a student at William and Mary College on the eve of the group's departure for England and heard Ostenaco make "his great farewell oration to his people." Though he did not understand the substance of the speech, which was delivered in Cherokee, Jefferson appreciated the performance style, as he recalled in a letter to John Adams dated 11 June 1812:

The moon was in full splendor, and to her he seemed to address himself in his prayers for his own safety on the voyage, and that of his people during his absence; his sounding voice, distinct articulation, animated action, and the solemn silence of his people at their several fires, filled me with awe and veneration, although I did not understand a word he uttered. (Whitman n. d., 277)

But in the speech by Ostenaco that Timberlake reported in his *Memoirs,* we have perhaps the best single source for the oratory of a public speaker who enjoyed respect and celebrity from both his own society and the colonial officials of Virginia and the Carolinas. The speeches that appear in the colonial documents are divested of much of their context, and they may not reflect Ostenaco's powers at their fullest. In addressing an audience that consisted of very few of his countrymen, he may even have adjusted his rhetoric. But the Timberlake document reports a speech in a fully traditional situation with the British observer as an interested onlooker. Even though Timberlake's text is dependent on the interpreter John McCormack, characterized as a "renegade" by one historian (Corkran 1962, 191), and even though interpreters seldom provided word-for-word translations (Davis 1978, 221–30), Timberlake was apparently sensitive to the possibility of encountering the artistic in Native American discourse. That such artistry characterized the speech is suggested by Jefferson's comments about a speech that Ostenaco delivered a few months later. In this case, we should be able to trust that we have the gist of the text and to assume—based on Timberlake's other work with Cherokee verbal art and reinforced by Ostenaco's experience as an orator, on his established record as a Cherokee politician, and on Jefferson's youthful assessment—that it evinced the appropriate esthetic for the situation and the context.

Newspapers

The texts of some of the most well-known speeches attributed to Native Americans appeared first in contemporary newspapers. For example, that of Tahgahjute, which generated such controversy when Thomas Jefferson used it to counteract the Comte de Buffon's contention that the western hemisphere and its inhabitants were constitutionally inferior to the "Old World," first came out in the *Virginia Gazette* in February 1775, and Sealth's famous address to Isaac Stevens, the first governor of Washington Territory, was published originally in the *Seattle Sunday Star* for 29 October 1887. The texts of both these speeches have been called into suspicion—the first by contemporaries of Jefferson and the other by recent scholars. Yet many journalistic records of Native American oratory should not be automatically dismissed, particularly when the writers of those records were first-hand witnesses. An example that may bear up under closer scrutiny is another well-known case: the speech which the Oglala Lakota Red Cloud delivered at the Cooper Institute in New York City on 16 June 1870. The advantages that the record of Red Cloud's oration has over those for Logan's and Seattle's addresses are that the reporters who wrote the accounts, which appeared in the *New York Times,* the *New York Herald,* and the *New York Daily Tribune,* indeed actually witnessed the oration, the newspapers printed a text of the speech on the day after it was delivered, and no one at the time apparently found anything amiss in what was printed.[10]

Though not much is known of his early life, Red Cloud, who was probably born in 1822, continues to receive some of the considerable attention he enjoyed especially during the latter part of his lifetime. At least three scholarly biographies of him were published in the twentieth century (Hyde 1957; Olson 1965; Larson 1997). He is heralded as the only Native American leader actually to have won a war against the federal government, an accomplishment that made him more or less a household name during the late 1860s. Having been received by President Grant with hospitality but without satisfaction for his grievances when he made his 1870 tour of the east—the first of several visits he was to make during his lifetime—Red Cloud enjoyed some celebrity status when he arrived in New York City on 14 June. Though he had been so disappointed by the failures of his diplomatic mission in the nation's capital that he planned not to speak publicly while in New York, the Indian commissioners, including Peter Cooper, convinced him that doing so would benefit his people's cause. Accordingly on 16 June, the lecture hall at the Cooper Institute was "besieged" by "an eager throng" estimated by the *Herald* reporter to number five thousand.

According to the *Times,* the program began with a prayer by the Reverend Dr. Howard Crosby. The audience then heard speeches by Cooper, who advocated compensation for any land that had been taken from the Oglalas, and by Crosby, who addressed Red Cloud directly, urging him to accept the protection of "good white men" such as the members of the Indian Commission. Then it was Red Cloud's turn. The Oglala orator "arose and faced the audience, drawing his blankets around him majestically." As soon as the "tumult" of applause had subsided, he began "on a somewhat high key and with a rapid utterance," speaking through two interpreters, John Richard Jr. and a "Mr. Beauvais," who sat on either side of him.

The text of the speech as reported in the *Times,* the *Herald,* and the

Tribune on 17 June consists of three parts. Red Cloud began by stressing his common humanity with his Euro-American listeners, while noting the real differences between their ways of life: "The Great Spirit made us poor and ignorant. He made you rich and wise and skillful in things which we know nothing about. The good Father made you to eat tame game and us to eat wild game" *(Times)*. Then, Red Cloud spoke of the history of treaty making between his people and the federal government. He focused on the Treaty of 1852, which he and his people had upheld scrupulously: "We kept our word. We committed no murders, no depredations, until the troops came here. When the troops were sent there trouble and disturbance arose" *(Times)*. The treaty section of his "talk" progressed to some comments on the recently negotiated document of 1868, which he had signed without being truly apprized of its significance. In fact, he claimed, he had not understood its full implications until Grant had explained them to him a few days previously. The third section of the speech spells out what he and his people desire: "We do not want riches, but we want to train our children right. Riches would do us no good. We could not take them with us to the other world. We do not want riches, we want peace and love" *(Times)*. He asked that instead of the whiskey-laden traders that represented Euro-American civilization to his people, the federal government send men "whom we know and can trust." He took his leave of his audience by expressing his gratitude for their attention.

The account in the *Herald* stressed the prudent care that had gone into the preparation of Red Cloud's address. No spontaneous effusion of natural eloquence, the speech had taken the orator most of the morning, assisted by his escort General John E. Smith and an interpreter—probably John Richard Jr.—to work out. Red Cloud was aware of the significance of the moment and of the role of the media by which his words "would speedily find their living impress upon the sy[m]bolic leaves of the press." The effort, when he emerged from his morning's labors, left Red Cloud's face "a shade paler than before—sicklied o'er, in fact, as it was with the pale cast of thought."

Though the newspaper had no way of knowing what had really gone into the preparations of the speech, the fact that such preparations are mentioned at all reminds us that the art of oratory might indeed require some planning, that it was not an automatic effusion of savage wisdom and eloquence. Moreover, having three texts of the same speech—though coming to the recipients through interpreters who translated Red Cloud's words for the Reverend Howard Crosby, who, in turn, used his "stentorian voice" to broadcast them to the crowd—serves as some check on the accuracy of the records "taken down by the swiftly cunning fingers of phonographic reporters"—again as the writer for the *Herald* put it. The general content of the texts is virtually identical, though they differ in details of wording. For example, the *Herald* writer has Red Cloud saying, "The Great Spirit made us both. He gave us lands. You came in here; we gave you those lands, and received you as brothers." In the *Times* the same passage from the oration becomes "The Great Spirit made us both. He gave us land, and he gave you land. You came here and we received you as brothers." The *Tribune* has Red Cloud denominating the giver as the "Good Spirit," who "gave us these lands." The *Herald* suggests that all the land held by Euro-Americans in the western hemisphere has come from Indians, while the *Times* and the *Tribune* texts have the "Great [or Good] Spirit" allocating lands to both Native Americans and Euro-Americans. The *Times* version anticipates perhaps what Red Cloud sees as a natural, Great Spirit–derived demarcation between his people and Euro-Americans: "You belong in the East, and I belong in the West" (*Times* text, virtually identical in the *Herald* but missing from the *Tribune*). The *Times* and *Tribune* texts seem to personify the federal government more as the "Great Father"—presumably President Grant—than does the *Herald* writer. When Red Cloud distinguishes himself from his political rival Spotted Tail of the Brulés, he says, according to the *Times,* that he cannot be "bought for a pin" to change his mind and recant on his word. The *Herald* cites a "fish" as the price of Spotted Tail's perfidy. While noting Red Cloud's invidious remarks about Spotted Tail, the writer for the *Tribune* makes no mention of the low price for which the orator accuses his rival of having sold out. Most of the differences among the newspaper accounts are similarly slight. What is surprising is the degree of identity between these texts, recorded without benefit of mechanical devices, though one supposes that pauses for translation by an interpreter may have resembled the process of dictation that was used when ethnologists began to record Native American verbal art a few years later.

Perhaps the really important difference is that the *Herald* writer provides the most complete sense of Red Cloud's oration as performance. Prefacing the transcription of the translation of the speaker's words, for instance, the writer reports that Red Cloud "pointed with his finger to the roof [of] the building, and with a charm of manner and an elegance of gesture that might be imitated with advantage by civilized and highly educated pale faces," began his speech. Both the *Herald* and the *Tribune* accounts even precisely note audience reactions, parenthetically placing at appropriate spots in the text "Applause," "Laughter," "Hear, hear," "Laughter and Applause," and "Great applause"—though the writers do not always place these responses at the same points in Red Cloud's speech.

Not only do these interpolations suggest the idea of oration as event more fully than simply reproducing Red Cloud's words, they also reflect something of the speech's immediate efficacy. That the speech accomplished what Red Cloud intended finds further support in a brief editorial that appeared in the *Herald* on 18 June under the title "The Indians—Try the Proposition of Red Cloud":

> Would it not really be a good plan to try the experiment of sending honest men to deal with the Indians? We have tried nearly everything else, from strychnine to the palaver of Quakers, and nothing gives us a satisfactory result. In the recent Indian speeches [Red Cloud's and that of his colleague Red Dog] the burden of the cry is that they have been cheated, right and left, on all occasions, and in every way. Now as the nation certainly has a disposition to exhaust fair means, why not try the proposition of Red Cloud and deal with the red man through honest agents? At least make it certain that the Indian hostility is not because of his discontent over dishonest practices.

The editorialist for the *Tribune* was equally effusive in praising the performance, calling it "one of the most striking incidents in the history of the aboriginal race." Noting the disadvantages that Red Cloud faced in the situation—his "grotesque costume" and "the fact that he was compelled to stop at the close of every sentence during the time required for its translation from Ogalalla into English"—the writer believed that the orator acquitted himself admirably. "His manner was natural and graceful," he wrote. Moreover, the interruptions did not destroy the speech's unity, and Red Cloud "stood statuesque and impressive" while awaiting the interpreters. The newspapers had also printed the text of a brief speech by Red Dog, "an orator by profession" (according to the *Tribune*'s characterization) and "the orator for the party" (in the *Herald*'s view). The editorialist for the former paper, though, believed that, "as a speaker, Red Cloud stood eminent and preeminent, though he displayed only the art of nature and the eloquence of truth."

Red Cloud's speech may have been instrumental in the appointment of a commission to try to effect an agreement in the West. It certainly averted an immediate outbreak of hostilities. However, the commission failed to produce any real results, and Red Cloud, perceived as a conciliator, lost some of his prestige at home. An assessment of its efficacy by a recent student of the speech perceives it as a failure "from a long-range viewpoint," though it had some immediately felt success (Ek 1966, 262).

Considering what is more to the point here—the success of the newspaper reporters in producing a useful record of the event—I believe that their journalism yielded a valuable record, which, though unappreciative of the full artistry of what the Oglala leader said and how he said it, nevertheless provides an accurate account of the delivery and reception—and perhaps even the preparation—of his speech.

ETHNOLOGICAL DOCUMENTS

Though the title "father of American ethnology" usually goes to Henry Rowe Schoolcraft, who began recording translations and some Native-language textualizations of Anishinaabe verbal art during the 1820s, the real emergence of a scientific anthropology of American Indian expressive culture probably should be associated with the founding of the Bureau of Ethnology in the Smithsonian Institution in 1879 or perhaps with the work of Harvard's Peabody Museum. Under the direction of John Wesley Powell, the Bureau of American Ethnology (or BAE) sponsored field research especially in the Southwest. From the beginning Powell encouraged his field-workers to pay particular attention to language, a concern that had figured in the work of the BAE's precursors all the way back to the time of the colonial divine Roger Williams (Hinsley 1981, 47–49). In the "Introductory" to the first of the Bureau's *Annual Reports,* Powell stressed the centrality of language for understanding all the cultural forms and practices which would fall under the agency's attention. He realized that the time when language study might benefit from the publication of short vocabularies was past (except in the cases of heretofore unrecorded languages). The linguistic plan he set for the Bureau began with the collection of a series of "chrestomathies" (passages of discourse used for language learning). He also advocated the publication of grammars and dictionaries. Most important for present concerns, he concluded the brief language portion of the Bureau's mission statement by emphasizing, "In each case it is deemed desirable to connect with the grammar and dictionary a body of literature designed as texts for reference in explaining the facts and principles of the language. The texts will be accompanied by interlinear translations so arranged as greatly to facilitate the study of the chief grammatical characteristics" (Powell 1881a, xv). Accordingly, using a technique paralleled by the activities of the university- and museum-trained anthropology of Franz Boas, BAE researchers collected verbal art texts, at least partially to get a sense of language in action.

The result was a rich trove of material that began to see print with the publication of such collections of texts as Erminnie A. Smith's "Myths of the Iroquois" (1883). In some cases—Frank Hamilton Cushing's "Outlines of Zuñi Creation Myths," for example (Cushing 1891–92)—BAE publications included only free English translations of stories, songs, and orations, but the standard became to offer the Native-language texts, often written out in now-obsolete orthographies, with interlinear and free translations. By the end of the century the BAE collection had grown into a quantity sufficient enough for the British folklorist Andrew Lang to recommend that "some American man or woman of letters" incorporate them into an anthology of "Red Indian poetry and prose" (Lang 1900, 163).

Strongly negative comments especially by literary enthusiasts for Native Americana in the 1910s and 1920s criticized the BAE publications and other scientific vehicles that presented American Indian verbal art texts for their inattention to English literary style (e.g., Henderson 1917). For the most part, also, the material was collected in nonperformance situations: the laborious dictation by a Native-language speaker to an ethnographer who used phonetic symbols to record patterns of sound that he or she often did not understand (e.g., Boas 1901). But the various series that began coming out shortly before 1900 preserve a vast amount of material: the BAE *Annual Reports* and *Bulletins,* the *Journal of American Folklore,* the *International Journal of American Linguistics, Publications of the American Ethnological Society,* and series and occasional papers from the Peabody Museum, the American Museum of Natural History, the Field Museum in Chicago, and the University of Pennsylvania Museum—to name just a few. By the 1920s enough textual material collected with a fair degree of anthropological rigor had been published for some work at synthesis to appear, such as Stith Thompson's *Tales of the North American Indians* (1929).

The student of Native American verbal art whose views and expectations have been informed by the ethnography of speaking and the ethnopoetics of the late twentieth century can find much to decry in this vast amount of data, which numbers literally thousands of texts. As noted, most of it was recorded under less than optimum circumstances, usually nonperformance situations. Little of it has anything beyond the barest sketch of what the actual recording situations were. Virtually nothing is known of the persons from whom the material came except their names, and we usually have no idea when and where the stories, songs, and orations would have been expressed under natural conditions. In other words, the very features that I have found to commend in most of the examples treated thus far were totally absent or treated cursorily in the BAE and other early ethnological publications.

But such material continues nonetheless to have value, as an example will show. Based on fieldwork done between November 1901 and June 1902, when he was in residence at Sacaton, Arizona Territory, Frank Russell produced the first full-scale ethnography of the Pima, which appeared in the BAE *Annual Report* in 1908. He obtained information on a range of cultural practices from ten informants and worked with five interpreters. For present purposes, the most important portion of the ethnography is the transcription of the texts of ten ritual orations (all but one of which have direct associations with warfare) which concludes the work. Russell presents free, prose translations of the speeches with the original Pima and interlinear translation at the bottom of each page.

Russell does not directly attribute any of the speeches, but all may in fact come from Ka'maltkak, or Thin Leather. Russell describes him, apparently his principal informant, as "an old man . . . said to be the most popular of the few remaining narrators of myths and speeches, or 'speakers.'" A prominent figure in councils, Ka'maltkak had been an important influence in maintaining the vitality of traditional Pima values. He was Russell's source for "the cosmogonical myth of the tribe, many speeches, songs, and much general information" (Russell 1908, 17).

Russell introduces the ten speeches with the following headnote:

> Set speeches which recited portions of the cosmogonical myth were a feature of many ceremonies and were especially important in the preparation for war. They were slightly adapted for each occasion but their general content remained the same. Highly figurative language is used and in consequence it is extremely difficult to obtain even an approximately correct translation. The free translation offered is the result of many discussions with older men. (339)

Russell also benefited from the translation services of José Lewis Brennan, a Papago (Tohono O'odham) who had lived among the neighboring Pima since childhood. The BAE was paying Brennan to prepare a Pima dictionary as well as to assist in other linguistic research. In fact, he was responsible for what is apparently the oldest available text of a Piman speech, a salt oration he textualized in 1897 (Bahr 1975, 8).

The only speeches for which Russell provides more specific information are the "Opening of the Rain Ceremony," for which he offers a two-paragraph headnote that places the oration in its customary ceremonial situation and context (347); and "War Chief Urging the People to Go on the Warpath Against the Apaches," which has a footnote stating, "This speech is believed to be based upon an adventure in which a Pima gambled with the Apaches and lost all his property. Overcome by the passion for gambling, he wagered the life of his brother and lost. The striking figures of speech indicate the speaker's greed" (357). For the other speeches, Russell offers occasional notes that explain linguistic usages.

Most of the items in Russell's collection of oratorical materials deal with warfare. Eight (perhaps nine) of the ten speech texts come from military ritual, and elsewhere in his ethnography of Pima culture Russell provides some idea about how the speeches figured into ritual procedure. His data can be supplemented, moreover, by information gathered by Frances Densmore (1929) and by Ruth M. Underhill (1938, 1979), whose work with the Papago a generation or so later than Russell's among the Pima treats verbal art including oratory extensively.

Traditionally, Pima military activity had been directed primarily against the Apache, who might raid their communities to commandeer produce from gardens. Retaliatory expeditions by the Pima occurred when a leader wanted to exact vengeance or to provide an opportunity for himself and his followers to attain the prestige that came with military successes. "[C]onventional speeches of magic character" figured into the assembling of a fighting force, since the leader depended on his oratorical skills to recruit men from several communities to form a band of warriors of sufficient size. Once the party had assembled and the material preparations had been made, "a man whose office it was to keep appropriate speeches in memory" delivered the first of a set of speeches that repeated what the gods had said in mythic time. These speeches, carefully sequenced according to when during the military expedition they were to be spoken, described great martial exploits for the purpose, Russell believed, of building morale. Furthermore, he recognized that the words of the speeches were spiritually efficacious—a point strongly reiterated by Underhill regarding Papago oratory and song (Underhill 1938, 11–19). They afforded warriors access to the power that the gods had possessed. By translating the present military campaign into the realm of myth, they transported participants into sacred time (Russell 1908, 202–203), as we know oratory was apt to do.

The real value of Russell's volume lies not so much in this information about context and situation, which is treated too cursorily to be very useful. The ethnography's enduring significance is in the speeches themselves. While José Lewis Brennan most likely deserves credit for the Pima texts and interlinear translations and at least partial credit for the free translations, Russell as ethnographer of record must have had some input into what appeared in the published product of his six months of fieldwork. Though written in an orthography that has become obsolete in the recording of Piman languages and translated in ways that do little justice to the literary style, even when they are successful at capturing the content, the oratory texts in *Pima Ethnography* are valuable raw material for contemporary translators more sensitive to matters ethnopoetic.

An example is the work of Donald Bahr, who has, in fact, retranslated one of Ka'maltkak's speeches in a way that does reflect some of the style of the original. In *Pima and Papago Ritual Oratory* (1975), one of the few book-length treatments of Native American oratory from an ethnographic and ethnopoetic perspective,[11] Bahr has reworked, retranslated, and analyzed three variants of the same ritual oration. Only one of the variants—that which Russell and Brennan had obtained from Ka'maltkak—had been previously published. The principal purpose of Bahr's book is to make available to Native speakers, few of whom are literate in Piman, a supply of textual material, but the work actually serves a larger purpose: that of presenting oratory as verbal art on its own terms. Moreover, it illustrates the continuing usefulness of sources such as those issued by the BAE.

Bahr begins with the assumption that ritual oratory among Pimans is a narrowly defined genre of artistic discourse in which the narrative of a shamanic journey that occurred in mythic times is retold. Much of what we know of the ways in which such oratory worked in traditional contexts comes from Ruth Underhill's work with the Tohono O'odham, among whom it functioned as one way of connecting participants not only in warfare but also in the salt pilgrimage and other sacred activities with the power associated with the time of myth. Simply put, the orator described a mythic paradigm for what the ritual participants were going through. Bahr emphasizes that the controlling structure of Piman ritual oratory is a journey and shows that one way of poetically organizing texts that were originally cast by translators in prose is by focusing on "journey words." Such words, which deal with the shaman-hero's departure, travel, and arrival, enable the textmaker to divide the oration into parts. Each of these parts consists of a single sentence base containing four verbs and two nouns. The orator elaborates on this base using parallelism or a construction Bahr labels "There was/he did." The latter is a statement that consists of a pair of lines, one stating the existence of something and the second describing what the shaman-protagonist did to it.

The oration that Bahr treats was apparently used during war ceremonies, probably during preparations for a campaign against the Apaches. It relates events that happened to I'itoi or Elder Brother Shaman, a second-generation marplot in the Piman theogony who also served as a culture hero. After an apocalyptic flood, Elder Brother Shaman had created a new race of people, whom latter-day Pimans identify as the Hohokam (Bahr et al. 1994, 6–11). Despite his services to them, the Hohokam were dissatisfied with Elder Brother Shaman, and another god, Buzzard, kills him. The oration begins with Elder Brother Shaman's resurrection. It relates his return to strength as he journeys about the countryside and ends with references to the mythic first war in which Pimans participated when, led by Elder Brother Shaman, they displaced the Hohokam from the territory which they now occupy.

Russell's free translation of the concluding portion of the oration, which depicts Elder Brother Shaman's war of vengeance against the Hohokam, is as follows:

> The people were now ready to do whatever Elder Brother desired of them and, like fierce predatory animals or raptorial birds, they poured out of the underworld and fell upon the inhabitants of the upper world, whom they conquered without difficulty. The victors swept the property and everything relating to the conquered from the face of the earth.
>
> Consider the magic power which abode with me and which is at your service. (Russell 1908, 345–46)

Bahr's rendering of the same section of the speech reflects the allusive quality of the original:

> then really stepped and stood my grown boys, like animals, like birds and they flew and poured against it [the enemy] and wrestled nothing and took it smoothly;
>
> there lay various of his possessions;
>
> they gathered it and slowly bundled it and slowly turned me around;
>
> thus you may wish and plan, it was a good life, and I took it and I brought it here. (Bahr 1975, 49–51)

Bahr performs an act of "ethnocriticism" (see Krupat 1992) through careful consideration of the language of three oration variants (this one by Ka'maltkak, one collected from Thomas Vanyiko by George Herzog in 1929, and one recorded from Juan Gregorio, a Tohono O'odham, by Underhill in the 1930s) and shows how stylistic analysis is a necessary foundation for an understanding of how the oration works in literary terms. One value of Bahr's book, which parallels what Dell Hymes has done with similar material primarily from the Northwest Coast (1981), lies in its showing that instances of discourse collected, textualized, and even translated before the emergence of ethnopoetics in the 1960s and 1970s can still be made to yield material that has indigenous artistic value. Without the Native-language text that appears in Russell's ethnography, the recovery of that artistic value would be impossible.

When Franz Boas began editing the *International Journal of American Linguistics* in 1917, the practice of collecting verbal art texts for linguistic purposes was a firmly established field technique. He noted, "[L]arge masses of texts are needed to elucidate the structure of the languages" as supplements to vocabularies and grammatical notes (Boas 1940, 199). Perhaps his comments on texts in the introduction to the first issue of *IJAL* can stand as a final word on this approach to textualization. Though Boas and his students recognized that the slowness and awkwardness of dictation inhibited speakers from employing "that freedom of diction that belongs to the well-told tale [or well-delivered speech]," thus producing an unnatural simplicity in syntax, he remained firm in his belief that dictated texts provided data that could not be obtained otherwise. When Native speakers learned to write their own languages, they might use a more natural style than that which emerged in dictation, but it was often a personal style, not reflecting common cultural usage. Moreover, those who learned to write were often young, highly acculturated, and thus unfamiliar with traditional speech patterns (Boas 1940, 200). So the dictated text remained crucial for the Boasian mode of linguistic research—a mode, of course, that Frank Russell and José Lewis Brennan (though coming at it through the BAE) were employing in their work.

While today we might wish that these early ethnologists had been more mindful of J. Walter Fewkes's example when he employed a cylinder recorder to capture the sounds of Passamaquoddy and then Zuni singing (Fewkes 1890), we should be happy to have what has come down to us: scrupulously recorded Native-language texts that can be used by contemporary translators who are sensitive to the demands of ethnopoetics. In those cases where we have contextual and situational information as well—even if not from the same source that documented the texts—our records of verbal art, including oratory, become fairly complete. When the Russell-Brennan texts can be reworked by Bahr and combined with the background provided by Underhill, we have as thorough an ethnography of oratory in spoken performance as we may get even from some contemporary contextualizers.

From the ethnographic, ethnopoetic perspective of the start of the new millennium, most of the kinds of sources which have been treated somewhat favorably here do not appear to be very promising. A number of factors worked against the presenters' providing anything really useful for one who is interested in Native American oratory. For example, in many cases the contact which the Europeans and Euro-Americans who wrote of oratory had with American Indian societies was superficial. Individuals might spend very little time with a group, visiting them for a day or two before they went on their way. Even when visitors were more than tourists, they often lived on the periphery of the community in a military, administrative, or missionary compound. Except for missionaries the person who could operate without an interpreter was rare. In addition to its superficiality, contact with Native Americans might have an air of the adversarial, especially if the intent was to subdue and govern (the case for soldiers and other government representatives) or to destroy and supplant (the case for many missionaries). Yet even if a visitor had a real desire to learn about the Indians' culture, that learning was secondary (except in the case of ethnologists such as Russell) to trading, governing, missionizing, or whatever task the visitor had been sent to accomplish. The lack of training in how to observe, in knowing what to look and listen for, militated against the value of the kinds of sources we have been examining. Moreover, at the end of a career a soldier, missionary, or bureaucrat might prepare his memoirs, perhaps stimulating his recollection with journal entries written at the time. But when a significant stretch of lifetime lay between the writer and his subject, the tendency would be to manufacture from whole cloth or from tattered rags of memory what a more contemporaneous account might have included.

What is amazing, I think, is that these sources have as much value as they do. That value has to be approached on a case-by-case basis, though. Generalizing that sources are either valuable or worthless contributes less to our understanding of oratory and other verbal behavior at particular times and places than does a careful examination of sources with a mind open to their potential usefulness.

I want to stress in the next two chapters what we can learn from such sources about Native American oratory, and I believe it is important. First, we can learn that the artful manipulation of figurative language was not a compensatory mechanism for the lack of abstraction in Native American intellects and concomitantly in their languages. Metaphor especially be-came a device by which a skilled speaker could draw upon the richness of his or her language to accomplish the ends of oratory. Second, we can learn something of how oratory worked: what besides the bare-bones text con-stituted its realization in performance, how that performance emerged in a dialogic dynamic, and what that performance could accomplish. We have explored some of the probable reasons behind the ascendancy of oratory in outsiders' depictions of American Indian cultural behavior, and we have surveyed a range of literary genres in which those outsiders presented what they encountered. Now, we are ready to learn some of what their presenta-tions can teach us.

CHAPTER 3

THE PLAY OF TROPES IN NATIVE
AMERICAN ORATORY

"T his country is now but a dried skeleton without flesh, without veins,
without sinews, and without arteries,—like bones that hold together
only by a very delicate thread." Thus, according to a Jesuit missionary
report, did a Huron orator begin his plea for forgiveness from the imported
officialdom of New France for the murder of one of their countrymen
(Thwaites 1959a, 30:235). He and others whose speeches the Jesuit missionaries heard and recorded tended to refer to themselves in figurative terms: as
"a poor little animal, crawling on the ground" (Thwaites 1959a, 2:205); as a
"great beast . . . who has the boldness to speak in the presence of Cap-
tains" (Thwaites 1959a, 9:267); as "only a dog" (Thwaites 1959a, 9:267); as
"the mouth for the whole of my country" (Thwaites 1959a, 27:253). These
few examples, which could be multiplied exponentially from any of the
kinds of sources surveyed in chapter 2, suggest how Indians came to be
identified with metaphor in the European and Euro-American mind (Murray 1991, 42).

By a large margin, the feature of Native American speech most frequently mentioned by commentators has been the use of metaphor and
other tropes of language. Abstractions such as truth and beauty, justice and
brotherhood appear infrequently in the published texts of Native American
orations. Instead, the orators of record larded their discourse with concrete
language that reflected the natural and cultural worlds of the speakers and
their listeners. The association between metaphorical speech and Indianness

became so ensconced in American iconography that one of the markers of "playing Indian" in the late eighteenth and early nineteenth century was speaking in metaphors. This became a "given way of signifying Indianness" (Deloria 1998, 33).

Pro-Indianists might cite the use of figurative language to support their belief in the essential humanity of the North American Natives, for artistic manipulation of language could be said to reveal highly developed intellects—"a sign of genius," as Aristotle's *Rhetoric* has it (quoted in Basso 1976, 93). Some commentators did indeed see the use of tropes from this perspective, but a stronger tradition developed that suggested that this apparent penchant for the figurative represented a weakness in intellect, an inability to communicate with precision in the language of abstract concepts, a "designative inadequacy" in Native American vocabularies that exceeded that of European languages (Basso 1976, 107). As David Murray has summarized this view, "The perceived lack of abstractions, reflecting a lack of intellectual development on the part of the Indians, means that concepts must be built up from objects and their qualities or associations" (Murray 1991, 42).

I do not know who first suggested that the tendency to rely heavily on figures of speech represents a "poverty of language." Though the idea had currency long before he wrote his *New Science* in the early eighteenth century, Italian philosopher Giambattista Vico certainly worked the idea fully and used it effectively as a basis for his conception of stages in historical development. A polemic on Descartes's *Discourse on Method,* the *New Science* affords an example of how the poverty-of-language idea could provide a received foundation for a complex argument. It figures in Vico's insistence that the most proper scholarly endeavor was the study of human history.

Vico begins his argument by noting the differences in two kinds of knowledge: *verum* and *certum.* The former is universal, a priori knowledge arrived at through a rigorous rational process in which each step is logically demonstrated. Cartesian geometry provided an excellent example, as did poetics and esthetics. These also shared the feature of being products of the human mind, where, in fact, they had their sole existence. The search for verum is *scienza.* Certum, on the other hand, is consciousness of truths gained through the senses and experiences, through *conscienza.* For Descartes, verum was vastly superior to certum, because the latter was subject to sensory unreliability.

Descartes had explicitly rejected the study of history from his scheme of verifiable knowledge, but Vico suggested that the study of human culture should be the principal activity of scholarship. Following the Cartesian insistence on the superiority of verum, Vico noted that the only areas of knowledge (e.g., mathematics and poetics) that could be legitimately categorized as verum were human-derived. "Verum et factum convertuntur," he wrote in one of the key aphorisms of the highly gnomic *New Science*. The civil world, Vico argued, has been made by humans—that is, customs and institutions are products of the human mind. The principles of civil development are consequently to be found in the modifications of the mind. Since God made the natural world, only he knows it as verum, but since mankind has made the civil world, humans can come to know it as verum. Furthermore, customs and institutions, unlike the theorems of geometry, have existence in the world outside the human mind and are also accessible as certum. Historical and ethnographic knowledge is thus superior to the mathematical and other branches of learning that found Cartesian favor because that knowledge is accessible as both verum and certum. Vico's new science of human development combined philosophy (knowledge as verum—i.e., general principles of historical change) with philology (knowledge as certum—i.e., the particulars of a specific culture's situation, especially as revealed through linguistic clues). Vico rejected the abstract theorizing of natural law philosophers (pure verum) for historical principles (verum) derived from cross-cultural historical knowledge (certum).

Vico believed that historical principles should be studied genetically because human nature was dynamic. He rejected what he called "the conceit of scholars," the notion that "primitive" humans thought in the same way as seventeenth-century natural philosophers. Instead, mankind in the earliest stage of development (what Vico called "the Age of Gods") thought "poetically," and here we return to the poverty-of-language idea. Primitive mankind represented the childhood of human development. Vico held that using his reconstructive imagination he was able to "descend" to a primitive mental state. What helped him was the fact that people in that condition were incapable of abstract thought and, consequently, expressed themselves concretely, specifically, and anthropomorphically—using figurative tropes, in other words.

According to Vico's historical scheme, the descendants of the survivors of Noah's flood did not hear thunder for many generations. The ground and air were too saturated for that meteorological phenomenon to occur. When enough drying took place for thunder to happen, awestruck humans assumed that it was the voice of a powerful being—hence, the thunder deities that figure in mythologies around the world, including Native North America. To understand the Age of Gods, the primitive developmental stage in a culture, Vico suggested, one should examine the concrete images in its visual and verbal art. Those images represented the institutions and customs about which people could not speak more directly due to their limited ability to think abstractly. The historical principle that mankind in the early stage of development was a child in intellect provided the verum for Vico's historical scheme, while the specific figures he encountered in artistic expression offered the observable data, the certum.[1]

The idea that figurative language signaled poverty of thought long preceded Vico, and he drew for most of his examples upon early Italian history rather than from observations of visitors to American Indian communities. But his scheme and its supporting epistemology suggested how widely and unquestioningly held the poverty-of-language idea was among European thinkers. Moreover, it persisted well into the nineteenth and even twentieth centuries with Native Americans sometimes appearing as exemplary specimens of folk whose "prelogical," "preabstract" mentality forced them to rely on metaphor, metonymy, and other figures of speech.

Perhaps the most influential of the poverty-of-language advocates of the mid-nineteenth century was the mythologist Max Müller, who based his interpretation of European mythology on the notion that the prehistoric Aryans—the cultural progenitors of the Indo-European societies—had been incapable of abstract thought and expression. They were also fascinated by the daily cycle of light and darkness, which they had to characterize in concrete phrases. After generations had passed, according to Müller, the meanings of these phrases had become obscure through a process he called the "disease of language." Myths developed to explain what these obscure phrases might mean—hence, the elaborate mythological systems of the Greeks, Norse, Celts, and other European peoples (Dorson 1958).

Müller's ideas made their way into the discourse on Native American traditions through the work of Horatio Hale and Daniel Garrison Brinton. Brinton, for example, showed that the root in the Algonquian trickster's name was one of those polyvalent words meaning light, heat, warmth, and the like. Thus, Manibozho became another solar deity, and tales of his escapades were a concrete way of representing the abstract contestation of light and darkness (see Clements 1986, 61–73). Another important thinker who espoused the idea that "primitive" mankind was incapable of abstract thought was the French philosopher Lucien Lévy-Bruhl, who suggested that the lack of abstraction in their languages produced rich and copious vocabularies, which could be exploited figuratively (Cazeneuve 1972, 3–11).

Possibly the first (certainly the first fully articulated) application of the concept to Native North Americans appeared in one of the earliest Jesuit documents, written by Pierre Biard, who arrived in Acadia in 1611. His lengthy statement is worth presenting in its entirety:

> [R]ude and untutored as they [the Native Acadians] are, all their conceptions are limited to sensible and material things; there is nothing abstract, internal, spiritual, or distinct. *Good, strong, red, black, large, hard,* they will repeat to you in their jargon; *goodness, strength, redness, blackness*—they do not know what they are. And as to all the virtues you may enumerate to them, *wisdom, fidelity, justice, mercy, gratitude, piety,* and others, these are not found among them at all except as expressed in the words *happy, tender love, good heart.* Likewise they will name to you a wolf, a fox, a squirrel, a moose, and so on to every kind of animal they have, all of which are wild, except the dog; but as to words expressing universal and generic ideas, such as beast, animal, body, substance, and the like, these are altogether too learned for them. (Thwaites 1959a, 2:11)

Biard was not alone among the Jesuit missionaries in noting a lack of abstractions in Native American languages. His successors such as Francesco Bressani, the only Italian among the French Jesuits, wrote of the Hurons that they "have no abstract nouns, and few substantives, and these indeclinable,—using for adjectives verbs instead of nouns, which last among them are conjugated not declined" (Thwaites 1959a, 39:121).

Bressani's attempt at grammatical analysis of the Huron language may suggest why the Indians appeared to be incapable of speaking abstractly—that is, the stumbling, fumbling nature of the missionaries' mastery of the Native languages. Imagine the contact situation. A missionary from Europe has encountered a group of people with whom he needs to communicate, but their language has very little in common with any language he has encountered either as a vernacular or in formal learning situations. He begins to learn the language, as he must, by asking its speakers to name things for him. The things they will name will be those that both they and he can apprehend with their senses. He can elicit—to build upon Biard's examples—their word for "dog" by pointing to an example of the pertinent animal (though he might get the equivalent of "Fido" rather than the word for a class by singling out an individual specimen), and he can elicit their word for "hare" by indicating the spoils of a recent hunting trip. But how can he move to a more general level: a word that would apply to both the living, domestic companion of the fireside and the dead, wild ingredient for the stewpot? To confuse matters more, these two phenomena need not be members of the same categorical domain. Dogs might very well be classed with humans, and dead hares might share a domain with other edibles such as wild blackberries. Cognitive anthropologists have sometimes proceeded in just the opposite way from the hypothetical illustration advanced here: beginning with generic headings which their Native collaborators are expected to fill in (cf. D'Andrade 1995, 58–62; Lakoff 1987). Moreover, in learning a language without a *written* grammar, it takes some time to figure out in a way that is comprehensible to European preconceptions how nouns and pronouns are declined and verbs conjugated, provided that any of those concepts have relevance at all to the language in question.

Communication between Europeans and Native Americans at the early stages of contact emphasized concrete terms because those were the easiest upon which to find common ground. Translation of abstractions remains problematical even when considerable work done with modern linguistic rigor has been undertaken—an example being the well-known case of the Navajo word *"hózhó,"* which can be (and has been) translated into English as "holiness," "wholeness," "harmony," "balance," "beauty," "symmetry," and "health"—to cite only some possibilities (Witherspoon 1977, 24–27). Surely many frustrated Navajos have attempted to clarify this elusive concept for Euro-American interlocutors by invoking specific concrete examples. Neither the Navajo (or "Acadian" or "Huron") nor the European mind is incapable of abstraction. They are simply incapable of communicating in abstractions at least in the early stages of linguistic contact.

Finally, we should note that "dead" metaphors often come to be conventional ways of linguistically representing abstractions. When Christians pray to "Our Father" in heaven, they are following convention. Doing so is no indication that they are "prelogical" or incapable of abstraction. Perhaps some of the concrete figures that appeared repeatedly in Native American discourse—terms like "covenant chain" used by the Iroquois—were similar traditional locutions that had become efficient ways of referring to an abstract concept—in this case, an intercultural political alliance. What they might lose in proving the ability of their speakers to think in abstractions they gained in bringing to bear a rich trove of connotations on the matter at hand. As a matter of fact, discourse on particular topics may depend so heavily on metaphor—some of which may be "dead" remnants of past usage and others of which may reflect and shape the way those topics are conceived—that its use becomes virtually subconscious (Lakoff and Johnson 1980). George Lakoff has suggested that in English (and with presumed application to other languages) use of metaphor is commonplace, especially when one is treating domains of information "where there is no clearly discernible preconceptual structure" (Lakoff 1987, 303). To use metaphor is to be human, not to be "primitive" or "childlike."

At least one source of the poverty-of-language assumption, the edifice upon which philosophers from Vico to Lévy-Bruhl and beyond have erected their conceptions of human intellect, must lie in the simple exigencies of interlingual contact and the lack of sophistication of commentators regarding the languages about which they were offering opinions. One wonders if Indians or Africans or Australians who participated in such contact were assuming that Europeans lacked the capacity to think abstractly because they only spoke of dogs and hares and other sense-accessible phenomena.

But this does not explain the extensive use of metaphor and other figures in oratory. For even when they were speaking to Europeans, Native American orators usually had the advantage of interpreters, who, though perhaps linguistically unsophisticated in many respects, had probably gotten the basics of mastering vocabulary. Yet, if we are to trust the accounts of early commentators, whose ideas, in this regard at least, are reinforced by recent anthropologists, linguists, and folklorists, American Indian speech makers did rely frequently on figurative tropes in their public discourse. Was it because they could not communicate abstractly, or was it part of a set of linguistic strategies that tropes have been reported as serving in many language contexts? I will argue the latter and suggest that the use of figurative language in Native American oratory served several fundamental purposes: to make clear otherwise nebulous concepts (which may seem to support the poverty-of-language hypothesis); to create memorable impressions not only of the conveyed message but also of the speaker him- or herself; to cloak ideas, sometimes unpleasant or inflammatory, in as pleasant a format as possible (that is, to achieve indirection); to ground what is said in the authority of tradition; to move referents through quality space with as much subtlety as possible (thus serving the ends of persuasion); and to integrate the diverse phenomena of the experienced environment into a satisfying whole.

Undoubtedly, the early commentators were correct to assume that Native American orators used such figures as metaphor and metonymy to communicate about abstractions. For example, the phrase "To open a path from one nation to another, by removing the logs, brush and briars out of way," which Moravian missionary John Heckewelder included in his glossary of Indian (primarily Lenapé) metaphorical expressions, conveys with vivid clarity the sentiments by which Heckewelder defined it: "To invite the nation to which the path leads, to a friendly intercourse; to prepare the way to live on friendly terms with them" (Heckewelder 1876, 139). To communicate his despair and frustration, Hin-mah-too-yah-laht-ket (Chief Joseph) could say his "heart" was "sick and sad." And to cite some examples that have become cliches in the representation of Indian speech: a unit of time reckoning may be tied to the concrete phenomenon of a "moon," a long period of time (some twelve or so moons) might be referred to as a "winter," the president of the United States became the "Great White Father," and putting an end to hostilities was rendered as "burying the hatchet." When dealing with matters of diplomacy and time-reckoning, frequent subjects for the oratorical encounters between Native Americans and Euro-Americans, public speakers often had recourse to figurative language for the sake of clarity.

But if this reflects unsophisticated intellects and a concomitant poverty of language among Indians, what are we to make of the ways in which the Christian missionaries referred to the members of the Trinity they were presenting to the Indians: a father, his son, and a third party represented perhaps as a dove or as a tongue of flame? In fact, a couple of pages before he offers his analysis of the deficiencies of the Huron language, Jesuit Francesco Bressani refers to the father figure in the Trinity as an "Author" (Thwaites 1959a, 39:119). In the speech of missionaries, the son in the Trinity might be alternately represented as a lamb, a bridegroom, or even a bright morning star, and the visual art that filled the Jesuits' places of worship back home (and later in America) depicted him as a nut, pelican, rainbow, rose, fish, or phoenix—to name only a few of the ways in which conventional iconography portrayed Jesus. These same missionaries, and certainly the government officials who accompanied them, worked for the "crown" or "scepter." The point is that the use of tropes to communicate about the abstract is not a distinctly "primitive" phenomenon, but a common practice.

As Lakoff has noted, "Metaphor provides us with a means for comprehending domains of experience that do not have a preconceptual structure of their own. A great many of our domains of experience are like this. Comprehending experience via metaphor is one of the great imaginative triumphs of the human mind. Much of rational thought involves the use of metaphoric models. Any adequate account of rationality must account for the use of imagination and much of imagination consists of metaphorical reasoning" (Lakoff 1987, 303). To render the unvisualizable in visual terms becomes especially important when the concepts involved lie at the root of what it means to be human—the domain of what James Fernandez calls "the inchoate" (Fernandez 1986, 235).

Lewis Cass, who, though recognized as an authority on Indians by his contemporaries, exhibited little sensitivity to Native American cultures, wrote in an 1826 essay:

> The range of thought of our Indian neighbors is extremely limited. Of abstract ideas they are almost wholly destitute. They have no sciences, and their religious notions are confused and circumscribed. They have but little property, less law, and no public offences. They soon forget the past, improvidently disregard the future, and waste their thoughts,

when they think, upon the present. The character of all original languages must depend, more or less, upon the wants, means, and occupations, mental and physical, of the people who speak them, and we ought not to expect to find the complicated refinements of polished tongues, among those of our Indians. (Cass 1826, 79)

Based on the use of figurative language in the speech of missionaries and other Euro-Americans, though, the same set of judgments could be rendered against them. When dealing with matters inchoate, such as the foundational abstractions characteristic of all human groups, people often resort to an "argument of images" that emerges not from the language used in formal logic but from the familiar, routine phenomena of everyday life. Part of the "mission of metaphor" is to "provide identity" for inchoate subjects (Fernandez 1986, 31; cf. Lakoff and Johnson 1980, Lakoff 1987); the need for metaphor remains consistent in the human experience whenever the ambiguity of the inchoate is encountered.

If Indian orators used metaphors and metonyms to communicate the incommunicable, they also employed figures of speech because they recognized that what they were saying was supposed to be artful and to be a showcase for their own wit. The "man of words" (a term used by African Americanists to denote the verbal artist in black western-hemisphere cultures [see, e.g., Abrahams 1970, 37–56]) can demonstrate this verbal agility through effective use of orally expressed metaphors. In various cultures, especially nonliterate ones, their employment may serve as badges of a speaker's position as orator, as competent political leader, as someone who should be listened to. Among the Maori, for example, the ability to manipulate the formal devices of oratorical tradition as well as "the fire and drama of delivery, the appropriateness of content, and their general entertainment value" is a principal source of status for the public person (Salmond 1975, 52). The most highly lauded orators are those with the most extensive repertoires of poetic devices (Salmond 1975, 55). For the Melpa of Papua New Guinea, figurative language functions, in part, as a basis for the orator's "showing his skills in speech-making and thus enhancing his general status" (Strathern 1975, 193). To speak well is to use effectively the communicative medium exclusive to humanity, and in nonliterate cultures, where verbal communication is completely oral, verbal ability and agility may very well be the foundation of what it means to be fully human.

Another widely noted feature of figurative language in oratory is its role in gilding the potentially unpleasant and defusing the potentially confrontational. Oratory often occurs in emotionally charged situations. Councils in which decisions affecting an entire group's livelihood may showcase oratory, individuals may use oratory to make cases for their own self-worth, leaders may use oratory to maintain their positions and discourage the success of rivals, and oratory may prevent or generate physical manifestations of hostility: these are but a few of the possibly explosive and sensitive circumstances during which this verbal art form may take place. Commonly, orators have used indirection to counteract the dynamics of the situations in which they speak. Using figurative language is one device of indirection. Donald Brenneis has referred to oratory that relies upon tropes as "oblique oratory," which, he argues, occurs frequently in what anthropologists call "egalitarian" societies as a way of preserving the appearance of equality and avoiding conflict (Brenneis 1984, 69-70). As Michelle Rosaldo has written of Ilongot oratory, "[T]he crooked and complex language of oratory is a means of reaching understanding when all know it will be difficult" (Rosaldo 1973, 219). Moreover, the use of indirection through tropes or another device allows the speaker to save face. Should someone accuse an orator of advocating a foolish position or of taking an unpopular stand, metaphor and metonymy allow the speaker a degree of deniability. The accuser has simply misunderstood the intent of what was said. This is probably one reason for the popularity of royal spokespersons in some West African societies. The "hazards of the spoken word" are deflected from the chief by his orator, who speaks in ways that afford some wiggle room (Yankah 1995, 179).

Some figurative language also carries with it an aura of authority. Students of Iroquois diplomacy have noted several recurrent images that appear in the speeches made by orators for the Six Nations (Jennings et al. 1985, 115–24). These include not only the well known "chain" to denote an alliance, but such figures as "eating" to refer to all manner of consumption, a house and its various components (e.g., doors and gables) to refer to the league itself, "mat" to refer to domesticity, and "tree," which was used to mean peace and security. The Iroquois orator who employed these figures invested his speech with the power of the group both synchronically and (since the tropes were traditional) diachronically. His images identified him with the group, and the argument that he used the traditional figures to advance seemed to come from that group and to have the implicit endorsement not only of the speaker's contemporaries but of previous generations who had employed the same figures as well. The use of traditional metaphors in oratory might carry the same weight as the epigraphs that essayists sometimes use to introduce their written arguments or the supporting quotations from recognized authorities with which academics bolster their scholarly publications.

Oratory is most often persuasive discourse. In those tribal contexts where other means of getting people to act in certain ways are not available and where authority is an ad hoc, consensus-based phenomenon, the persuasive function of oratory may loom large. It may be the principal means by which leaders assume and maintain their positions and by which they generate communal activities—be those effecting peaceful relationships with former foes, going to war, organizing a hunt, or moving camp. Figurative language can be an efficacious device in persuasion.

James Fernandez has demonstrated one way in which metaphor operates persuasively: by moving inchoate subjects along continua in "quality space," a hierarchy. The foundation of his argument lies in a definition of metaphor as the "strategic predication upon an inchoate pronoun . . . which makes a movement and leads to performance" (Fernandez 1986, 8). Equating an adversary with some phenomenon that is regarded as of low status can invest the adversary with some of that status. Calling a warrior a "woman," for example, might imply (even in a culture that has not traditionally devalued women) that the person lacks the requisite skills and/or temperament to carry out the status-enhancing, gender-based activities of his culture. Often speakers may use metaphor in this way ironically—to appear to move themselves or their adversaries around in "quality space" for the sake of gaining rhetorical advantage. Such may happen when a speaker begins—as many Native Americans addressing Europeans did—by characterizing himself negatively: as a "dog" or as a "child" dependent on a "Great White Father," for instance. The adoption of this meek persona—analogous to the "grammatical markers of uncertainty" that occur in Ilongot oratory (Rosaldo

1973, 216)—seemingly moves the speaker down the continuum, placing another referent, perhaps the listener or whomever he or she represents, in a position to be magnanimous. Or the device may be insinuative, the speaker moving himself lower in quality space in order to cause someone else's guard to come down. Another instance that seems to demean the speaker is the use of metaphors as performance disclaimers, which lower audience expectations so that what the orator does have to say will not be judged too harshly. Because metaphors possess connotations that direct characterizations may lack and because they open up the possibility of deniability, they are particularly effective in the persuasive dimension of oratory.

Metaphor is not the only persuasive figure used in oratory. Native American speechmakers often made use of irony to attain their rhetorical goals (Robie 1982). In 1829, the *Niles Weekly Register* published a speech attributed to a Muskogee, Speckled Snake, in response to President Andrew Jackson's efforts to get the people to move from their traditional land base to Indian Territory. Speckled Snake—apparently a fictional figure created by the Muskogee leader John Ridge, who wrote out the speech (see Debo 1941, 97)—began with a fairly conventional metaphorical predication: the president was a "Great Father" who ostensibly loved his "red children." The apparent movement in quality space here has Jackson, the hostile adversary who has made an unpopular recommendation (that will eventually become more than mere recommendation), cast as the benign paternal guardian. Meanwhile, the Muskogee move to a hierarchical niche beneath him—one in which they are dependent on his benignity. Speckled Snake then rehearsed the history of Native American relations with Euro-Americans and their ancestors. That had begun when Europeans, "cramped" by their journey over the "wide waters," needed some room to stretch—a need the Indians accommodated by providing them with land and other material assistance. He added, though, that the "little man" the European had been had become "very large" and required more land. Gradually the initial hierarchy had been reversed: the "little man" had become the "Great Father" while his early benefactors had been reduced to being "his children." Again and again, the Great Father had asked the red children to move westward, despite promising each time that no more removes would be necessary. President Jackson, though, now said, "Go beyond the Mississippi; there is game; there you may remain while the grass grows and the rivers run." Speckled Snake offered this comment: "Will not our Great Father come there also? He loves his red children, and his tongue is not forked." By this time his listeners knew, of course, that the original metaphorical predication did not coincide with the facts of history and that they should regard with circumspection anything suggested by such a "Father." Moreover, irony allowed Ridge, through Speckled Snake, to offer this advice with indirection. He could not be accused of calling Jackson a malicious liar; in fact, he had said just the opposite.[2]

Finally, metaphor can have a transcendent function. It can be a way of bridging categorical chasms and effecting what Fernandez calls "returning to the whole" (Fernandez 1986, 188–213). The use of kinship terminology as oratorical metaphor illustrates this. By referring to the president in Washington as the "Great White Father," the Native American public speaker could temporarily gloss over obvious cultural differences. By referring to his own community as an aggregation of "fires," rather than "wigwams" or "tepees" or "longhouses," he uses a homely image that would not only be acceptable to his own people but would also resonate with Europeans who treasured the domestic hearth. The gap between the two groups narrows— maybe disappears—at least momentarily.

Keith Basso has noted the way in which metaphor reveals "the existence of relationships where previously none were perceived" in the "wise words" used by Western Apache elders. Speech acts of this genre "are *creative* in the fullest and most genuine sense, for they presuppose and exemplify an ability to arrange familiar semantic features into unfamiliar combinations, to form fresh categorizations of not so fresh phenomena—in short, to generate new categories of meaning" (Basso 1976, 110–11). Moreover, Basso notes, the creator of metaphor "glimpses new categories of meaning before anyone else and, realizing that the linguistic resources at his disposal are inadequate to express them directly, turns to metaphor as a way to escape from his dilemma" (111). Though many oratorical metaphors—and those in Western Apache "wise words"—have been traditional, the use of even cliched metaphors signals a recognition that conventional categories may be inadequate for the situation at hand, that one must find some way to transcend categorical gaps.

The play of tropes in public speaking need not represent poverty of intellect, but can be a careful strategy that, while possibly reflecting traditional practice, evinces the skill of each orator. To see how the skillful manipulation of figurative language might work itself out in a single speech, we will look at an oration delivered by Thanayieson, also known as Tanaghrisson, "Half King" of the Ohio Indians allied with the English during the mid-eighteenth century. A text of the speech appears in the journal of Conrad Weiser (Thwaites 1966, 1:33–35; see also Wallace 1945, 267–68), who had learned the Iroquois language from the Mohawks, with whom he had lived for some time. Weiser, who was highly respected for his linguistic abilities by both Six Nations people and colonials, served as principal interpreter during the first official embassy by British colonial authority to Native Americans living west of the Alleghenies. The purpose of the embassy was threefold: to try to secure an alliance for the British with Indian groups who were becoming dissatisfied with their French connections; to deliver a monetary gift voted by the governments of Pennsylvania and Virginia; and to obtain some explanation for attacks by "northern" Indians on settlements in the Carolinas that had resulted in several persons being taken prisoner. On 12 September 1748, about a month into the expedition, Weiser elicited a response from Thanayieson to a request for information about those prisoners. Born a Catawba but reared by the Senecas, Thanayieson held a position of leadership among the Mingo, perhaps in part because of his oratorical abilities. He spoke "in the presence of all the Deputies of the other Nations" (Thwaites 1966, 1:33). Weiser's journal presents an English translation of the speech with occasional references to how the orator manipulated wampum during the performance.

Thanayieson began by using what his European listeners would have perceived as a metaphor, though the Seneca term which Weiser translated as "Brethren" might have had literal significance:

Brethren, You came a great way to visit us, & many sorts of Evils might have befallen You by the way which might have been hurtful to your Eyes & your inward parts, for the Woods are full of Evil Spirits. We give You this string of Wampum to clear up your Eyes & Minds & to remove all bitterness of your Spirit, that you may hear us speak in good Chear. (33)

Thanayieson's use of body lore as a way of articulating the spiritual harm that might have befallen his listeners during their arduous journey over the mountains is an efficient means of communicating cross-culturally about the inchoate. Iroquoian and Christian concepts of spiritual evil might have certain features in common, but to ensure that his solicitations for their comfort were comprehensible the orator chose to deal in very material terms. Morever, selecting the eyes as the physical focus for danger allowed him to move easily to where the real peril lay—in the minds of his hearers, whose receptivity to his message was paramount in his concerns.

Thanayieson next introduced a conventional image for the growth of the European (in this case, British) presence in Six Nations territory—an image reminiscent of that used by John Ridge in his "Speckled Snake" persona to convince his Muskogee hearers of the inevitable increments that would figure in white men's incursions into Indian lands. Thanayieson said,

> Brethren, when we and you first saw one another at your first arrival at Albany we shook Hands together and became Brethren & we tyed your Ship to the Bushes, and after we had more acquaintance with you we lov'd you more and more, & perceiving that a Bush wou'd not hold your Vessel we then tyed her to a large Tree & ever after good Friendship continued between us. (33)

Not only did the European presence increase in size, requiring a larger stake to tie to, but the links to the "New World" also required strengthening. Moreover, the reference to "tree" may have been carefully chosen, since conventional figurative language in Iroquois oratory might equate a tree with peaceful relationships. Again, Thanayieson employed a conventional image:

> [A]fterwards, you, our Brethren, told us that a Tree might happen to fall down and the Rope rot wherewith the Ship was tyed. You then proposed to make a Silver Chain & tye your Ship to the great Mountains of the five Nations' Country, & that Chain was called the Chain of Friendship; we were all tyed by our Arms together with it, & we Indians of the five Nations heartily agreed to it, & ever since a very good Correspondence have been kept between us. (33)

According to Cadwallader Colden, "The Indians always express a League by a Chain by which two or more things are kept fast together" (Colden 1958, 30), and this rope/chain image has received considerable attention from modern commentators on Iroquois diplomacy (e.g., Jennings et al. 1985). Orators used the image to refer to the series of treaties that predated Thanayieson by at least a century. According to one gloss, "rope" was used conventionally to apply to a nonaggression pact for purposes of trade between the Mohawks and Dutch at Fort Orange. The rope became an "iron chain" in about 1643, when treaties connected the Mohawks with all the Dutch in New Netherlands in a bilateral mutual assistance alliance. The British, as well as non-Mohawk members of the Iroquois League such as the Senecas, entered into the iron chain alliance later in the seventeenth century. In 1677 the iron chain became "silver" and thus the famous Covenant Chain when the Iroquois League and various British colonies formed a multilateral confederation. Massachusetts Bay tried to identify its link in the chain as superior to the others by calling it "golden," but that extension of the metaphor never entered general currency (Jennings et al. 1985, 116).

Whether Thanayieson knew of the complexity of this series of linkage metaphors and could expect his listeners to share his familiarity is uncertain. If so, it meant that he was establishing through the argument of images a series of precedents for continued good will. If not, it meant that he was using the same argument to suggest in imagistic terms the progressive strengthening and increasing value of a relationship that should not be undermined by a minor disruptive incident.

Having done what he could metaphorically to ensure that his listeners would be in proper mind and spirit to hear what he had to say and having reminded them of the tradition of cooperation that had existed for many years between their nations, Thanayieson got down to the business of the moment:

[B]ut we are very sorry that at your coming here we are oblig'd to talk of the Accident that lately befell you in Carolina, where some of our Warriors, by the Instigation of the Evil Spirit, struck their Hatchet into our own Body like, for our Brethren the English & we are of one Body, & what was done we utterly abhor as a thing done by the Evil Spirit himself; we never expected any of our People wou'd ever do so to our Brethren. (33–34)

Modern readers, sensitive to the role of tropes in discourse, should notice three features of this passage. First, Thanayieson blames the incident on an Evil Spirit—perhaps the same kind of spiritual force that could have led the British embassy astray as they journeyed across the mountains to reach the site of their conference. If their eyes, "inward parts," and minds could have been affected by the Evil that lurks in rank wilderness, so then could the perpetrators of the acts for which the embassy is seeking explanation and redress have been bewildered and misled into wrongdoing. Second, we should note the use of "Hatchet" as a metonym for physical violence. Once again, the Six Nations orator is relying upon a traditional image, for the hatchet became virtually an icon for peace (if it was buried) or for war (if it was taken up). Third, Thanayieson has "brethren" become one "body"; for the hatchet is implanted in *"our"* body: the injury has been done not only to the Euro-Americans wounded directly during the hostilities but also to members of the Iroquois League, since all are equally links in a chain of precious metal. He has covered over the categorical distance that would separate even members of the same figurative family. He feels his interlocutors' pain, for it is his own pain.

Thanayieson proposed redress:

> We therefore remove our Hatchet which, by the influence of the Evil Spirit, was struck into your Body, and we desire that our Brethren the Govr. of New York & Onas [the Pennsylvania governor] may use their utmost endeavours that the thing may be buried in the bottomless Pit, that it may never be seen again—that the Chain of Friendship which is of so long standing may be preserv'd bright & unhurt. (34)

At this point in the negotiations, the speaker is relying totally on the play of tropes. His people will remove the metonymic hatchet from the metaphorical body of the British so that the "thing" (a concrete term for a far-from-concrete situation) may be cast into the metaphorical pit where it will not be able to weaken the metaphorical chain of alliance. The point, of course, is that whatever ill will may have generated the Carolina incidents should no longer exist.

But Thanayieson apparently realized that more than manipulation of figures was needed to heal the imminent breach between the British and the Iroquois League, so he promised appropriate restitution:

> Brethren, as we have removed our Hatchet out of your Body, or prop-erly speaking out of our own, We now desire that the Air may be clear'd up again & the wound given may be healed, & every thing put in good understanding, as it was before, and we desire you will assist us to make up everything with the Govr. of Carolina; the Man [apparently William Brown] that was brought as a Prisoner we now deliver to You, he is yours. (34)

Lest his listeners think that they and theirs have been the only victims in this unfortunate incident, the speaker again pointed out their shared wounding. Healing of that wound (a reiteration of the physical imagery that previously had been used to represent spiritual discomfiture) and "clearing the air" (an image that implies the necessity of purifying from taint a substance vital to life) of anything that might obscure the history of the alliance should follow the restoration of the prisoner.

To this point Thanayieson has used traditional figurative language to urge his British listeners not to allow the working of evil (which might affect the judgment of anyone) to interfere with an alliance that has been in place for over a century. But he ends by suggesting that his people are not the only ones whose malfeasance might contribute to weakening that alliance. The British will have to share some of the culpability:

> [T]he Six Nation Warriors often meet Englishmen trading to the Ca-tawbas, & often found that the Englishmen betrayed them to their Enemy, & some of the English Traders had been spoke to by the Indian Speaker [presumably himself] last Year in the Cherrykees Country & were told not to do so; that the Speaker & many others of the Six Nations had been afraid a long time that such a thing wou'd be done by some of their Warriors at one time or other. (34–35)

No figurative language here: plain speech suggests that in addition to the "Evil Spirit" that might have possessed Iroquois raiders on the Carolina settlements, the British had provided some provocation by failing to honor their side of the obligations of alliance.

What Thanayieson's speech shows—among other things—is the *effective* use of metaphor and other figures of speech in an argument of images that appealed to tradition and attempted to create a picture of shared humanity— both in susceptibility to evil influences and in the consequent suffering. Instead of poverty of language and thought, the speech manifests careful calculation using verbal artistry to defuse a potentially inflammatory situation, one that could lead to the dissolution of an alliance that was benefiting all those involved in it. Basso, in fact, insists that the use of metaphor by speakers proves they are not "linguistic cripples." Only those with considerable competence in a language can experiment with words in the unorthodox ways that metaphor requires (Basso 1976, 116). We might add that a language must be *rich,* not poor in resources in order for metaphor to flourish.

Although metaphor was not the only verbal artistic device that Native American orators employed, it was that upon which early reporters commented most frequently. This situation may have arisen, in part, from the ability of metaphor to survive the process of translation and entextualization more successfully than other manifestations of verbal art. Sound devices such as parallelism, alliteration, and anaphora would be lost on European and Euro-American listeners who did not understand the language being used. Even when—as was the case with Conrad Weiser—they were conversant with the language in which an orator spoke, it would be difficult to capture such manifestations of verbal artistry without a tape recorder or video camera. Metaphor was something that they were familiar with and might be memorable enough to stick in their minds long enough for them to write down an approximation of what they had heard or of what their interpreters had told them.[3]

Let us consider one other example, one in which the textmaker does not recognize the use of figurative language and takes a statement by the orator at face value—partially because that statement confirms his own sense of cultural superiority. Thomas James ("General" James from his position in the Second Brigade, First Division of Illinois Militia) made three trips west from his home in what were called the "American Bottoms," the alluvial floodplain of the Mississippi River in Illinois south of Saint Louis. All were accomplished for commercial purposes, though the spirit of adventure also characterized his first trip, made as a rifleman in a Missouri Fur Company expedition that reached the upper Missouri River in 1809 and 1810. After returning home and traveling back east for awhile, James set up as a shopkeeper in Harrisonville, Illinois, in whose vicinity he lived the rest of his life. He interrupted his sedentary existence on two other occasions, both of which involved attempts to boost his sagging commercial fortunes. In 1818 a drought lowered the waters of the Ohio River so much that needed goods could not be shipped to him. To avoid bankruptcy, James embarked on a trading journey to Santa Fe. Though he brought back tales of his adventures, James soon found himself again in financial straits. So he spent the winter of 1822 and 1823 trying to establish commerce with the Comanches.

James's three trips, which provide the subject for his book *Three Years among the Indians and Mexicans* published in 1846, brought him into contact with Indians, and like most travelers who had such contact experiences, he wrote of the Natives' oratorical skills. For example, he characterized the Indians of the Upper Missouri, primarily Mandans and Blackfeet, as "proud, haughty, simple minded warriors and orators" (James 1953, 93). Though not particularly well educated himself and with little knowledge of any rhetoric but the bombastic variety of frontier politicians and preachers, he still felt qualified to offer special praise for those Native Americans who possessed "the eloquence of real orators":

> Their manner of speaking is extremely dignified and energetic. They gesticulate with infinite grace, freedom, and animation. Their words flow deliberately, conveying their ideas with great force and vividness of expression deep into the hearts of their hearers. Among their speakers I recognized all the essentials in manner of consummate orators. (94)

When James describes his trip to Santa Fe in 1818, he considers Indian oratory in more specific terms. One instance recounts a speech delivered by a Ute called Lechat ("a young man of about thirty and of a right princely port and bearing" [160]), who had led a party to the city to seek trade with the Americans visiting there. James wrote that he performed like "a true stump orator." The speech—denominated a "harangue" by James—was a response to some insults from the Santa Fe Spanish, for whom the American businessman had considerable distaste. Thus, he lauded the "independent and lordly manner" affected by Lechat: "He looked like a king upbraiding his subjects for being poor, when they might be rich, and his whole conduct seemed to me like bearding a wild beast in his den" (161–62).

The speech reported by this commercial traveler which I want to consider more fully had occurred earlier on the trip, shortly after the party had reached their destination. The speaker is Cordaro, a Comanche who had been instrumental in insulating James's party from harm as they were making their way toward the principal city of northern New Spain. Cordaro, a leader among the Kotsoteka, the major Comanche band, had become friends with the traders at Nachitoches, Louisiana, and had pledged to protect them as they traversed Comanche country. The speech occurred after the group's arrival in Santa Fe sometime during the winter of 1821–1822, when Cordaro appeared on the scene to assure himself, he claimed, that they had gotten there safely. At the Comanche's request a meeting convened in the Spanish Council House on the public square. Before the Spanish officers and magistrates as well as the community's principal citizens, he voiced his satisfaction that Spanish officials and American traders had formed a friendship that would promote the continuation of trading parties making their way through Comanche country. He noted that while good trading relations existed between Americans and the Osages, who were receiving powder, lead, and guns which they used against his people, no such commercial benefits had accrued to the Comanches—a situation that he hoped the United States and Spanish governments would rectify. James inserted some direct quotation from Cordaro's speech, but because he was harking back over almost a quarter century to words that he had heard through an interpreter, we might hesitate to trust his reliability about exactly how Cordaro expressed himself verbally:

> They [the Osages] steal our horses and murder our people, . . . and the
> Americans sell them the arms and ammunition which they use in war
> upon us. We want your trade, and if you will come among us we will
> not cheat nor rob you. I have had a talk with my nation and told them
> they had done a great wrong in treating you as they did, and they

promised never to do so again. They say they will pay you in horses and mules for the goods they took from you on the Canadian, if you will only come once more into our country. Come with your goods among us; you shall be well treated. I pledge you my word, the word of Cordaro, that you shall not be hurt nor your goods taken from you without full payment. Each of my nation promises to give you two of the best horses in the nation. Come to our country once more and you shall find friends among the Comanches. Come and you shall be safe. Cordaro says it. (150–51)

Even if James is only representing the fundamentals of what Cordaro had said, he did recall that "[t]he old warrior spoke like an orator and looked like a statesman" (151).

This account from the work of an uneducated, ethnocentric commercial traveler who was recalling what he had experienced many years previously seems to have little to recommend it to the serious student of Native American oratory. It would indeed be foolish to argue its more than cursory reliability. But it does suggest the extent to which an American Indian orator was able to manipulate language so as to accomplish his purpose. In this case, that manipulation managed to mislead the person documenting the speech.

Unlike the speech of Thanayieson reported by Conrad Weiser, Cordaro's speech is remarkably straightforward. No apparent metaphor occurs in the "direct" quotation which James presents, something that apparently impressed the commercial traveler. James was also impressed by Cordaro's humility, for he was "conscious of the vast superiority of the whites, or rather of the Americans [not the New Mexicans!], to his own race and desired the elevation of his countrymen by adopting some of our improvements and customs" (151). No doubt Cordaro recognized that some aspects of Euro-American technology and perhaps other aspects of the culture were desirable, but one familiar with Native American oratory (and, in fact, persuasive discourse in probably most cultures) recognizes that the speaker is employing a trope. He plays that trope in such a way as to position himself lower in the hierarchy of images than those whom he is cajoling. Adopting a stance of humbleness—as John Ridge had had Speckled Snake do by casting President Jackson as "father" to his Muskogee "children"—affords the speaker several advantages: his audience may lower its guard and consequently become more receptive to what the orator has to say, the sincerity of the speaker's neediness is made apparent, the paternal concern of the audience is elicited. Cordaro, who had in fact enjoyed the position of superior a few months previous when he had served as the James party's protector as they passed through Comanche country, has adroitly upended the hierarchy by adopting the persona of the humble speaker. One is reminded of the self-abasing postures that orators may adopt while speaking, for example in Bali (Hobart 1975, 77–78) and among the Merina of Madagascar (Bloch 1975a, 7).

Like that of any orally expressed verbal art, artistry in Native American oratory manifested itself in more than what was said. The art of oratory is more than metaphors and other figures of speech. By definition, oratory is a very public art form, and the orator had to recognize the public situation as he or she spoke. The effective orator succeeded often as much by how the speech was rendered as by what the speech said. The performance situation—particularly the fact that the orator had to play to an audience—received considerable treatment by early commentators. Some of what we can learn from them makes up the subject of the next chapter.

CHAPTER **4**

FROM PERFORMANCE THROUGH
DIALOGISM TO EFFICACY

Though figurative language might survive the rigors of translation into a European language and subsequent reproduction in print, early records of Native American oratory most often fail to capture accurately the words uttered by public speakers. Considered on the level of message, they do not successfully effect the esthetic transaction between languages, cultures, and media (see Fine 1984). Whatever strengths they have lie in their treatment of other components of oratorical events. Some of what they reveal about such events provides the focus for this chapter.

Oratorical discourse is formal discourse. Not only is its register evident in its frequent invocation of cultural history and mythological time, but it becomes manifest in the special linguistic flourishes, not limited to metaphors and other figures of speech, that characterize oratory cross-culturally. For example, when people orate they may speak in more regular and stately rhythms than they do in normal conversation. The rhythmic sermons preached largely by African Americans and analyzed by Bruce E. Rosenberg (1988) and Gerald L. Davis (1985) from the perspective of the Parry-Lord hypothesis show this tendency in an extreme form, and Michael K. Foster (1974) has applied a similar oral formulaic perspective to Iroquois oratory. The formality of oratory also encourages a special, perhaps archaic vocabulary ("Fourscore and seven" rather than "eighty-seven," for example), which speakers employ sometimes at the expense of total intelligibility for all present. These features—regularized rhythm and special vocabulary—

appear in Native American oratory, though it may take a perceptive translator such as Dell Hymes (1981), Michael Foster (1974), or Donald Bahr (1975) to reveal them fully.

The formality of oratorical discourse is further evident in the special situations where it occurs. No study that I know of has placed oratory within the full context of other speech genres in a Native North American culture, but such work has been done among the Chamula in the Mexican state of Chiapas. There, according to Gary H. Gossen, oratory represents a marginal genre between the categories of "everyday language" used in conversation and "pure words"—the "stable genres that comprise Chamula oral tradition" and have "formal and contextual constraints of many kinds" (Gossen 1974, 47). The Chamula refer to marginal categories of speaking as "language for people whose hearts are heated" because these discourse genres employ stylistic features, especially repetition and other devices of redundancy that suggest intensified emotions. The marginal genres share these stylistic features with pure words, but unlike the latter, *what* is said is not necessarily formularized. The content of a speaker's utterance is not predictable (48, 57). That oratory meets these criteria is evident from Gossen's description: Speakers who address crowds at festivals "are not constrained by tradition with regard to what they say. They improvise as the situation dictates. Only the style of speech, which is loaded with repetition and metaphor, and its public setting distinguish oratory from ordinary language" (65–66).

Situations for oratory among the Chamula and elsewhere are public in the sense that they usually involve more than the speaker's usual group of casual interlocutors and occur at sites and in circumstances different from the routines of profane space and time. For example, one does not usually deliver an oration for members of one's family seated around the domestic fire or the kitchen table. One would not want to argue, as Colonel Dodge did, that Indians could speak effectively only in those situations that allowed for oratory (Dodge 1882, 246–47), but it is plausible to suggest that speaking reached its most intense in those situations. Special places and special times elicited special uses of language.

Like all orally expressed verbal art, Native American oratory finds its realization in performance, the assumption by the speaker of responsibility for rendering discourse artfully (Bauman 1984; Hymes 1981, 79–259). He or she speaks in a way that calls attention to how the message is rendered. Many early accounts of American Indian speech making stressed its performance features and appreciatively noted the speakers' mastery of them. As Edwin T. Denig suggested, writing of Assiniboine public speakers during the mid-nineteenth century, "A great deal of the effects of their oratory is due to posture, gesture, and accent" (Denig 1930, 526). In fact, much of the value of these early reports lies in their accounts of performance. While later, more scientifically oriented ethnographers trained by John Wesley Powell or Franz Boas may have represented *what* was said more scrupulously, the early accounts, which often describe first-hand experience of oratory in relatively natural situations, sometimes provide fuller descriptions of the manner of delivery, including paralinguistics, proxemics, and kinesics. Though they seldom applied relevant, culture-specific criteria in their descriptions of performance, perhaps the inability of the commentators to understand the languages being used—often the case, and hence the dependence on interpreters—caused them to concentrate on what they could observe, much of which did indeed signal performance according to indigenous standards. But while their descriptions of performance provide us with some valuable ethnographic data, those descriptions usually emerged from and were consequently shaped by either an admiration of the Indians' performance skills or a generally dismissive attitude toward performance that perceived it as a substitute for substance.

Several fairly thorough descriptions of performance appear in the account of Stephen H. Long's exploring expedition to the west conducted in 1819 and 1820. The narrative, written by the expedition botanist and geologist Edwin James, presents descriptions of oratorical events the Long party encountered at various points during their travels. One such event occurred near Council Bluffs in what is now Iowa. Six Kansa (or Kaw) Indians, under the sponsorship of the interpreter John Dougherty, visited an encampment of Otos, Missouris, and Iowas to sue for an end to hostilities of several years' standing. Arriving at dusk, they entered the hostile camp, but were treated with traditional hospitality. The next day at noon a "joint and grand council" took place. Herochshe, leader of the Kansas, had responsibility for addressing a none-too-friendly audience.

He began with a period of silence while he sat "immovable for the space of three-fourths of an hour" (Thwaites 1966, 15:102). Then, according to

James, who had apparently not witnessed the incident first-hand but was relying on Dougherty's account,

> [H]e arose, pointed the stem of the calumet towards each of the three nations successively, then towards heaven, and the earth, after which he stretched out his arm, with the palm of the hand towards the members of the council, moving round with his body so as to present the palm towards each of the members in succession. He then proceeded to shake each individual by the hand, after which he returned to his place, and renewed the motion of his hand as before. (103)

The commentator characterizes these actions as "introductory formalities," then notes that Herochshe assumed an orator's stance, "firm and erect, though perfectly easy and unconstrained." Thus he addressed the council "with a bold expression of countenance, loud voice, and emphatical gesticulation" (103). The text of the speech, which takes a couple of pages in the Thwaites edition of James's narrative, follows. Herochshe expressed conventional disclaimers stressing his own unworthiness (a stance similar to that which Cordaro had assumed while addressing the Thomas James party), emphasized how he expected to suffer death for his imprudent visit to his enemies (undoubtedly to point up the depth and sincerity of the Kansas' desire for peace), and proposed that the disputed territory, which separated the Kansas from the Otos, Missouris, and Iowas, be traversed by a connecting roadway over which even "squaws" could pass unmolested.

After he had finished speaking, Herochshe presented the stem of the calumet to Wasacaruja, an Oto, who touched it and asked, "Is all true that you have spoken[?]" Upon receiving an affirmation from the orator, Wasacaruja accepted the pipe and smoked "whilst Herochshe courteously held the bowl of it in his hand" (105). He performed the same polite ceremony with other council participants.

James closes his second-hand account of this oratorical performance with an evaluation:

> It is impossible to convey an adequate idea of the energy, and propriety, with which this speech was delivered, or of the dignity and self-possession of the speaker. Before he commenced, he hesitated and

looked around upon his enemies, probably in order to trace in the lineaments of their countenances, the expression of their feelings towards him. He then began his address, by raising his voice at once to its full intonation, producing a truly powerful effect upon the ear, by a contrast with the deep and long continued silence which preceded it. He was at no loss for subject or for words, but proceeded right onwards to the close of his speech, like a full-flowing, bold, and impetuous stream. (105)

Keeping in mind that the characteristics of communication that qualify it as performance are culture-specific (though not so much so that they could not be exploited in intercultural situations such as this one described by James), we can nevertheless note features of Herochshe's oration that seem to have been encountered throughout much of Native North America, were deemed worthy of remark by early commentators, and were considered by them to be indicators of performance. Three particularly important performance features of the Kansa's speech delivery that found their way into many early descriptions of oratory are the paralinguistic devices he employs, his manipulation of objects, and the way in which he presented himself kinesically.

Commentators often wrote of the ways in which Indian orators used "body language" in performance. The kinesic dimension of oratory that they noted involved two major components: posture and gesture. Posture dominates a brief description of speech making written by D. C. Poole, who served as agent to the Brulé and Oglala Lakota in 1869 and 1870. Poole generalized about his charges: "They were natural orators, and always at home as they rose to speak in council; standing in a finely poised attitude, their blankets drawn over one shoulder, the other left bare, giving full play to their graceful gestures" (Poole 1988, 43). Among Iroquois orators, according to Jesuit missionary Pierre Millet, the typical postures were "either standing erect, or, more frequently, walking about" (Thwaites 1959a, 58:185). James Adair claimed that orators always assumed a "standing posture" when speaking in councils (Williams 1930, 460).

Writing in generalities, Edwin James characterized the gestures used by the Native American speech makers encountered by the Long expedition as "extravagant," noting that such "gesticulation" was "one of the prominent features of Indian oratory" (Thwaites 1966, 15:239). Gestures figure prominently in the descriptions of oratory found in the Jesuit *Relations.* For example, Barthelmy Vimont wrote of an Iroquois orator who "made use of a thousand gestures, as if he had collected the waves and had caused a calm, from Quebec to the Iroquois country" (Thwaites 1959a, 27:259). From the same group came the speaker who "spread out his arms and raised them aloft, as if addressing himself to Heaven; he knelt down and danced in that posture, raising his eyes and arms to Heaven" (Thwaites 1959a, 27:243). A spokesman for the Huron, according to François le Mercier, "made as much use of gestures as of his tongue" (Thwaites 1959a, 49:227). The same Jesuit missionary held that Iroquois orators spoke "not less by gesticulation than by language" (Thwaites 1959a, 51:205). The famous orator Keokuk, according to Prince Maximilian zu Wied, made effective use of kinesics: "gesticulating . . . in harmony with his thoughts" (Thwaites 1966, 22:227). Writing about the tribes of the Upper Missouri, whom he had visited a decade or so before the Long expedition, Thomas James noted how "[t]hey gesticulate with infinite grace, freedom, and animation" (James 1953, 94).

Many writers who encountered oratory around council fires echoed Edwin James's description of Herochshe's use of the calumet. William Clark, writing in his journal of the Corps of Discovery for 26 September 1804, described the scene at a council with the Tetons. Several elders had spoken when the "great Chief" assumed a speaking posture "with great State." After his address, the orator "with great Solemnity took up the pipe of Peace & after pointing it to the heavins[,] the 4 quarters of the Globe & the earth," resumed his discourse. Then the Teton speaker presented the pipe to members of the Lewis and Clark party to smoke (Thwaites 1959b, 1:167). Similar accounts appear in the journal account for 13 August 1805, when the Corps encountered the Shoshone (Thwaites 1959b, 2:341), as well as elsewhere during the two-year period of exploration treated in these valuable resources.[1]

Other objects that received attention in descriptions of oratory included the wampum belts that the Iroquois and other northeastern orators often used to validate and reinforce the points they were making and the post that some Plains societies erected apparently as a way of certifying the truth of an orator's remarks. Edwin James describes this latter practice among the Otos and Iowas at a meeting at Council Bluffs: "In the intervals of their dances, a warrior would step forward and strike a flagstaff they had erected with a stick, whip, or other weapon, and recount his martial deeds. The ceremony is called *striking the post,* and whatever is then said may be relied upon as rigid truth, being delivered in the presence of many a jealous warrior and witness, who could easily detect and would immediately disgrace the *striker* for exaggeration or falsehood" (Thwaites 1966, 14:231). James noted a similar practice at an Omaha calumet dance (Thwaites 1966, 15:125).

The role of wampum in speech making has received considerable attention from modern scholars on Indian diplomacy, especially among Iroquoians (e.g., Foster 1985). The trader John Long reported various oratorical uses for wampum belts among Algonquians as well: "When a council is held, they are given out with the speeches, and always proportioned in their size, and the number of rows of wampum which they contain, to the idea the Indians entertain of the importance of the meeting." The use of black-and-white shell beading to create designs on the belts might serve to regulate treaty negotiations. Long described how Sir William Johnson would take a belt by one end while his counterpart on the Native American side held the other. When the Indian diplomat was making a point, he would run his finger along a line of white beads, and when Johnson's turn came, he would point to the diamond-shaped design of white beads in the center of the belt, which, according to Long, signified "the council fire." Wampum belts also served as records of previous treaties and were "easily deciphered by the Indians, and referred to in every treaty with the white people" (Thwaites 1966, 2:83–84).

Frank G. Speck, an early twentieth-century anthropologist, suggested that wampum among the Abnaki, Algonquian speakers in the Northeast, served as a kind of guide to what a speaker was to say, especially if that speaker was a messenger for a tribal council: "With almost religious seriousness the messengers who carried the belts on their missions were instructed in the speeches they were to deliver, the symbols on the belts corresponding to the content of the messages" (Speck 1915, 492–508). Suffice it to say here that wampum belts figured significantly in oratorical performances, often being handled by the speaker in particularly dramatic ways to reinforce the solemnity and significance of points he or she might be making. Moreover, traditional patterns for using wampum might carry over to manipulation of other objects. For example, archival records describe an Iroquois speaker who punctuated an indictment of a Euro-American entrepreneur by using liquor bottles in lieu of wampum. George Klock had tricked Indians into making their marks on deeds of sale by getting them drunk (Nammack 1969, 49).

Commentators also remarked frequently on the paralinguistic features of oratorical delivery, especially volume dynamics and vocal timbre. The latter feature of performance interested Jesuit Pierre Millet, who noted the careful adjustment of tone of voice to rhetorical purpose: "At times, he [the Iroquois orator] speaks in lugubrious tones, drawling out his words; at others, in a sharp tone calculated to produce emotion; sometimes in a joyful voice, intermingled with songs, which the other elders repeat in harmony" (Thwaites 1959a, 48:185–87). The Moravian missionary David Zeisberger characterized the tone of Iroquois speakers as "very pompous and boastful" (Hulbert and Schwarze 1910, 142). Paul Le Jeune was impressed by the way in which speakers manipulated the volume of their delivery. About a Montagnais speaker whom he had not personally heard, he reported that witnesses "told me how he raised his voice according to the subjects he treated, then lowered it with so much humility, and with such an attitude of submission, that he won the hearts of all who looked at him, though they did not understand him" (Thwaites 1959a, 5:211). Huron speakers were known to "raise and quaver their voice, like the tones of a Preacher in olden times" (Thwaites 1959a, 10:257). Edwin James noted how the Omaha orator Big Elk began a speech "in a low tone, the voice gradually rising as the speaker proceeded, until it attained its full intonation" (Thwaites 1966, 14:261).

These glimpses of some performance attributes of American Indian oratory, like much else that was written on the subject by early commentators, might cut two ways. On one hand, performance skills might be a component in the package of eloquence that signaled the Indians' possession of a common humanity that manifested itself in the effective use of language. But, on the other hand, the reliance on gesture, vocal embellishments, and other features of performance might be another indication of how little the Indians really had to say because of the poverty of their intellects and the consequent poverty of their languages. The controversial John Dunn Hunter generalized, for example, that Native American languages are "pantomimic, and . . . their poverty is, to a considerable degree, made up for by those impressive and common [kinesic] auxiliaries" (Hunter 1973, 86). Garrick Mallery cites several examples of commentators who assumed that gestures used by Indians compensated for linguistic deficiencies. Writing of the Arapahos, for instance, Richard Burton suggested that gestures were so essential as an augmentation of their scanty vocabulary that speakers could hardly talk to each other in the dark (quoted in Mallery 1881, 315). Mallery rejected this connection between use of gestures and poverty of language and, in fact, perceived gestures as ways of "keying" performance (cf. Bauman 1984, 16–22). To counteract the position taken by Burton, he cited a talk made by the Ute leader Ouray to his delegation after a disappointing interview with the Secretary of the Interior in Washington:

> He spoke without pause in his own language for nearly an hour, in a monotone and without a single gesture. The reason for this depressed manner was undoubtedly because he was very sad at the result [of the interview], involving loss of land and change of home; but the fact remains that full information was communicated on a complicated subject without the aid of a manual sign, and also without even such change of inflection of voice as is common among Europeans. (Mallery 1881, 315)

Ouray was clearly not speaking in a performance mode in this situation.

Though Mallery's subject was the intercultural gestural language that allowed cursory communication among representatives of different ethnic groups in Native North America, he recognized the role of kinesics in oratory. He noted that "modern public speakers" needed to develop gestural skills as part of their training in oratorical delivery (311). Presumably, he would apply the same ideas to the ways in which Indian orators came to master their art.

Most commentators agreed that Indian orators were effective actors, but for many all they were doing was playing a part. One repeatedly encounters statements about how appealing speeches might be, but not because of the ideas they presented—ideas whose full significance was generally inaccessible to Europeans and Euro-Americans for linguistic reasons. Histrionics supplanted ideas as they supposedly did on the popular stages of Europe and Euro-America. Hence, one could refer to a skilled public speaker as a *"tabarin"* (a comic actor) as did Jesuit Barthelmy Vimont (Thwaites 1959a, 27:255), damning him with faint praise since the art of the actor, which for early commentators was inherent in the Native character, was at best superficial and at worst false and misleading. Peter Skene Ogden perhaps summed up the dismissive way in which some Euro-Americans came to regard the performance style of Native American orators in a comment about the interchanges between a group of Flatheads and Blackfeet over the theft of some horses: "[I]f they wanted the euphonial polish of a Cicero, [they] might have vied with Demosthenes in the energetic vigour of their language" (Odgen 1853, 32), invoking thus the conventional classical analogue but backhandedly identifying the Indian speakers with the least refined oratory of the ancients.

Yet what these performance descriptions of the art of oratory should recall to us is that this genre of verbal art, by definition, manifests itself *publicly*—a point that may be forgotten when one is confronted with only the unadorned literary texts of orations that have often been all that appears in print. It is important to stress that when an orator speaks, he or she has an audience that is as much a part of the performance as the orator. The presence of that audience recalls the fact that oratory, like every other kind of discourse, is dialogic, that the orator is always responding to and reacting to other discourse.

In an essay on a personal narrative tradition in an African American family in Florida, Allan F. Burns has contrasted the dialogic nature of conversation with what he views as oratory's "monologism." "In many conversations," he writes, "one person completes the thoughts and sentences of another. In more formal contexts, *including oratory,* this feature of 'dual thinking' is spurned and thought of as inappropriate to the flow of speech, or as rude." Moreover, oratory has a "more frozen and formal monologic style" than conversation (Burns 1996, 79; emphasis added). While oratory may appear, especially when represented as a text on a printed page, to be monologic, in performance it manifests the dialogism that Mikhail Bakhtin has noted as characterizing all verbal art (Bakhtin 1981). As Deborah Tannen notes in the same essay collection in which Burns's article appears, every utterance evinces a "polyphonic nature. . . . This polyphony derives from the multiple resonances of the people, contexts, and genres with which the utterance . . . has been associated" (Tannen 1996, 198). Or one could argue *contra* Burns, "[T]he so-called monologue . . . is always a dialogue [at least] with an imagined other" (Attanasi and Friedrich 1995, 34)

Anthropological literature on oratory in cross-cultural contexts notes, in fact, that dialogism appears in even its most obvious forms. Among the Kuna of Panama, for example, formal oratory takes the form of dialogic chanting. The person designated as principal chanter sits astraddle his hammock in the gathering house and begins to chant in a soft voice. After each unit of discourse, another person, designated as responder and also straddling his hammock, answers with a formalized affirmation—translatable as "Indeed" or "Yes" (Sherzer 1983, 73–76). Similar "stylized dialogicality" occurs among some Native South Americans such as the Shokleng of southern Brazil (Urban 1991, 123–47). Or one might note the competitive oratory substituted for warfare as a way of acquiring *mana* among the Maori (Salmond 1975, 48). Another example of dialogic oratory occurs in many parts of West Africa, where royal speech is articulated through a mouthpiece, the professional orator. Such a tradition protects the royal from face-challenging situations that might result from rhetorical slips or from direct confrontations. It also protects the principal's interlocutors from whatever spiritual power emanates from him. The role of the orator may be simply to repeat verbatim what the monarch dictates to him, but often he is expected to couch the royal message in the most effective rhetoric, a skill acquired through apprenticeship and experience (Yankah 1995).

A similar case of overtly dialogic oratory was reported by Lewis Cass, no great admirer of Native Americans or their verbal art. In dismissing the oratorical abilities of Tecumseh, Cass claimed that "the public delivery of the speech is a mere act of memory on the part of the orator" because he or she was merely a spokesperson for what the tribal council had prepared and instructed the orator to say (Cass 1826, 99n). In fact, in many eastern groups the role of "orator" was a relatively formal office, and figures such as Sagoyewatha (Red Jacket) achieved considerable prestige from the speaking ability they employed to present perspectives of the people they represented. Even when they used the first-person singular, they spoke for the collectivity (Ganter 2001)—a convention their European and Euro-American interlocutors often misinterpreted.

One component of our operational definition of oratory in cross-cultural perspective stresses its *public* nature. That is, oratory must have an audience, probably a human one. In fact, Wick R. Miller draws a distinction between oratory and ceremonial speech in American Indian traditions by suggesting that the former is "almost always directed to other people," while the latter "may be directed to other speech or to supernaturals" (Miller 1996, 231). Of course, even in ceremonial speech ostensibly targeted at spiritual beings, the performer is probably so aware of the presence of other people listening in that they become at least a secondary audience; the distinction drawn by Miller perhaps does not work totally. But it does remind us that the essential dialogism in oratory occurs between speaker and audience, whose presence and responsiveness or lack thereof is part of the performance.

Orators, like other verbal artists, shape what they say and how they say it to the expectations generated by the particular generic tradition in which they are operating. Note, for example, the ways in which expectation shapes the method and style of Iroquois orators in a generalized description prepared by the Jesuit missionary Josephus Aubery:

> A speaker rises in their midst, and pronounces a discourse. If he perorates aptly, eloquently, or cleverly, he wins his cause; if timidly, hesitatingly, inelegantly, his cause is lost. They are swayed by reason, and the eloquence of him who would convince them on any point depends upon one condition only,—to wit, that he place his argument in a good light, and explore it without ornament or disguise. (Thwaites 1959a, 66:177–79)

One dimension of the performer-audience dialogism in Native American oratory, then, involves the speaker's sense of an esthetic heritage, the culture-specific conventions of the genre that he or she acknowledges by following or, more rarely, by violating during the discourse.

Unfortunately, those conventions are among the most difficult to ascertain from the available literature, since almost always the commentators invoked their own sense of what a good oration should be rather than articulating any sort of indigenous esthetic. Note, for example, Aubery's use of the vocabulary of Western rhetorical criticism ("to perorate") in his description of an Iroquois oratorical esthetic. The very features that make oratory verbal art, some of which were treated in chapter 3, constitute a major component of the tradition with which the orator is in dialogue, and—as already noted—what we know of those features represents, for the most part, a European perspective.

Many—perhaps most—European and Euro-American commentators apparently believed that knowledge of traditional oratorical behavior was inherent. The term "natural eloquence" became virtually a cliché in treatments of Indian speechmaking. Barthelmy Vimont's praise of the thespian skills of an Iroquois verbal artist, for example, cites him as "a very good Actor, for a man who has learned but what nature has taught him, without rule and without precept" (Thwaites 1959a, 27:267) and reflects conventional wisdom.[2] Nevertheless, an occasional observer realized that the ability to speak effectively derived from enculturation not genetics, from nurture not nature. David Zeisberger, the Moravian missionary who did not always find the performance style of Native American oratory appealing, was one such rare observer. "Young men are being constantly trained for" oratorical duty, he wrote. "They are admitted as hearers to the council, to familiar intercourse with the chiefs, who instruct them faithfully, and are employed as ambassadors to give them an opportunity to exercise themselves in public speaking" (Hulbert and Schwarze 1910, 143). Another nineteenth-century commentator, George E. Foster, realized the necessity of training in order for an orator to be in a truly dialogic relationship with his or her tradition. Writing particularly of Cherokee orators such as Attacullaculla and Oconostota, he outlined some of the training that orators underwent:

> To improve their minds, they listened hours together to the historical legends of the aged warrior and patriot, and treasured up the events he related or sentiments he uttered. The student in oratory was careful to remember the best figures of rhetoric, which were used by the aged in illustrating their sentiments; hence a set of phrases have descended among them for ages. (Foster 1889, 15)

Here Foster listed several tropes, such as "To bury the hatchet," that he argued had become so standardized that their meaning was unquestionable.

Charles Alexander Eastman had personal knowledge of how young men might be trained for verbal artistry. *Indian Boyhood,* his account of growing up as a Santee in southern Canada during the 1860s, emphasizes that part of the Santee youth's enculturation focused on learning verbal artistry:

> Very early, the Indian boy assumed the task of preserving and transmitting the legends of his ancestors and his race. Almost every evening a myth, or a true story of some deed done in the past, was narrated by one of the parents or grandparents, while the boy listened with parted lips and glistening eyes. On the following evening, he was usually required to repeat it. If he was not an apt scholar, he struggled long with his task; but, as a rule, the Indian boy is a good listener and has a good memory, so that the stories were tolerably well mastered. The household became his audience, by which he was alternately criticized and applauded. (Eastman 1902, 51)

Eastman believed that this early training in verbal art had shaped his own skills as an orator. During the first two decades of the twentieth century, he devoted much of his time to speaking engagements. He attributed his success at those events to having developed "the native gift of oratory in some degree" (Eastman 1936, 186).

The most obvious dimension of the dialogic nature of American Indian oratory in performance involves the direct, responsive role of the audience. As William F. Hanks has noted, "[R]eception is the evaluation and investment of discourse with meaning" (Hanks 1987, 679). Since public speakers intended for their words to have efficacy in bringing about some desired behavior, in establishing their own prestige, or simply in augmenting group knowledge, they had to take into account how listeners were evaluating and investing their words with meaning. This meant, of course, that the orator had to follow the conventions relevant to public speaking in whatever the situation might be. But it also meant an awareness of how a specific audience was reacting. Traditional ways for an audience to acknowledge a speech were reported by many early commentators, with the Jesuits in New France as usual taking the lead. On several occasions Paul Le Jeune related how the hearers of speeches delivered by Huron orators would signal their approval by drawing from the "depths of their stomachs" a series of aspirated syllables, which he variously represented as "ho," "hau," or "haau"

(Thwaites 1959a, 5:249, 295; 9:267; 10:259). Le Jeune reported that one of his missionaries, Jean de Brebeuf, had stated that at a Montagnais council each orator would end

> his advice in these terms, *Condayauendi lerhayde cha nonhwicwahachen:* that is to say, "That is my thought on the subject under Discussion:" then the whole Assembly responds with a very strong respiration drawn from the pit of the stomach, *Haau.* I noticed that when any one has spoken to their liking, this *Haau* is given forth with much more effort. (Thwaites 1959a, 10:259)

When these aspirations occurred in a series, the last one might emerge at a higher pitch than that of its predecessors (Thwaites 1959a, 5:249).

Other observers also reported how audiences responded to Native American oratory. The diarist for the Lewis and Clark Expedition, for instance, reported in an entry for 28 May 1806 that the women of a Chopunnish community constantly "cryed[,] wrung their hands, tore their hair and appeared to be in utmost distress" throughout a "loud animated harangue" in which their leader urged cooperation with the Corps of Discovery (Thwaites 1959b, 5:79). An Indian sitting for a portrait by George Catlin, who characterized himself as "the greatest orator in the Sioux nation," claimed that he consciously manipulated audience responsiveness: "[I]t was a very easy thing for him to set all the women of the tribe to crying" (Catlin 1841, 1:223). In a very thorough description of the dialogic quality of performance, Edwin James described how oratory during Omaha councils was "uniformly conducted with the most perfect good order and decorum":

> Each speaker carefully abstains from militating against the sensibility of any of his hearers, and uncourteous expressions towards each other on these occasions, are never heard. Generally at each pause of the speaker, the audience testify their approbation aloud, by the interjection *heh;* and as they believe that he has a just right to his own opinions, however absurd they may appear to be, and opposite to their own, the expression of them excites no reprehension, and if they cannot approve, they do not condemn, unless urged by necessity. (Thwaites 1966, 14:292)

Or we might consider the way in which the Baron Möllhausen described how an audience reacted to a Choctaw orator's low-key performance:

> From his first word the most breathless stillness reigned, and every one listened with profound attention, even those among his auditors who were entirely ignorant of the language in which he spoke. He had no time for preparation, but he knew what he wished to say; there were no theatrical gestures, or attempts to excite the passions of his hearers, but merely a light movement of the hand occasionally accompanying the most emphatic words, which although uttered in deep guttural tones, were distinctly audible to the most distant of the assembly. He spoke with ease and freedom, and was interrupted neither by applause nor contradiction; only a unanimous *Hau!* followed on certain questions that he asked, and when he had ended there was a short murmur of remarks among his auditory, and then another orator took his place. (Möllhausen 1858, 1:40–41)

The end of this passage from Möllhausen suggests a way in which the entire situation for speech making might be considered dialogic, for it was often customary for speeches to follow one another in reaction or response to what had just been said. Alexander Ross described how an Okanagan elder would open a council with a speech, "closing every sentence with great emphasis, the other councillors vociferating approbation." He continued: "As soon as the chief is done speechifying, others harangue also; but only one at a time" (Ross 1849, 293). Such give and take of public speaking often adhered to rule-bound protocols. One only has to examine documentation of treaty negotiations such as those printed by Benjamin Franklin in the mid-eighteenth century to determine that oratory was not only dialogic, but also dialectic, various speakers responding to one another until a consensus of opinion could be reached.

Only when reduced on the printed page to merely the words spoken does oratory seem to be monologic. Certainly it involves performer-audience distinctions that are more clearly demarcated than those for conversational genres of discourse, but oratory nevertheless depends upon the presence of an audience and the recognition by the speaker of that presence. With that audience in mind, the orator utilizes the performance devices that disappear from many entextualizations: paralinguistics, kinesics, and the manipulation of objects. As I have argued throughout this study, the performance, not the text, is the fundamental unit in an orally expressed verbal art such as oratory. And that performance encompasses not just the multi-channel communicative behavior of the principal speaker, but the responsive activities of the audience as well. It also involves the ambience of the situation, for oratory does not occur at any time and in any place.

Though it need not consist of performatives, as J. L. Austin (Austin 1962) conceives of that term, oratorical discourse demonstrates the equation "saying is doing" (Paine 1981b, 11). It has practical ends. And though listeners may be taken by the artistry of the performance and appreciate it from an esthetic perspective, oratory usually has the clear purpose of generating definable ends. For listeners, it may arouse them to action, confirm them in the opinions that lead to such action, or change their minds and redirect them to a new course of action. For speakers, oratory has the effect of establishing their status and assisting them in maintaining that status.

A successful orator is one who accomplishes a specific purpose. He or she may employ artistic touches to attain that purpose, but the end justifies the means (realizing, of course, that means which violate the protocols of the genre will not produce the desired goals). We might consider a speech delivered by Broken Arm, a Chopunnish leader, to the members of the Corps of Discovery. Lewis (or Clark) recorded the incident in the journal for 12 May 1806. A council of Chopunnish leaders had just met to consider the Corps's interest in establishing trading posts in their territory. After the proceedings, which had been held apart from the rest of the people and which approved of the Corps' presence, Broken Arm delivered a "harangue[,] the purport of which was making known the deliberations of their council and impressing the necessity of unanimity among them and a strict attention to the resolutions which had been agreed on in the councill" (Thwaites 1959b, 5:23). He sweetened the call for approval by offering a feast to any who would agree to abide by the council's decisions and forbidding those who would not so agree from partaking. Broken Arm's speech was efficacious. The diarist noted, "I was told by one of our men who was present, that there was not a dissenting voice on this great national question, but all swallowed their objections if any they had, very cheerfully with their mush" (23). We do not know what Broken Arm said or how he said it.

Nothing of his style of performing is recorded in the journal entry, nor do we know if he couched his argument in metaphor or other figurative tropes. But we do know that in this case Broken Arm was an accomplished orator, since he achieved his purpose. The promised feast, described as consisting of "the roots of cows [i.e., camas]" (23) used to make a thick soup, probably had little to do with the people's consent to the council's recommendations. It served primarily as a way of ratifying publicly what Broken Arm's words had persuaded the people to do.

Commentator after commentator on Native American politics has stressed that leaders ruled by creating consensus, and the way that they could do that most effectively was through oratory. A potential leader might attain status through deeds of martial valor or by developing a reputation for commonsensical behavior in routine community life. But he could make his will known and generate support for it among a group of people most easily by effectively orating. The distinction between "man of action" and "man of words" did not exist in many American Indian societies. Colonel Dodge's characteristically ethnocentric comments about the Indians of the Northern Plains nevertheless capture the importance of oratory as a way of effecting desired goals: "As among our highly civilized American citizens nothing, however trivial, can be done without a preliminary letting off a vast amount of verbiage; so the Indians can never do anything without speech-making" (Dodge 1882, 76).

Broken Arm's speech changed minds. Other orations were aimed at stimulating action. Among the Cherokee and many other American Indian groups, for example, those who wanted to lead a party into war had no apparent authority to force anyone to join them. Consequently, they had to rely upon the persuasive force of rhetoric, their ability to convince potential warriors not only of the justness of their cause, but of the need for them to take up arms and assist in the war party. James Adair, writing primarily of the Cherokees, described in general terms how someone hoping to form a war party might go about it. After circumambulating "his dark winter-house" three times while beating a drum, singing a war song, and giving forth war whoops, the person seeking recruits "speaks to the listening crowd with very rapid language, short pauses, and an awful commanding voice." The import of his oration is to specify clearly the perfidy of the enemy, who have returned kindnesses with cruelty. Drawing upon his store of tropes, the orator asserts that "as the white paths have changed their beloved colour, his heart burns within him with eagerness to tincture them all along, and even to make them flow over with the hateful blood of the base contemptible enemy." He urges his male listeners to assume the war-path "with manly cheerful hearts." He reminds them of the value of vengeance, the need "to hazard their lives to revenge the blood of their kindred and country-men." Though Adair credits "their own greedy thirst of revenge, and intense love of martial glory," he also recognizes the power of oratory in persuading enough of a hopeful leader's listeners to begin the three-day purifying process that must precede going to war (Williams 1930, 167–68).

Oratory works its way upon its audience. It persuades them to accept ideas and to take action. The successful orator is not necessarily the one who is most artistic in his use of language, though art probably plays a part in what makes him successful. The only measure of success in oratory must be in terms of efficacy. If it works, the oratory can be deemed good. Practicality must take precedent over esthetics, though the two usually (perhaps invariably) go together. The first measure of efficacy is the effect of the speech making on the audience. If they are persuaded to think or to act as the speaker suggests, then the oration has passed the first test. Then, the other side of efficacious speech figures into the equation. The speaker gains a reputation, becomes a person of stature, one to be reckoned with in the community if his speeches have their intended effect upon his listeners. The speech becomes a way not only of influencing immediately the direction in which others think and act; it becomes a way for the orator to gain prestige and political power. This is the way oratory works among the Ilongot of the Philippines: "[F]or men, a poised command of witty and beautiful ways of talking means that one has 'knowledge,' the right to leadership, and the political power which comes with an ability to persuade and understand" (Rosaldo 1973, 194). This is the way oratory works among the Melpa of Papua New Guinea: "Prominent men are speech-makers. A man can raise numerous pigs and give many away in *moka* [ceremonial exchange], but he cannot effectively influence his fellow-men unless he can use speech persuasively" (Strathern 1975, 187). Among the Kuna of Panama, "political success, not only of community leaders but of all women and men, depends on the ability to speak well in the village 'gathering house.' . . . [A] really successful 'chief' must be an excellent and often extraordinary speaker" (Sherzer 1983, 109). Among the Shuar of Ecuador, "a man who speaks well has great power" (Hendricks 1993, 80). In Bali local council leaders assume their positions of political authority based on speaking ability (Hobart 1975, 71). And, to conclude a list that could be extended exponentially, oratory represents "one of the tools of a politically influential man" among the Mursi of East Africa (Turton 1975, 163).

These examples come from contemporary anthropological literature, which has become more and more sensitive to the importance of reporting how language is used cross-culturally. They offer comparative confirmation that the reiterated claim made by commentators, many of whom made no attempt to transcend their ethnocentrism and most of whom had little skill in observation, that oratory was one of the most important, if not the most significant skill that a successful American Indian political leader could possess. It gained his position for him and maintained that position once it had been attained. Writing of twentieth-century Iroquois orators, Michael K. Foster has noted the profundity of the assumption of the oratorical role:

> Speakers begin speaking at different times in life; they view the moment of assuming the role for their moiety as a sudden one of crisis. They feel that they have been able to fill the role because of the special gift they have received from the Creator, but this does not preclude their seeking guidance from experienced men. They know who their mentors were, and there is a distinct impression of speaker "lineages" at the different longhouses. (Foster 1974, 40)

Undoubtedly, oratory functioned and continues to function in many Indian communities as a major way of effecting action and of establishing personal prestige. But was it really as important as early commentators suggest? And what does their insistence on its centrality in Native American political affairs mean? I believe that their emphasis on the importance and efficaciousness of Indian oratory, though it had basis in fact, also reinforced opinions about *"le pensée sauvage"* that dominated thinking about Indians— whether from sympathizers such as Jefferson or dismissers such as Cass.

In *Notes on the State of Virginia,* Jefferson championed the cause of the Indian by citing the eloquence of Tahgahjute. He prefaced his reprinting of the famous "Logan's Lament" by noting, "The principles of their society forbidding all compulsion, they are to be led to duty and to enterprise by personal influence and persuasion. Hence eloquence in council, bravery and address in war, become the foundations of all consequence with them" (Jefferson 1982, 62).

Eloquence is good, from the Jeffersonian perspective, and those who practice it effectively have elevated intellects. On the other hand, though, people who can be swayed by an orator's verbal agility so as to follow unthinkingly the charismatic speaker may be weak-minded. That oratory is efficacious may demonstrate the superiority of those who practice it, but it also illustrates the inferiority of those who are swayed by it. As Paul Le Jeune wrote, "These barbarians [Hurons] often place more value upon a great talker than upon a man of good sense" (Thwaites 1959a, 16:135). About the Algonquian speakers whom he had encountered soon after his arrival in New France, Le Jeune had written somewhat disparagingly of the efficacy of oratory among them: "All the authority of their chief is in his tongue's end; for he is powerful in so far as he is eloquent; and, even if he kills himself talking and haranguing, he will not be obeyed unless he pleases the Savages" (Thwaites 1959a, 6:243).

Examined in situ, oratory begins as multichanneled performance, takes shape in dialogic relationship with factors in its immediate setting as well as in its verbal art tradition, and produces results. Despite their ethnographic failings, the early reporters of Native American oratory often captured this enactment process. While ethnocentrism might color the accounts and while the verbal component of performance might not be rendered with accuracy and comprehensiveness, the judicious student can still find useful information on how oratory manifested itself and on how it functioned for both speakers and audiences in works by missionaries, explorers, soldiers, and others who encountered Native American public speaking as they went about their business of conquest.

EPILOGUE

WHITHER ORATORY?

Arnold Krupat has noted that the necessary prerequisite for the development of literary criticism in the Western sense is a body of accepted textual material—a "canon," so to speak (Krupat 1992, 175–76). The first order of business for the study of American Indian oratory requires identifying texts and assessing their reliability and comprehensiveness. Texts that respond to the exigencies of the ethnography of speaking, performance folkloristics, and ethnopoetics will ideally provide the spoken words, their texture, the situation where and when they were spoken, and the pertinent contexts for appreciating their emic significance. As we have noticed in most of the examples presented above, it is virtually impossible to identify texts that meet those criteria. But researchers can begin to sift through the available material and determine as far as possible on a case-by-case basis exactly what each representation of Native American oratory has to offer.

Some excellent work has shown the way in this regard. For example, a good treatment of the textual authenticity of a frequently reprinted speech attributed to an American Indian is Harry Robie's analysis (Robie 1986) of the standard text of the oration delivered in 1805 by the Seneca Sagoweyatha (Red Jacket) to Christian missionaries among the Six Nations in western New York. To ascertain whether the record of this speech can be considered reliable, Robie examines it from four perspectives: the reputed abilities of the orator, the reputation of the translator/interpreter, the text's publication history, and the text's conformity to Iroquoian oratorical conventions. The strongest element of his argument addresses the third issue, and Robie endorses what was apparently the first printed version of the speech, that which appeared in J. D. Bemis's *Native Eloquence* in 1811,[1] because of Bemis's standing in the region where the speech had been delivered and where witnesses to it could have easily corrected any inaccuracies in the printed account. Moreover, Robie shows how sixteen other published versions of the speech derive more or less accurately from Bemis's publication. Robie also considers the place Sagoweyatha had in Seneca society and the reputation of the interpreters, Israel Chapin and Jasper Parrish. The major weakness in Robie's essay is his failure adequately to consider how traditions of oratory in Iroquois culture were manifested in Sagoweyatha's speech, but his work represents an approach that must be taken in regard to every early record of a Native American speech event if we want to be able to consider its place in the documentation of this verbal art.

Often the tendency in studies of individual speeches has been to "debunk" messages attributed to Indians as largely or completely the projects of the translators/textmakers/transcribers. Both Rudolph Kaiser and Albert Furtwangler have used methods similar to Robie's publication history to demonstrate that the ecological oratory attributed to the Duwamish Sealth (Seattle) apparently has little relationship to what the orator might have said when he supposedly spoke to territorial governor Isaac Stevens in the 1850s. Thomas E. McElwain (2001) has backtranslated from the words of "Logan's Lament," praised for its eloquence by Thomas Jefferson and sanctified in textbooks throughout the nineteenth century, to show that the language could not faithfully represent an Iroquois source either linguistically or culturally. Such studies are important as long as researchers recall that their principal aim is to create a corpus of authentic texts, not to search out materials that may be fabricated—what Robie, borrowing from the folklorist Richard M. Dorson, calls "fakelore" (Robie 1986, 99–100).

The main problem with investigations of the documented reliability of individual speeches lies in students' concentrating exclusively on the linguistic message and not on the other components of the oratorical event that the text purports to represent. In addition to establishing the fidelity to the oral original of what the speaker said, researchers should consider whether texts provide textural, situational, and contextual information or whether that information can be culled elsewhere.

To some degree, this occurs in Bruce E. Johansen's study of Canassatego's closing speech at the Lancaster treaty negotiations between the Haudenosaunee and Pennsylvania on 4 July 1744. Based on the reputation of the parties involved in the proceedings—especially interpreter Conrad Weiser and printer Benjamin Franklin—Johansen assumes the reliability of the record of the oration, which has become well known because of the speaker's suggestion that the British colonies form themselves into a union similar to that of the Six Nations—a suggestion that Franklin took up and which apparently influenced postrevolutionary federalism. His purpose is to make the complete speech available to modern readers and to place it in appropriate contexts. To the latter end, he describes the political situation that generated the Lancaster council, the nature of Iroquoian diplomacy, and the orator's background. A substantial essay—necessary for providing the reader with the information necessary to appreciate the speech—introduces the "first time that this famous treaty speech has been set in type by digital means and made available to libraries nationwide for research at all levels of scholarship" (Johansen 2001, 84). Originally published by Franklin as a chapbook and then reissued as part of a limited edition reprint of treaty proceedings which Franklin had published between 1736 and 1762 (Van Doren and Boyd 1938), the complete text of the speech has been difficult to find. Johansen's reproduction attempts not only to represent the sense of the original (as printed by Franklin), but also to reflect Franklin's manipulations of font size, spacing, capitalization, and italicization, which provide the printed transcription of Weiser's interpretation of Canassatego's oration "a linguistic subtext of its own" (96). Though he pays only limited attention to literary matters, Johansen's presentation represents what must be done with Native oratorical texts if they are to be comprehended at all in terms of their original contexts and situations.

Barbara Alice Mann has done something similar with the speech by which the Lenapé orator Hopocan ("Captain Pipe") defended Moravian missionary John Heckewelder from charges of espionage before a British tribunal on 9 November 1781. Based on the assumption that Heckewelder, whose familiarity with the Indians was longstanding, correctly represented Hopocan's speech, Mann notes several of the specific strategies that the orator employed and reproduces the speech as it appeared in the missionary's *History, Manners, and Customs of the Indian Nations* (Mann 2001a, 153–57).

Studies of individual speeches are most likely to be published in academic vehicles, as journal articles or as chapters in essay collections. Ultimately the findings may make their way to general readers, but the route can be long and circuitous. Another focus for research should be the preparation of anthologies of speeches—from single groups, from culture areas, and from Native America in general. Such collections can focus on oratorical materials alone, or they may include oratory as one genre of verbal art that has flourished and flourishes in American Indian communities. Of course, many such anthologies already exist, but for the most part they have flaws that a new generation of collections should address.

A couple of recent anthologies devoted more or less exclusively to oratory suggest the problems that can arise with such collections. One such book, John Bierhorst's *In the Trail of the Wind: American Indian Poems and Ritual Orations* (1971), suffers from what I have called elsewhere "the art museum approach" to presenting Native American verbal art (Clements 1996, 179–98). Here is a collection of texts—just the sung or spoken words—organized by a theme identified by the anthologist and presented with virtually no contextual data except the group of which the singer or speaker was a member. Notes, tucked away at the end of the volume, provide the bibliographic source and some clarifying information. In many cases, the reader is not given sufficient information to know which texts are "ritual orations" and which are the words of songs. The assumption that the words can speak for themselves to readers with no familiarity with general cultural background or specifics of performance situation discourages appreciation from any perspective but that which the reader brings to the material, and, of course, that perspective may profoundly misapprehend what is said. A similar problem, lack of sufficient contextual and situational background, mars Virginia Irving Armstrong's *I Have Spoken* (1991), though her volume includes a generous number of texts—some from sources not available to many readers.

Meanwhile, W. C. Vanderwerth's *Indian Oratory* (1971), an anthology of speeches delivered between 1758 and 1910, also presents some hard-to-find materials. The editor introduces each speech with some historical background and a little information about the orator. So this volume cannot be considered guilty of following the "art museum approach" in presenting its texts. But Vanderwerth is too uncritical in accepting texts at face value and provides no information that might be useful to the student of oratory in any way but getting a Native point of view on various historical events. Nor is Vanderwerth always scrupulous in presenting material as it appeared in his sources, making some changes in wording and punctuation silently.

Oratory also appears in general anthologies of Native American verbal art, both oral and written. For example, Frederick W. Turner's *Portable North American Indian Reader* (1974) includes a dozen oration texts—each presented with a headnote of only a couple of sentences at most. The half-dozen speeches in the revised edition of Alan R. Velie's *American Indian Literature* (1991) receive slightly more lengthy introductions, but far from adequate for an understanding of the material except from the outsider's perspective that Velie seems to advocate throughout his anthology. The only general anthology that comes close to presenting oratory ethnographically and ethnopoetically is Brian Swann's *Coming to Light* (1994), but only a few oratorical materials appear in the volume.

What is needed are anthologies informed by the perspectives advocated here and consisting of material that has been evaluated in terms of its reliable reflection of the full oratorical event. The texts will consist of transcriptions and translations of the spoken words amplified by signals that indicate the textures of the performances and set them in pertinent contexts and situations.

Once a "canon" has been established and made accessible to readers, the work of literary assessment can proceed more meaningfully than it has been able to do thus far. One analytical approach examines orators as *auteurs,* individual manipulators of and contributors to generic traditions. An exemplary study that might point the direction for such efforts is Granville Ganter's examination of several speeches by Sagoyewatha, "You Are a Cunning People without Sincerity" (2001). Arguing for the reliability of available texts because of their consistency in various sources and because Sago-yewatha's knowledge of English helped to guarantee accurate translation, Ganter identifies recurrent devices that this spokesperson for the Senecas regularly employed: irony and sarcasm, wit, and an ability to exploit Euro-American cultural values for his polemical ends. The result of Sagoyewatha's use of these stylistic features in the orations that are available was to express cultural differences in ways that were accessible to his interlocutors (see Ganter 2001, 189). Since Sagoyewatha's speeches were seldom accompanied by descriptions of the complete oratorical event, Ganter must address only the message portion of those speeches, but his study provides a useful idea of what can be done. We probably do not have sufficient textual material that has been evaluated punctiliously enough for its reliability to provide similar treatments of very many other orators, but when such material does become available through efforts such as those of Robie and Johansen, other Native American speech makers should receive similar treatment.

Researchers should not fall into the trap of assuming that American Indian orators—even those like Sagoyewatha from societies where it was customary for an appointed speaker to present the views of the collectivity—were not individually responsible for the verbal art they produced. But another focus for research should be to identify oratorical conventions in particular cultures. To date, the oratorical traditions of three societies have received the kind of analytical attention that should be directed toward as many such heritages as possible.

Historians, literary critics, and ethnographers have worked to present a fairly comprehensive depiction of oratory among the Five (later Six) Nations of the Iroquois. Some studies of individual speeches and speakers from this tradition have been noted above. Comprehensive overviews of Iroquois oratory in the seventeenth and eighteenth centuries appear in *The History and Culture of Iroquois Diplomacy* (Jennings et al. 1985). Michael Foster has examined contemporary Iroquois oratory in terms both of ethnographic context and situation and of literary style (see esp. Foster 1974; see also Swann 1994, 476–88). His work, that of historically oriented scholars, and even that of earlier scholars (e.g., Hale 1883) have opened up Iroquois oratory in a way that has not yet been done for any other Native American speech-making heritage.

Not yet as fully realized as scholarship on Iroquois oratory, because fewer scholars have been involved, are studies of oratory among the Pimans of southern Arizona and the Tlingit of southeastern Alaska. Frank Russell, whose work is treated above in chapter 2, was the first to publish an extensive body of Pima oratory. Ruth Underhill, who worked among the Tohono O'odham in the 1930s, included some oratorical material in her *Singing for Power* (1938) and *Papago Indian Religion* (1946), but the fullest treatment of the tradition appears in a reexamination of Underhill's data on oratory that appeared in 1979 (Underhill et al. 1997). Therein Donald Bahr, whose study of three Pima orations has also been treated above in chapter 2, presents the original-language texts recorded by Underhill of ritual orations that occurred in conjunction with the annual horticultural and foraging cycles, hunting, warfare, and the salt pilgrimage. New translations, literary analysis, and cultural context information make this volume an extremely valuable treatment of one society's traditional oratory.

Tlingit oratory has also received comprehensive treatment in a single volume: *Haa Tuwunáagu Yís, for Healing Our Spirit,* by Nora Marks Dauenhauer and Richard Dauenhauer (1990). A very thorough presentation of contextual information on Tlingit oratory introduces a series of speeches in Tlingit and ethnopoetic translation with extensive notes. Aside from a couple of speeches recorded on wax cylinders in 1899, all of the speeches come from the end of the twentieth century, when traditional oratory still flourished among the Tlingit. In addition to several orations from various occasions, the Dauenhauers present a series of speeches from one event, a memorial service held in 1968. Having provided a thorough ethnography of the memorial service tradition in their introduction (see also Kan 1983) and providing considerable explanatory notes, the Dauenhauers offer in this series perhaps the most comprehensive treatment from ethnographic and literary perspectives of a specific occasion for oratory in any of the literature on Native American verbal art. They also include a section of selected orations by Tlingit speakers at the First Sealaska Elders Conference held in Sitka, Alaska, in 1980.

What I have outlined here by citing several exemplary studies is a several-step program for research that begins with the evaluation of particular records of oratorical performances and makes them generally accessible. When a body of reliable material has been identified for individual orators, their work should be examined from the perspective of ethnopoetically-informed literary criticism. Then researchers can move to the examination of cultural traditions. Steps in this program have been already successfully undertaken, and probably they will continue. Larry Evers has written of "cycles of appreciation" of American Indian verbal art that recurred throughout the twentieth century (Evers 1983). The current "cycle" began in the 1970s (earlier for some scholars) and continues to flourish. Perhaps appreciating Native Americana has become less cyclic and will be a permanent feature of our intellectual and spiritual lives.

APPENDIX

Selected Documents for Sources and Resources for Native American Oratory

Treaties

The Five Nations Treat with Captain Ingoldsby

From Cadwallader Colden, *The history of the Five Indian Nations depending on the province of New-York in America* (1727; 1747; rpt. Ithaca: Cornell University Press, 1958), pp. 123–27.

The Governor of New-York, Colonel Slaughter's Death, soon after his Arrival, was very prejudicial to the Affairs of New-York; for Captain Ingoldsby, who had no other Commission but that of Captain of one of the Independent Companies of Foot, took upon himself the Government of the Province, without any Authority; and he having likewise highly offended a great Number of the People, by the Share he took in the late Party Quarrels, it was not easy for him to prosecute any vigorous Measures. He was reckoned to be much more a Soldier than a Statesman.

Captain Ingoldsby met the Five Nations at Albany, the sixth of June 1692. In his Speech, he told them of his vigorous Resolutions to prosecute the War, and then blamed them for not sending (according to their Promise) a Party down Cadarackui River, to join them that went from Albany against Montreal, and for their Carelessness in suffering themselves to be surprised last Winter in their Hunting. He desired them to keep the Enemy in perpetual Alarm, by the Incursions of their Parties into the Enemy's Country, and to give him timely Notice of all their Motions. He told them in the next Place, that he heard the French were still using their wonted Artifice, of amusing them with Offers of Peace; but the former Proceedings of the French sufficiently demonstrates, said he to the Brethren, that while Peace is in their Mouths, War is in their Hearts, and the late horrid Murder of the Brethren, after Quarter given, sufficiently shews the Perfidy and Rancour of their Hearts. It is in vain, said he, to think of any Cessation of Arms, much less of a Peace, while the two Kings are at War at Home. He added, Virginia is ready to assist us, and only waits the King's Orders, which are daily expected, and then renewed the Chain for Virginia. In the last Place he told them, that he heard the Dionondadas had sent two Prisoners Home, with a View thereby to procure Peace; and advised them by all Means to make Peace with that Nation.

The Five Nations answered by Cheda, an Oneydo Sachem:

"Brother Corlear,

The Sachems of the Five Nations have with great Attention heard Corlear speak; we shall make a short Recital, to shew you with what Care we have hearkened. After the Recital he continued.

We heartily thank Corlear, for his coming to this Place to view the Strength thereof, for his bringing Forces with him, and for his Resolution of putting Garisons into the Frontier Places. Giving five Bevers and a Belt.

Brother Corlear, as to what you blame us for, let us not reproach one another, such Words do not savour well among Friends. They gave nothing with this Article.

Brother Corlear, be patient under the Loss of your Men, as we are of the Mohawks our Brethren, that were killed at the same Time. You take no Notice of the great Losses we have suffered. We designed to have come to this Place to have condoled with you in your Loss, but the War took up all our Time, and employed all Hands. They gave five Bevers, four Otters, and one Belt, as a Gift of Condolence.

Brother Corlear, we are all Subjects of one great King and Queen, we have one Head, one Heart, one Interest, and are all ingaged in the same War. You tell us, that we must expect no Peace while the Kings are at War on the other Side the great Water. We thank you for being so plain with us. We assure you we have no Thoughts of Peace. We are resolved to carry on the War, though we know we only are in danger of being Losers. Pray do you prosecute the War with the same Resolution. You are strong and have many People. You have a great King, who is able to hold out long. We are but a small People, and decline daily, by the Men we lose in this War, we do our utmost to destroy the Enemy; but how strange does it seem to us! How unaccountable! that while our great King is so inveterate against the French, and you are so earnest with us to carry on the War, that Powder is now sold dearer to us than ever? We are poor, and not able to buy while we neglect hunting; and we cannot hunt and carry on the War at the same Time: We expect, that this Evil we so justly complain of be immediately remedied. Giving nine Bevers.

Brother Corlear, you desire us to keep the Enemy in perpetual Alarm, that they may have no Rest, till they are in their Graves; Is it not to secure your own Frontiers? Why then not one Word of your People that are to join us? We assure you we shall continue to carry on the War into the Heart of the Enemies Country. Giving eight Bevers.

We the Five Nations, Mohawks, Oneydoes, Onondagas, Cayugas, and Senekas, renew the Silver Chain whereby we are linked fast with our Brethren of Assarigoa (Virginia) and we promise to preserve it as long as the Sun shall shine in the Heavens. Giving ten Bevers.

But Brother Corlear, How comes it, that none of our Brethren fastened in the same Chain with us, offer their helping Hand in this general War, in which our great King is engaged against the French? Pray Corlear, how come Maryland, Delaware River, and New-England, to be disengaged from this War? You have always told us, that they are our Brethren, Subjects of the same great King. Has our King sold them? Or do they fail in their Obedience? Or do they draw their Arms out of our Chain? Or has the great King commanded, that the few Subjects he has in this Place, should make War against the French alone? Pray make plain to us this Mystery? How can they and we be Brethren, and make different Families? How can they and we be Subjects of the same great King, and not be engaged in the same War? How can they and we have the same Heart, the same Head, and the same Interest, as you tell us, and not have the same Thoughts? How comes it, that the Enemy burns and destroys the Towns in New-England, and they make no Resistance? How comes our great King to make War, and not to destroy his Enemies? When, if he would only command his Subjects on this Side the great Lake to joyn, the Destruction of the Enemy would not make one Summer's Work.

You need not warn us of the Deceit and Treachery of the French, who would probably insinuate Thoughts of Peace; but Brethren, you need not fear us, we will never hearken to them: Tho' at the same Time, we must own, that we have not been without Thoughts of your being inclined to Peace, by Reason of the Brethrens Backwardness in pushing on the War. The French spread Reports among us to this Purpose, and say, that they had in a Manner concluded the Matter with you. We rejoice to be now assured of this Falshood. We shall never desist fighting the French as long as we shall live. And gave a Belt of Wampum.

We now renew the old Chain, and here plant the Tree of Prosperity and Peace. May it grow and thrive, and spread its Roots even beyond Canada. Giving a Belt.

We make the House clean, where all our Affairs of Importance are transacted with these five Otters.

We return you Thanks for the Powder and Lead given us; but what shall we do with them without Guns, shall we throw them at the Enemy? We doubt they will not hurt them so. Before this we always had Guns given us. It is no Wonder the Governor of Canada gains upon us, for he supplies his Indians with Guns as well as Powder; he supplies them plentifully with every Thing that can hurt us. Giving five Otters.

As to the Dionondadas setting two of our Nation at Liberty, we must tell you, that it was not the Act of that Nation, but the private Act of one Person: We are desirous to make Peace with that Nation as soon as we can, upon honourable Terms. And gave a Belt.

The Mohawks, before they left the Place, desired a private Conference with the Governor, and told him, that they were all exceedingly dissatisfied, that the other English Colonies gave no Assistance, and that it might prove of ill Consequence. Captain Ingoldsby promised to write to them, and hoped it would have a good Effect.

Accounts by Travelers and Explorers

INDIAN BURIAL OF THEIR DEAD

From John Lawson, *A New Voyage to Carolina; Containing the Exact Description and Natural History of That Country: Together with the Present State Thereof. And a Journal of a Thousand Miles, Travel'd thro' Several Nations of Indians. Giving a Particular Account of Their Customs, Manners, &c.* (London: NP, 1709), pp. 179–83.

The Burial of their Dead is perform'd with a great deal of Ceremony, in which one Nation differs, in some few Circumstances, from another, yet not so much but we may, by a general Relation, pretty nearly account for them all.

When an *Indian* is dead, the greater Person he was, the more expensive is his Funeral. The first thing which is done, is, to place the nearest Relations near the Corps, who mourn and weep very much, having their Hair hanging down their Shoulders, in a very forlorn manner. After the dead Person has lain a Day and a Night, in one of their Hurdles of Canes, commonly in some Out-House made for that purpose, those that officiate about the Funeral, go into the Town, and the first young Men they meet withal, that have Blankets or Match Coats on, whom they think fit for their Turn, they strip them from their Backs, who suffer them so to do, without any Resistance. In these they wrap the dead Bodies, and cover them with two or three Mats, which the *Indians* make of Rushes or Cane; and last of all, they have a long Web of woven Reeds, or hollow Canes, which is the Coffin of the *Indians,* and is brought round several times, and tied fast at both ends, which indeed, looks very decent and well. Then the Corps is brought out of the House, into the Orchard of Peach-Trees, where another Hurdle is made to receive it, about which comes all the Relations and Nation that the dead Person belong'd to, besides several from other Nations in Alliance with them; all which sit down on the Ground, upon Mats spread there, for that purpose; where the Doctor or Conjurer appears; and, after some time, makes a Sort of *O-yes,* at which all are very silent; then he begins to give an Account, who the dead Person was, and how stout a Man he approv'd himself; how many Enemies and Captives he had kill'd and taken; how strong, tall, and nimble he was; that he was a great Hunter, a Lover of his Country, and possess'd of a great many beautiful Wives and Children, esteem'd the greatest of Blessings among these Savages, in which they have a true Notion. Thus this Orator runs on, highly extolling the dead Man, for his Valour, Conduct, Strength, Riches, and Good-Humour; and enumerating his Guns, Slaves and almost every thing he was possess'd of, when living. After which, he addresses himself to the People of that Town or Nation, and bids them supply the dead Man's Place, by following his steps, who, he assures them, is gone into the Country of Souls, (which they think lies a great way off, in this World, which the Sun visits, in his ordinary Course) and that he will have the Enjoyment of handsome young Women, great Store of Deer to hunt, never meet with Hunger, Cold or Fatigue, but every thing to answer his Expectation and Desire. This is the Heaven they propose to themselves; but, on the contrary, for those *Indians* that are lazy, thievish amongst themselves, bad Hunters, and no Warriours, nor of much Use to the Nation, to such they allot, in the next World, Hunger, Cold, Troubles, old ugly Women for their Companions, with Snakes, and all sorts of nasty Victuals to feed on. Thus is mark'd out their Heaven and Hell. After all this Harangue, he diverts the People with some of their Traditions, as when there was a violent hot Summer, or very hard Winter; when any notable Distempers rag'd amongst them; when they were at War with such and such

Nations; how victorious they were; and what were the Names of their War-Captains. To prove the times more exactly, he produces the Records of the Country, which are a Parcel of Reeds, of different Lengths, with several distinct Marks, known to none but themselves; by which they seem to guess, very exactly, at Accidents that happen'd many Years ago; nay two or three Ages or more. The Reason I have to believe what they tell me, on this Account, is, because I have been at the Meetings of several *Indian* Nations; and they agreed, in relating the same Circumstances, as to Time, very exactly; as, for Example, they say, there was so hard a Winter in *Carolina,* 105 years ago, that the great Sound was frozen over, and the Wild Geese came into the Woods to eat Acorns, and that they were so tame, (I suppose, through Want) that they kill'd abundance in the Woods, by knocking them on the Head with Sticks.

But, to return to the dead Man. When this long Tale is ended, by him that spoke first; perhaps, a second begins another long Story; so a third, and fourth, if there be so many Doctors present; which all tell one and the same thing. At last, the Corps is brought away from that Hurdle to the Grave, by four young Men, attended by the Relations, the King, old Men, and all the Nation. When they come to the Sepulcre, which is about six Foot deep, and eight Foot long, having at each end (that is, at the Head and Foot) a Light-Wood, or Pitch-Pine Fork driven close down the sides of the Grave, firmly into the Ground; (these two Forks are to contain the Ridge-Pole, as you shall understand presently) before they lay the Corps into the Grave, they cover the bottom two or three times over with Bark of Trees, then they let down the Corps (with two Belts, that the *Indians* carry their Burdens withal) very leisurely, upon the said Barks; then they lay over a Pole of the same Wood, in the two Forks, and having a great many Pieces of Pitch-Pine Logs, about two Foot and a half long, they stick them in the sides of the Grave down each End, and near the Top thereof, where the other Ends lie on the Ridge-Pole, so that they are declining like the Roof of a House. These being very thick-plac'd, they cover them (many times double) with Bark; then they throw the Earth thereon, that came out of the Grave, and beat it down very firm; by this Means, the dead Body lies in a Vault, nothing touching him; so that when I saw this way of Burial, I was mightily pleas'd with it, esteeming it very decent and pretty, as having seen a great many Christians buried without the tenth Part of that Ceremony and Decency. Now, when the Flesh is rotted and moulder'd from the Bone, they take up the Carcass, and clean the Bones, and joint them together; afterwards, they dress them up in pure white dress'd Deer-Skins, and lay them amongst their Grandees and Kings in the *Quiogozon,* which is their Royal Tomb or Burial-Place of their Kings and War-Captains.

This is a very large magnificent Cabin, (according to their Building) which is rais'd at the Publick Charge of the Nation, and maintain'd in a great deal of Form and Neatness. About seven foot high, is a Floor or Loft made, on which lie all their Princes, and Great Men, that have died for several hundred Years, all attir'd in the Dress I before told you of. No Person is to have his Bones lie here, and to be thus dress'd, unless he gives a round Sum of their Money to the Rulers, for Admittance. If they remove never so far, to live in a Foreign Country, they never fail to take all these dead Bones along with them, though the Tediousness of their short daily Marches keeps them never so long on their Journey. They reverence and adore this *Quiogozon,* with all the Veneration and Respect that is possible for such a People to discharge, and had rather lose all, than have any Violence or Injury offer'd thereto. These Savages differ some small matter in their Burials; some burying right upwards, and otherwise, as you are acquainted withal in my Journal form South to North *Carolina;* Yet they all agree in their Mourning, which is, to appear every Night, at the Sepulcre, and howl and weep in a very dismal manner, having their Faces dawb'd over with Light-wood Soot, (which is the same as Lamp-black) and Bears Oil. This renders them as black as it is possible to make themselves, so that theirs very much resemble the Faces of Executed Men boil'd in Tar. If the dead Person was a Grandee, to carry on the Funeral Ceremonies, they hire People to cry and lament over the dead Man. Of this sort there are several, that practise it for a Livelihood, and are very expert at Shedding abundance of Tears, and howling like Wolves, and so discharging their Office with abundance of Hypocrisy and Art. The Women are never accompanied with these Ceremonies after Death; and to what World they allot that Sex, I never understood, unless, to wait on their dead Husbands; but they have more Wit, than some of the Eastern Nations, who sacrifice themselves to accompany their Husbands into the next World. It is the dead Man's Relations, by Blood, as his Uncles, Brothers, Sisters, Cousins, Sons, and Daughters, that mourn in good earnest, the Wives thinking their Duty is discharg'd, and that they are become free, when their Husband is dead; so, as fast as they can, look out for another, to supply his Place.

BARRING THE WHITE MAN FROM PIPE STONE QUARRY

From George Catlin, *Letters and Notes on the Manners, Customs, and Condition of the North American Indians by Geo. Catlin; Written During Eight Years'*

Travel Amongst the Wildest Tribes of Indians in North America; in 1832, 33, 34, 35, 36, 37, 38, and 39 (London: by the Author, 1841), vol. 2, p. 172.

I mentioned in a former Letter, that we had been arrested by the Sioux, on our approach to this place, at the trading-post of Le Blanc, on the banks of the St. Peters; and I herein insert the most important part of the speeches made, and talks held on that momentous occasion, as near as my friend and I could restore them, from partial notes and recollection. After these copper-visaged advocates of their country's rights had assembled about us, and filled up every avenue of the cabin, the grave council was opened in the following manner:—

Te-o-kun-hko (the swift man), first rose and said—

"My friends, I am not a chief, but the son of a chief—I am the son of my father—he is a chief—and when he is gone away, it is my duty to speak for him—he is not here—but what I say is the talk of his mouth. We have been told that you are going to the Pipe Stone Quarry. We come now to ask for what purpose you are going, and what business you have to go there." ('How! how!' vociferated all of them, thereby approving what was said, giving assent by the word *how*, which is their word for yes).

"*Brothers*—I am a brave, but not a chief—my arrow stands in the top of the leaping-rock; all can see it, and all know that Te-o-kun-hko's foot has been there. ('How! how!').

"*Brothers*—We look at you and we see that your are Che-mo-ke-mon capitains (white men officers): we know that you have been sent by your Government, to see what that place is worth, and we think the white people want to buy it. ('How, how').

"*Brothers*—We have seen always that the white people, when they see anything in our country that they want, send officers to value it, and then if they can't buy it, they will get it some other way. ('How! how!')

"*Brothers*—I speak strong, my heart is strong, and I speak fast; this red pipe was given to the red men by the Great Spirit—it is a part of our flesh, and therefore is great *medicine*. ('How! how!')

"*Brothers*—We know that the whites are like a great cloud that rises in the East, and will cover the whole country. We know that they will have all our lands; but, if ever they get our Red Pipe Quarry they will have to pay very dear for it. ('How! how! how!')

"*Brothers*—We know that no white man has ever been to the Pipe Stone Quarry, and our chiefs have often decided in council that no white man shall ever go to it. ('How! how!')

"*Brothers*—You have heard what I have to say, and you can go no further, but you must turn about and go back. ('How! how! how!')

"*Brothers*—You see that the sweat runs from my face, for I am troubled."

Captivity Narratives

TE-CUM-SEH'S ADDRESS TO THE OSAGE PEOPLE

From John D. Hunter, *Manners and Customs of Several Indian Tribes Located West of the Mississippi, Including Some Account of the Soil, Climate, and Vegetable Productions, and the Indian Materia Medica: to Which Is Prefixed the History of the Author's Life During a Residence of Several Years Among Them* (Philadelphia: J. Maxwell, 1823), pp. 51–56.

Some of the white people whom I met, as before noticed, among the Osages, were traders, and others were reputed to be runners from their Great Father beyond the Great Waters, to invite the Indians to take up the tomahawk against the settlers. They made many long talks, and distributed many valuable presents; but without being able to shake the resolution which the Osages had formed, to preserve peace with their Great Father, the President. Their determinations were, however, to undergo a more severe trial; Te-cum-seh, the celebrated Shawanee warrior and chief, in company with Francis the prophet, now made their appearance among them.

He addressed them in long, eloquent, and pathetic strains, and an assembly more numerous than had ever been witnessed on any former occasion, listened to him with an intensely agitated, though profoundly respectful interest and attention. In fact, so great was the effect produced by Te-cum-seh's eloquence, that the chiefs adjourned the council, shortly after he had closed his harangue; nor did they finally come to a decision on the great question in debate, for several days afterwards.

I wish it was in my power to do justice to the eloquence of this distinguished man; but it is utterly impossible. The richest colours shaded with a master's pencil, would fall infinitely short of the glowing finish of the original. The occasion and subject were peculiarly adapted to call into action all the powers of genuine patriotism; and such language, such gestures, and such feelings and fulness of soul contending for utterance, were exhibited by this untutored native of the forest in the central wilds of America, as no audience, I am persuaded, either in ancient or modern times, ever before witnessed.

My readers may think some qualification due to this opinion; but none is necessary. The unlettered Te-cum-seh gave extemporaneous utterance only to what he felt; it was a simple, but vehement narration of the wrongs imposed by the white people on the Indians, and an exhortation for the latter to resist them. The whole addressed to an audience composed of individuals who had been educated to prefer almost any sacrifice to that of personal liberty; and even death, to the degradation of their nation; and who, on this occasion, felt the portraiture of Te-cum-seh but too strikingly identified with their own condition, wrongs, and sufferings.

This discourse made an impression on my mind, which I think, will last as long as I live. I cannot repeat it *verbatim,* though if I could, it would be a mere skeleton, without the rounding finish of its integuments; it would only be the shadow of the substance, because the gestures, and the interest and feelings excited by the occasion, and which constitute the essentials of its character, would be altogether wanting. Nevertheless, I shall, as far as my recollection serves, make the attempt, and trust to the indulgence of my readers, for an apology for the presumptuous digression.

When the Osages and distinguished strangers had assembled, Te-cum-seh arose, and after a pause of some minutes, in which he surveyed his audience in a very dignified, though respectfully complaisant and sympathizing manner, he commenced, as follows:

"*Brothers*—We all belong to one family, we are all children of the Great Spirit; we walk in the same path; slake our thirst at the same spring; and now affairs of the greatest concern, lead us to smoke the pipe around the same council fire!

Brothers—We are friends; we must assist each other to bear our burdens. The blood of many of our fathers and brothers has run like water on the ground, to satisfy the avarice of the white men. We, ourselves, are threatened with a great evil; nothing will pacify them but the destruction of all the red men.

Brothers—When the white men first set foot on our grounds, they were hungry; they had no place on which to spread their blankets, or to kindle their fires. They were feeble, they could do nothing for themselves. Our fathers commiserated their distress, and shared freely with them whatever the Great Spirit had given his red children. They gave them food when hungry, medicine when sick, spread skins for them to sleep on, and gave them grounds, that they might hunt and raise corn. Brothers, the white people are like poisonous serpents; when chilled, they are feeble and harmless, but invigorate them with warmth, and they sting their benefactors to death.

The white people came among us feeble; and now we have made them strong, they wish to kill us, or drive us back, as they would wolves and panthers.

Brothers—The white men are not friends to the Indians; at first they only asked for land sufficient for a wigwam, now, nothing will satisfy them but the whole of our hunting grounds, from the rising to the setting sun.

Brothers—The white men want more than our hunting grounds—they wish to kill our warriors; they would even kill our old men, women, and little ones.

Brothers—Many winters ago, there was no land—the sun did not rise and set: all was darkness. The Great Spirit made all things. He gave the white people a home beyond the great waters. He supplied these grounds with game, and gave them to his red children, and he gave them strength and courage to defend them.

Brothers—My people wish for peace, the red men all wish for peace: but where the white people are, there is no peace for them, except it be on the bosom of our mother.

Brothers—The white men despise and cheat the Indians; they abuse and insult them; they do not think the red men sufficiently good to live.

The red men have borne many and great injuries; they ought to suffer them no longer. My people will not; they are determined on vengeance; they have taken up the tomahawk; they will make it fat with blood—they will drink the blood of the white people.

Brothers—My people are brave and numerous, but the white people are too strong for them alone. I wish you to take up the tomahawk with them. If we all unite, we will cause the rivers to stain the great waters with their blood.

Brothers—If you do not unite with us, they will first destroy us, and then you will fall an easy prey to them. They have destroyed many nations of red men, because they were not united, because they were not friends to each other.

Brothers—The white people send runners amongst us; they wish to make us enemies, that they may sweep over, and desolate our hunting grounds, like devastating winds, or rushing waters.

Brothers—Our Great Father, over the great waters, is angry with the white people, our enemies. He will send his brave warriors against them; he will send us rifles, and whatever else we want—he is our friend, and we are his children.

Brothers—Who are the white people that we should fear them? They cannot fun fast, and are good marks to shoot at; they are only men; our fathers have killed many of them; we are not squaws, and we will stain the earth red with their blood.

Brothers—The Great Spirit is angry with our enemies—he speaks in thunder, and the earth swallows up villages, and drinks up the Mississippi. The great waters will cover their low-lands, their corn cannot grow, and the Great Spirit will sweep those who escape to the hills, from the earth with his terrible breath.

Brothers—We must be united; we must smoke the same pipe; we must fight each other's battles; and more than all, we must love the Great Spirit: he is for us; he will destroy our enemies, and make all his red children happy."

On the following day, Francis the prophet addressed the Osages in council, and although he repeated almost precisely the language of Te-cum-seh, and enlarged considerably more, on the power, and disposition of the Great Spirit; yet his discourse produced comparatively little effect on his audience. He was not a favourite among the Indians, and I am of opinion, that it did more injury than benefit, to the cause he undertook to espouse.

After they had concluded, I looked upon war as inevitable; and in its consequences contemplated the destruction of our enemies, and the restoration of the Indians to their primitive rights, power, and happiness. There was nothing I then so ardently desired as that of being a warrior, and I even envied those who were to achieve these important objects, the fame and glory that would redound as a necessary result. In a short time afterwards, however, the Osages rejected Te-cum-seh's proposals, and all these brilliant prospects vanished.

Newspaper Accounts

Three versions of red cloud's speech at the Cooper institute, 16 june 1870

Text from the *New York Times,* 17 June 1870

My Brothers and my Friends who are before me today: God Almighty has made us all, and He is here to hear what I have to say to you today. The Great Spirit made us both. He gave us lands and He gave you lands. You came here and we received you as brothers. When the Almighty made you, He made you all white and clothed you. When He made us He made us with red skins and poor. When you first came we were very many and you were few. Now you are many and we are few. You do not know who appears before you to speak. He is a representative of the original American race, the first people of this continent. We are good, and not bad. The reports which you get about us are all on one side. You hear of us only as murderers and thieves. We are not so. If we had more lands to give to you we would give them, but we have no more. We are driven into a very little island, and we want you, our dear friends, to help us with the Government of the United States. The Great Spirit made us poor and ignorant. He made you rich and wise and skillful in things which we know nothing about. The good Father made you to eat tame game and us to eat wild game. Ask any one who has gone through to California. They will tell you we have treated them well. You have children. We, too, have children, and we wish to bring them up well. We ask you to help us do it. At the mouth of Horse Creek, in 1852, the Great Father made a treaty with us. We agreed to let him pass through our territory unharmed for fifty-five years. We kept our word. We committed no murders, no depredations, until the troops came there. When the troops were sent there trouble and disturbance arose. Since that time there have been various goods sent forth from time to time to us, but only once did they reach us, and soon the Great Father took away the only good man he had sent to us, Col. Fitzpatrick. The Great Father said we must go to farming, and some of our men went to farming near Fort Laramie, and were treated very badly indeed. We came to Washington to see our Great Father that peace might be continued. The Great Father that made us both wishes peace to be kept; we want to keep peace. Will you help us? In 1868 men came out and brought papers. We could not read them, and they did not tell us truly what was in them. We thought the treaty was to remove the forts, and that we should then cease from fighting. But they wanted to send us traders on the Missouri. We did not want to go on the Missouri, but wanted traders where we were. When I reached Washington the Great Father explained to me what the treaty was, and showed me that the interpreters had deceived me. All I want is right and justice. I have tried to get from the Great Father what is right and just. I have not altogether succeeded. I want you to help me get what is right and just. I represent the whole Sioux nation, and they will be bound by what I say. I am no Spotted Tail, to say one thing one day and be bought for a pin the next. Look at me. I am poor and naked, but I am the Chief of the nation. We do not want riches, but we want to train our children right. Riches would do us no good. We could not take them with us to the other world. We do not want riches, we want peace and love.

The riches that we have in this world, Secretary Cox said truly, we cannot take with us to the next world. Then I wish to know why Commissioners are sent out to us who do nothing but rob us and get the riches of this world away from us? I was brought up among the traders, and those who came out there in the early times treated me well and I had a good time with them. They taught us to wear clothes and to use tobacco and ammunition. But, by and by, the Great Father sent out a different kind of men; men who cheated and drank whisky; men who were so bad that the Great Father could not keep them at home and so sent them out there. I have sent a great many words to the Great Father but they never reached him. They were drowned on the way, and I was afraid the words I spoke lately to the Great Father would not reach you, so I came to speak to you myself; and now I am going away to my home. I want to have men sent out to my people whom we know and can trust. I am glad I have come here. You belong in the East and I belong in the West, and I am glad I have come here and that we could understand one another. I am very much obliged to you for listening to me. I go home this afternoon. I hope you will think of what I have said to you. I bid you all an affectionate farewell.

Text from the *New York Daily Tribune*, 17 June 1870

My brethren and my friends who are here before me this day, God Almighty has made us all, and He is here to bless what I have to say to you to-day. [Applause.] The Good Spirit made us both; He gave you lands and He gave us lands; He gave us these lands; you came in here and we respected you as brothers. [Applause.] God Almighty made you, but made you all white and clothed you; when He made us He made us with red skins and poor; now you have come. When you first came we were very many, and you were very few, now you are many, and we are getting very few, and we are poor. [Applause.] You do not know who appears before you to-day to speak. I am a representative of the original American race—the first people of this continent. [Great applause.] We are good and not bad. The reports that you hear concerning us are all on one side. We are always well-disposed to them. You are here told that we are traders and thieves, and it is not so. We have given you nearly all our lands, and if we had any more land to give we would be very glad to give it. We have nothing more. We are driven into a very little land, and we want you now, as our dear friends, to help us with the Government of the United States. [Hear, hear.] The Great Father made us poor and ignorant—made you rich and wise, and more skillful in these things that we know nothing about. The Great Father, the Good Father in heaven, made you all to eat tame food—made us to eat wild food—gives us the wild food. You ask anybody who has gone through our country to California; ask those who have settled there and in Utah, and you will find that we have treated them always well. You have children; we have children. You want to raise your children and make them happy and prosperous; we want to raise ours and make them happy and prosperous. We ask you to help us do it. [Great applause.] At the mouth of the Horse Creek, in 1852, the Great Father made a treaty with us by which we agreed to let all that country open for 55 years for the transit of those who were going through. We kept this treaty; we never treated any man wrong; we never committed any murder or depredation until afterward the troops were sent into that country, and the troops killed our people and ill-treated them, and thus war and trouble arose; but before the troops were sent there we were quiet and peaceable, and there was no disturbance. [Applause, and Hear, hear.] Since that time there have been various goods sent from time to time to us, the only ones that ever reached us, and then after they reached us (very soon after) the Government took them away. You, as good men, ought to help us to these goods. Col. Fitzpatrick of the Government said we must all go to farm, and some of the people went to Fort Laramie and were badly treated. I only want to do that which is peaceful, and the Great Fathers know it, and also the Great Father who made us both. I came to Washington to see the Great Father in order to have peace, and in order to have peace continue. That is all we want, and that is the reason why we are here now. [Great applause.]

In 1868 men came out and brought papers. We are ignorant and do not read papers, and they did not tell us right what was in these papers. We wanted them to take away their forts, leave our country, would not make war, and give our traders something. They said we had bound ourselves to trade on the Missouri, and we said, No, we did not want that. The interpreters deceived us. When I went to Washington I saw the great Father; the Great Father showed me what the treaties were; he showed me all these points, and showed me that the interpreters had deceived me, and did not let me know what the right side of the treaty was. All I want is right and justice. I have tried to get from the Great Father what is true and just. I have not altogether succeeded. I want you to believe with me and to know with me that which is right and just. I represent the Sioux Nation; they will be governed by what I say and what I represent. I am no Spotted Tail, who will say one thing one day and do the opposite the next. [Great applause and laughter.] Look at me. I am poor and naked, but I am the chief of the nation. We do not want riches, we do not ask for riches, but we want our children properly trained and brought up. We look to you for your sympathy. Our riches will not do us no good; we cannot take away into the other world anything we have—we want to have love and peace. [Applause.] Who gave the riches that we have in this world? Secretary Cox rightly told me that anything we could not take away into the next world; if that is so, we would like to know why commissioners are sent out there to do nothing but rob them and get the riches of this world away from us? [Great laughter and applause.] I was brought up among the traders and those who came out there in those early times. I had a good time for they treated us nicely and well. They taught me how to wear clothes and use tobacco [laughter], and to use fire-arms and ammunition, and all went on very well until the Great Father sent out another kind of men—men who drank whisky. He sent out whiskymen, men who drank and quarreled, men who were so bad that he could not keep them at home, and so he sent them out there. [Great laughter.] I have sent a great many words to the Great Father, but I don't know that they ever reached the Great Father. They were drowned on the way, therefore I was a little offended with it. The words I told the Great Father lately would never come to him, so I thought I would come and tell you myself. And I am going to leave you to-day, and I am going back to my home. I want to tell the people that we cannot trust his agents and superintendents. I don't want strange people that we know nothing about. I am very glad that you belong to us. I am very glad that we have come here and found you and that we can understand one another. I don't want any more such men sent out there, who are so poor that when they come out there their first thoughts are how to fill their own pockets. We want preserves in our reserves. We want honest men and we want you to help to keep us in the lands that belong to us so that we may not be a prey to those who are viciously disposed. I am going home, I am very glad that you have listened to me, and I wish you good bye and give you an affectionate farewell. [Great applause.]

Text from the *New York Herald,* 17 June 1870

My brothers and friends who are here befor me to-day, the Almighty has made us all, and He is here to listen to what I have to say. The Great Spirit made us both. He gave us lands. You came in here; we gave you those lands, and received you as brothers. (Applause.) When the Almighty made you He made you all white and clothed you, and He made us with red skins, and made us poor. When you first came we were very many and you were very few. Now we are very few and you are very many, and we are very poor. You do not know who it is who appears before you to-day to speak. We are the representatives of the original American race, the first people of this continent. (Applause.) We are good and not bad. The reports you have heard concerning us are all on one side and from interested men. We are all good, although you hear we are all murderers and thieves. We have given you all the lands we had, and now we have no more, but a small island. If we had any more we would willingly give them. And now, our dear friends, we want you to help us with [the] government of the United States. (Applause.) The Great Spirit made us poor and ignorant, and made you rich and wise, and skilful in doing things about which we know nothing. He made you to eat tame game and us to eat wild. You ask anyone who has been across the continent to Utah whether we have not always treated him well. We have children to raise like you, and we want you to help us raise them. (Applause.) At the mouth of Horse creek, in 1852, the Great Father made a treaty with us which required that we should leave the country open for transit for fifty-five years. We kept that treaty. We never committed any depredations until the troops were sent into the country and killed our people. Then we could not do anything else. Since that time there have been goods sent us from time to time; but only once have they reached us. Very soon the government took away the only good man—Colonel Fitzpatrick—who ever helped us to goods. The government said we should go to farming. Some of our people went to Fort Laramie and worked, but got very poor. We only want peace and justice, and we went to Washington for that purpose, and that is the reason we are here now. In 1868 men came out and brought papers. We are ignorant and cannot read papers, and they did not tell us what was in those papers. We thought at first that the United States government would take away those forts and give us traders. They misrepresented and deceived us, and we did not know what the papers contained. When I went to Washington and saw the Great Father he told me what the treaty was, and that the interpreters had been false to me, and did not let me know what the real subject of the treaty was. (Applause.) I want no more than right and justice, and I did not succeed altogether in getting what I wanted. I want you to help me. I am the representative of the old Sioux nation. I am no Spotted Tail, that will say one thing one day and be bought with a fish. (Great applause.) Look at me, I am poor and naked, and yet I am the chief of the nation. We do not ask for riches. We do not want them, but we do want our children properly brought up. Riches bring no good. We can't take them with us to the other world, and all we want is love and peace. (Applause.) The riches that we have in this world—as Secretary Cox rightly told me—cannot be taken into the next life. Now, if that be so, I would like to know why the commissioners who are sent out to us do nothing but rob us all the time. (Laughter.) I was brought up among the traders and those who came out to us in the early times, and I had pleasure with them. They taught me to wear clothes, to smoke tobacco, the use of firearms, and all was well until the Great Father sent out to us men who sued to drink fire water; men who the Great Father could not keep at home, and so he sent them to us. (Laughter and Applause.) I have sent a great many words to the Great Father, but I do not believe that they ever reached him. Now I have had something to say, and I thought I would come and say it myself. I am going to leave you to-day, and go right home. I want to have men sent out to me and my people that we can trust. We do not want strangers. You belong to the East, and I to the West, and we ought to have an interest in one another. (Applause.) I do not want any more such men who are so poor that their only thought is to fill their pockets. We want honesty and honest men on our reservation, and want you to help keep us there. I am very much obliged to you for listening to me. I hope you have heard what I said. And now I bid you an affectionate farewell. (Great applause.)

ETHNOLOGICAL DOCUMENTS

THIN LEATHER'S ORATION: TEXT IN PIMA

From Frank Russell, "The Pima Indians," *Twenty-Sixth Annual Report of the Bureau of American Ethnology for 1904–1905* (Washington: GPO, 1908), pp. 339–46.

Komtâva Sis Makai spadâ âlitûk tatcoa. Ĭt tcʊwʊɹ tcʊkĭtc âĭtkʿ si-ĭmâĭtatcotkʿ am sʿap tcʊ-umâ-â. Ĭt tâ-âta-ak tcotcoatc âĭtkʿ si-ĭmâĭtatcotkʿ am sʿap ko-okiʿ. Ĭt rsârsânûkam rsorsokĭ tâtoatc âĭtkʿ si-ĭmâĭtcotkʿ am sʿap tcʊ-umâ-â. Ĭt os kʊ-ʊrsatc âĭtkʿ si-ĭmâĭtatcotkʿ am sʿap ko-okiʿ. Am ki-ĭkʿhâ tcʊx himĭtcotkʿ am tcoĭkâ kopal hʊtcʊlwoĭtc. Ka-am katckahimĭtc am ʊtcʊkĭta. Kaɹsi-ĭtatakrskʿ ivam(pi) am ʊvwʊkatc inyʊnhâk tcʊm nyʊĭ âvapĭ hʊkam haĭtco kanhastcoĭk. Ĭt wʊskʿ ap tcʊm ʊmatcĭamahimûk piʊnakâ. Ĭm hoɹĭnyĭk woĭ ʌâtʊvâ kʊs tcʊtakĭʿ ʊʌamatûta hokĭt am woĭhyamûk am puĭ vatak os. Am ki-ĭk hĭkomĭak am ʊwʊtcâ toak am sikommo. Kotak tânâlĭkatc am maorsatûkĭt siwoʌak towe katcĭm tcʊwʊɹ tam am kokoʌa. Towe katcĭm tcʊwʊɹ maskâ oltʿ; towe tcotcĭm tâ-âta-ak ʌʊpʊkĭomĭtkʿ tcotcoa. Tak hap tcoĭkam tcom nyʊĭtok am ʊta tcorsal ihʊhʊmĭâ. Ĭm hoɹĭnyĭk takĭŏ tcʊt ihimĭtc kʊs tcok ʊkâ-âmhaĭʌakĭta. Hʊk hʊkatc itakĭhonûk ʊta pimaskâ iolĭnûk sa-apĭʿ itâ-âtan. Ĭm katcĭm takĭŏ ihimĭtc kʊs ta-atʿkĭʿ ʊkâ-âmhaĭwakĭta hʊk hʊkatc isita-akĭhonûk ʊta pimaskâ iolĭnûk sa-ap itâ-âtan.

Ĭm sialĭk takĭŏ tcʊt ihimĭtc kʊs tântâm ʊkâhaĭʌakita hʊk hʊkʊtc sita-kĭhonûk ʊta pimaskâ iolĭnûk sa-ap itâtan. Ĭt tʊtamʊ tcʊt ihotony kʊs tcʊtakĭ ʊkâ-âmhaĭʌakĭta hʊk hʊkûtc sita-akĭhonûk ʊta pimaskâ iolĭnûk sa-ap itâtan. Ĭm hoɹĭnyĭk takĭŏ tcʊt himĭtc kʊs tcoak ʊʌamatûtak hʊk hʊkûtc isiʌotkʿ natâ. Ĭm katcĭm takĭŏ tcʊt ihimitc kʊs ta-atʿkĭʿ ʊʌamatûtak hʊk hʊkûtc isivotkʿ natâ.

Ĭm sialĭk takĭŏ tcʊt ihimĭtc kʊs tântân ʊʌamatʊtakʻ hʊk hʊkûtc isivotkʻ natâ. Ĭt tʊtamʊ tcʊt ihotĭny kʊs tcʊ-ʊtaki ʊʌamatatûk hʊk hʊkûtc isivotkʻ natâ. Am ivorsanyuk am siûkʊĭrs. Âva hʊpai taha kʊs makaitʻkam â-âtam kotak am sikʊĭhitcony ata-am pai-ĭtc siûkʊĭrs. Âva hʊpai taha kʊs nyiâkam â-âtam kotak am sikʊĭhitcony ata-am pai-ĭtc si-ikʊĭrs. Âva hʊpai taha kʊs siakam â-âtam tak am sikʊĭhitcony, âvawot iwʊs taam siûkʊĭrs. Âva hʊpai tahakʊ ofʻĭ stcopoi-hitûkam kʊ ofʻĭ stcotcûkitûkam kot hʊk hawʊnatkʻ am sikʊĭhitconyĭtkʻ am tco-opiʻ. Am kâmalm miarspahimûk sialĭk takĭŏ mâ-âkanyĭk am tcʊt kʊs tân-tâm ʊʌâkĭta ĭtcʊ. Kʊs kʊ-ukʊ-uĭtam tâ-âta-ak tcotcoatc ʊrsârsân ap vapaa-aʌany. Hʊk wʊsk ʊta vapʻkiʻhĭtc hʊkʊtc hʊk ʊipûtak ivaosĭtahĭm. Rsâr-sânûkam rsorsokĭ tâtoatc haakĭa nanûkâtcoĭkam mămăthăt katcpʻ ʊi-ĭntc wʊo(f)ʊtck hʊk wʊsk ʊt mawopĭtc hʊkʊtc hʊk ʊi-ipʊtak ivaosĭtahĭm. Kʊs kʊ-ukʊtam o-os tcotcoatckʻ hʊk wʊsk ap mawopĭtc hʊkatc hʊk ʊipʊtak ivaosĭtahĭm. ʌataʌa tcʊmâ-â hʊkʊ Pa-ak ʊmoa-akŭt woĭtcotkʻ pitcĭmûk woĭt-cotkʻ napatoʌak vi-ĭtckŭt tcoĭk tcivĭa. Hastco pŭhimʊtkʻ tcivĭak vi-ĭtckŭt tcoikʻtcʻ tcivĭa. Hi-ĭks, nanypĭm akĭt spathâlĭtkʻ tatcoa tcʊwʊɹ ltcukĭ hʊmata tarsa. Ta-am sialĭk woa ki-ĭk aprsârs, ʌataʌa tcʊ-umâ-â taɹs tcʊtcrsatckŭt ki-ĭk ap (m)âĭtam kâvâtltkʻ ki-ĭk ap (m)âĭtam tcʊtany. Âvaʌŭt kʊĭrspakutatc wʊs kâs hʊwʊlhâkĭtak wʊs kâs tcʊʌakitak tcŭm pipapakʻĭ hʊk ʊta takʊĭrspan ʊtco kotak ʊta ap siʊkʊĭrs. Âvawot takrspakŭtatc wʊs kâs hʊvʊhâkĭtak wʊs kâs tcʊʌakĭtak tcompipapakʻĭ hʊk ʊta apta takrspam ʊtco kotak ʊta ap si-ĭtakrs. Am iʌorsanyĭk koiwoa i-ipoĭʌoak koĭwoa itakʻtcʻkowa paitcok koiwoa i-ipoi-woa koiwa itakkʻtcʻkowa. Am pai-ĭtcok koĭwa i-ipoĭwoak koĭwa itakkʻtcʻ koĭwa Âvawot iwʊrs ta-am i-ipoĭwoak koĭwa itakkʻtcʻkowa. Âvawot ʊta kat-cĭm vâkĭtatc kotak iâĭ katcĭm takĭŏ vâkĭtatc wʊs kâs payokatak wʊs kâs nahakiâtak a-an kiatûta hokĭtûk vi-ĭk kiatûta hokĭtûk os hiktcʻka hiasĭtastc hokĭtûk kak sivantc koʌatc sikopal woihĭm. Nanûkʻĭ âĭt takĭŏ vâkĭtatc wʊs kâs payokatak wʊs kâs nahakiâtak a-an kiatûta hokitak vi-ĭk kiatûta hokĭtuk os hikutcʻka hiâsitastcʻ hokĭtûk kak sihopanytc.

Sitcuxhĭm tcotahĭm. Kahupai taha kʊs makaĭtʻkam â-âtam kak am sitcux-hĭm tcotahĭm. ʌatava tcʊ-umââ kʊ nyiakʊtam os. Woĭtcotkʻ pitcĭmûkʻ woĭt-cotkʻ napatoʌak viĭtckŭt tcoĭkʻtcʻ tcivĭa. Hastco pŭihĭmʊtkʻ tcivĭak viĭtckŭt tcoĭkʻtcʻ tcivĭa. Hi-ĭks, nanypĭm akĭt spathâlĭtkʻ tatcŏa tcʊwʊɹ ltcukĭ hʊmata tarsa. Pʻata kaĭtam tcʊtcʊa aʌawŏt ʊta kʊkam vaokatc tak siâm kioʌltʻkatkʻ ap isi kâmʊrspĭtcʻ avawot kâsĭvoltatc tak ap vanytcʻkʻ kʊ sialĭk ʌʊkĭomĭlĭkatc wʊs ka itakĭhonûk ʌʊnatkʻ ap isi kamʊrspĭtcʻ âvawot ʊlʊtatcʻ kas siâm tcokŭt matsĭk akʻtcʻ korsâ ĭpʻ takĭtcony vi-ĭkam ap isi kakâmhaĭtckakat. Ĭm mot katcĭm takĭŏ mamhakatc tak ap molinûk siâm âmĭna vʊpatkʻ sikapĭtckatkʻ rsak. Âvawot ʊta katcĭm vâkĭtatc kotak iâĭ katcĭm takĭŏ vâkĭtatc wᴜs kas payokatak wᴜs kas nahakĭâtak a-an kina-atᴜta hokĭtuk vi-ĭk kiatûta hokĭtûk os hikᴜtcʻka hiasĭtastc hokĭtuk kak sivantcʻkoʌatc sikopal woĭhĭm. Nanûkĭ âĭt takĭŏ ʌakitatc wᴜs kas payokatak wᴜs kas nahakiâtak a-an kiatûta hokĭtuk vi-ĭk kiatûta hokĭtuk os hikĭtcʻka hiasĭtastcʻ hokĭtŭk kak sihopanytcʻ sitcᴜxhĭm tcotahĭm. Ka hᴜpai taha kᴜs nyâkam â-âtam kak am sitcᴜxhĭm tcotahĭm. ʌataʌa tcu-umâ-â kᴜ tars i-ĭkŭt rsotakĭʻ kaot tan woĭkotatc wᴜs kas hᴜwᴜlhakĭtak wᴜs kas tcuʌakĭtak. Tcᴜm pipapakĭ hᴜk ᴜta apta tân woĭm ᴜtco tak ᴜta ap sitânwoa. Kaot takrspa-kotatc wᴜs kas hᴜʌulhâkĭtak wᴜs kas tcuʌakĭtak. Tcᴜm pipapakĭʻ hᴜk ᴜta apta takrspam ᴜtco tak ᴜta ap si-ĭtakrs. Am i-ĭtcomalkatkʻ am i. Am tcᴜm nyuĭ kᴜk ᴜta am kᴜk stcᴜ-utakĭ hâtaĭ tapĭnya. Kot hᴜk wᴜtcâ am maorsk am takĭthâ hᴜk Â-âpsʻ kam uâmĭna. Nyĭâkŭtam os uâmĭna viak hᴜk rsa-ak iâĭ. Âʌawot-ᴜta katcĭm vâkĭtatc kotak iâĭ katcĭm takĭŏ vâkĭtatc wᴜs kas payokatak wᴜs kas nahakiâtak a-an kia-atᴜta hokĭtak vi-ĭk kiatᴜta hokĭtvk os hiktcʻka hiâsĭtastcʻ hokĭtvk kak sivanĭtckovatc sikopaɬ woĭhĭm. Na-anki âĭt takĭŏ vâkĭtatcʻ wᴜs kas payokatak wᴜs kas nahakĭâtak a-an kiatᴜta hokĭtvk vi-ĭk kiatᴜta hokĭtvk os hikʻtcka hiâsĭtastcʻ hokĭtvk kak sihopanytcʻ sitcᴜxhĭm tcotahĭm. Kahᴜpaĭ taha kᴜs siakam â-âtam kak am sitcᴜxhĭm tcotahĭm. ʌataʌa tcu-umâ-â kᴜ taɹs hotokot ki-ĭk ap mâĭtam sᴜtapĭonytc katc kotak âĭtkʻ ki-ĭkhâ itapĭonyĭk ĭmho tuʌᴜtca sʻpapaki tcu kᴜ sis makaĭ. Woitcotkʻ pitcĭmkʻ woitcotkʻ ɲapatoʌak vi-ĭtckŭt tcoi-ĭkʻtcʻ tcivĭa. Hastco pŭĭhimûtʻkʻ tcivĭa, hastco pŭĭhĭmûtʻkʻ tcivĭa, hastco pŭĭhĭmŭtʻkʻ tcivĭa, hastco pŭĭhĭmûtʻkʻ tcivĭak vi-ĭtckŭt tcoĭkʻtcʻ tcivĭa. Hi-ĭks, nanypĭm akĭt spathâlĭtcʻ tatcoa tcᴜvᴜɹ nytcukĭ hᴜmata tarsa pʻata kaĭtam tcᴜtcu. Ata-im hoɹĭnyĭk takĭŏ tcut âĭtktcut tcivĭa.

Ĭm sialĭk woĭ tcᴜxhĭmtcotkʻ sialĭk parsâĭnâtkĭtkʻ opam tarsowa ĭm katcĭm takĭŏtcŭt âĭtktcut tcivĭa. Na-ankĭ âĭt woĭ tcᴜxhĭmtcotkʻ na-ankĭʻ âĭt parsâĭpâtkĭtkʻ opam tarswoa. Ĭm sialĭk takĭŏtcŭt âĭtkʻtcut tcivĭa. Hoɹĭnyĭk woĭ tcᴜxhĭmtcotkʻ hoɹinyĭk parsâinâtkĭtkʻ opam tarswoa. Ĭt tamᴜtcut âĭtktcut tcivĭa. Tam atcĭm woĭ tcᴜxhĭmtcotk tam atcĭm parsâinâtkĭtkʻ opam tarswoa haapa-tavâĭtâ-âta. An wᴜkatc hᴜk tcᴜwᴜɹ itakĭŏmk hastcoprs alĭ wᴜpâtkʻ ikâmûk hᴜk ᴜta am tarswoa. Kawot kᴜ kâkâĭ tax aɹĭtcĭkĭtcᵃ pawoĭs tax aɹĭtcĭkĭtc kotak ap parsâ i-ĭpûĭhuĭʌoa kota siâm uiʌakitat kavaot kᴜs kâmakĭ tcufha rsâikatc kotak ap imúk rsârsoâ. Kota am tcopĭnyk am sialĭk takĭŏ mâ-âkanûk am kᴜs tântâm rso-otakĭʻ tcᴜ. Kᴜ Pa-ak pahĭwoa katc am simaĭrsk tcᴜ. Am pai-ĭtc tcopĭnyĭk am mâ-âkanyĭk am kᴜs tcok rso-otakĭʻ tcᴜ. Kᴜ haʌany a-an katc maĭrsk am tcᴜ. Am pai-ĭtc tcopĭnyk am mâ-âkanyk am kᴜs tcᴜ-utakĭ rsotakĭ tcᴜ. Hᴜʌatcot a-an katc naĭrsk am tcᴜ. Am pai-ĭtc tcopĭnyk am mâ-âkanyk am kᴜs soam rso-otakĭ tcᴜ. Kᴜ ʌatcokok a-an katc maĭrsk am tcᴜ. Am tcopĭnyk am mâ-âkanyk am ikoatcĭtkˁ am tcᴜm nyuĭ. Ĭt ᴧâkᴜta katcĭm pipapakĭ hastco katc tcoitcĭm tcoi-ĭk. Âvak tcom sitaĭrstc takatkˁ ᴜ-ᴜlĭt hᴜk makai. Kota am wᴜkatc katcĭm na-ankâ tcoi-ĭtckatc sisârspâl ki-ĭkomĭa. Pᴜk am opam tcopĭˁ. Ki-ĭk ap mâ-âkanyk makaĭ na-ata tcᴜ-ᴜmûk hokĭt an takĭtâ. Sˁmakai-ĭtakam â-âtam vaksĭtkˁ tam tarswoa. Tak ᴜta hᴜk isi kuĭrsk kukĭᴧak nyuĭ ᴧiapâkᴜ-ulĭka tcᴜwᴜ꜔â mᴜ-tᴜtam ᴜᴧᴜpâkiˁ o-ofĭk ta-atam ᴜᴧᴜpâkitkˁ nyuĭnyk tam ap ᴜiaᴧak ap piatco tatkĭtcotkˁ ap sᴜtapam puĭ. Am ᴧᴜkûtc katcĭm nananûka tcoĭtckatc si-ĭnasĭk sˁpapakĭˁ kaᴧolkatkˁ sˁpapakĭˁ hahâk inyᴜ woa.

Hapkvk hᴜmŭs ᴜhitkˁ tatcoa âᴧaot kᴜs kᴜ-ᴜk toakak konta ap pᴜk antaᴧaĭoapa.

THIN LEATHER'S ORATION:
FREE TRANSLATION BY RUSSELL AND JOSÉ LEWIS BRENNAN

You people desired to capture Elder Brother so that you might destroy him. You secured the assistance of Vulture, who made a miniature earth; you saw him at his home engaged in this work. He shaped the mountains, defined the water courses, placed the trees, and in four days completed his task. Mounting the zigzag ladders of his house he flew forth and circled about until he saw Elder Brother. Vulture saw the blue flames issuing from Elder Brother's heart and knew that he was invulnerable. In his turn Elder Brother knew that Vulture wished to kill him and had made the miniature earth for that purpose.

Elder Brother, as he regained consciousness, rose on hands and feet and swayed unsteadily from side to side. He thought of the world about him and it seemed but a barren waste around him; as he recovered from his bewilderment he saw the true condition of things.

Looking about him he saw a river toward the west along which grew arrow bushes. From these he cut four magic sticks; placing his hand on these he blew cigarette smoke over them, whereupon magic power shone forth from between his fingers. He was much pleased with this and laughed softly to himself. He rubbed his magic bag of buckskin four times with each of the four sticks and then put them in and tied it. He then arose and stamped down all mortal magicians and even ground his own house into the earth. He stamped upon the orator, the warrior, the industrious, and the provident woman, and crushed them down. Then he sank beneath the surface of the earth. He reappeared in the east and made from the point of emergence a transparent trail to the place where he had gone down. About the base of his mountains the water began to seep forth; entering, he came out with spirit refreshed. Taking all waters, even those covered with water plants, he dipped his hands in and made downward passes. Touching the large trees he made downward sweeps with his hands. Going to the place where he had killed Eagle he sat down looking like a ghost. A voice from the darkness asked, "Why are you here?" He answered that notwithstanding all that he had done for them the people hated him. Renewing his power four times in the east at the place where the sun rises, he blew his hot breath upon the people, which like a weight held them where they were. He accompanied the Sun on his journey, traveling along the south border of the trail where there was a fringe of beads, feathers, strings of down, and flowers. He jerked the string holding these so that they fell and made the magicians jump. In the north he saw a trail bordered like the one in the south and overturned it.

On his journey along the Sun's orbit Elder Brother came to Talking Tree. "Why do you come like a ghost?" asked Tree. He replied, "Notwithstanding all I have done for the people they hate me." Tree broke one of its middle branches and cut a notch around it to form a war club and gave it to him. Then Tree broke a branch on the south side and made a bundle of ceremonial sticks from it for him. He saw a trail toward the south and another toward the north bordered with shells, feathers, down, and flowers, which he overturned.

Arriving at the drinking place of the Sun, he knelt down in the tracks made by the Sun to drink, and saw a dark-blue stone. He left there the arrow-bush ceremonial sticks containing his enemies' power, but retained in his grasp the sticks cut from Talking Tree. Toward the south were strewn necklaces, earrings, feathers, strings of down, and flowers, all of which he jerked and threw face down. Toward the north he threw down the same objects, and as they struck the earth they caused the magicians to jump. Reaching the place where the sun sets he slid four times before he reached the place where Earth Doctor lived.

"Why do you come looking like a ghost?" asked the god. "Notwithstanding all that I have done for them the people hate me," he answered. By Earth Doctor's order the wind from the west caught him up and carried him far to the east, then brought him back and threw him violently down. . . . The south wind carried him to the north; the east wind carried him to the west; the wind from the zenith carried him to the sky; all returned to throw him violently down. From his cigarette containing two kinds of roots Earth Doctor blew smoke upon the breast of Elder Brother, whereupon green leaves sprang forth and he gained consciousness. Earth Doctor cleared the ground for a council and then picked up Elder Brother as he would have taken up a child and put him in his house.

Earth Doctor sent Gray Gopher up through the earth to emerge in the east by the white water where lay the eagle tail. He came out by the black water where lay the raven feathers. He came out by the blue water where lay the bluebird's feathers. He came out by the yellow water where lay the hawk feathers. He found so many people that he feared they could not be conquered. But he gnawed the magic power of their leader until he weakened it. Then he returned to the council in the nether world, where his power as a magician was recognized, and he was placed on a mat with Elder Brother.

The people were now ready to do whatever Elder Brother desired of them and, like fierce predatory animals or raptorial birds, they poured out of the underworld and fell upon the inhabitants of the upper world, whom they conquered without difficulty. The victors swept the property and everything relating to the conquered from the face of the earth.

Consider the magic power which abode with me and which is at your service.

TRANSLATION BY DONALD M. BAHR

From Donald M. Bahr, *Pima and Papago Ritual Oratory: A Study of Three Texts* (San Francisco: Indian Historian Press, 1975), pp. 35–51.

Prelude

So for Elder Brother Shaman you had ill will and planned;
this one [Buzzard], land he put down and continued and planned much and completed;
this one, mountains he stood up and continued and planned much and ended;
this one, water sources he put down and continued and planned much and completed;
this one, wood he stood up and continued and planned much and ended, there four times he shot him and there face-down he lay, there he lay and there regained his senses, pressed [with his hands] and arose, there around himself looked and tried to see;
there were none of those things that used to be;
all this he tried to figure out and couldn't;
westward lay a blue snake of his making [a river];
beside it there he peered and got a wet stick [an arrowweed], there in fourths he cut it and beneath himself he placed it and really blew on it, its rays between the fingers really came out and our opposite-lying land, to it they reached;

our opposite-lying land they clearly held;

our opposite-standing mountains they reddened and stood up, that was
    the kind of thing he wished to see and softly inside himself he
    laughed;

there from the west he started a black haze of his making, with it he wiped
    it [the four pieces of reed] and inside invisibly held it and well he did;

there from the south he started a yellow haze of his making, with it he
    wiped it and inside invisibly held it and well he did;

there from the east he started a shining haze of his making, with it he
    wiped it and inside invisibly held it and well he did;

here from above us descended a blue haze of his making, with it he wiped
    it and inside invisibly held it and well he did;

there from the west he started a black snake of his making, with it he tied
    it [the bundle] and finished;

there from the south he started a yellow snake of his making, with it he
    tied it and finished;

there from the east he started a shining snake of his making, with it he tied
    it and finished;

here from above us descended a blue snake of his making, with it he tied it
    and finished.

Part 1

There he set out and

there stepped;

someplace sat the shaman man, on him he really stamped, on him took
    the next step;

someplace sat the talker man, on him he really stamped, on him took the
    next step;

someplace sat the warrior man, on him he really stamped, on all of them
    he stepped;

someplace sat the woman who gathers much [wild food], the woman who
    stores much, those together he really stamped and.

Part 2

There sank, there thinly he was buried and

eastwards popped out and

from there a shining road of his making he found;

large mountains he stood up, their bases seeping, in all of that he entered
and with it his heart was moistening;
sources of water he put down, with many kinds of water plants
covered they lay, in all that he dipped and with it his heart was
moistening;
big trees he stood up, at all those he dipped and with it his heart was
moistening;
then reached his eagle killing place;
approached it straight and circled and approached it straight, "Are you
going to come in, being something blown by the wind and arrived
here, what do you want to get and arrive here, being something
blown by the wind and arrived here?" "Yes, because I tell you, ill will
and plans, land put down, people I set."

Part 3

Next eastwards he made four moves;
then reached the sun rising place;
quadruply [it was] hollowed and
quadruply [he was] thudding;
there was its stepping place, all windy and all cloudy, it was not a thing to
step in slowly;
and in it he really stepped;
there was its grasping place, all windy and all cloudy, it was not a thing to
grasp in slowly;
and in it he really grasped.

Part 4

There set out and
breathed and pushed;
next he breathed and pushed;
there next he breathed and pushed;
it was on all of it he breathed and pushed;
there was its [the sun's] center-lying road;
and he followed [it];
its south-lying road, all beaded, all earringed, wing feather bowstring
sided, down feather bowstring sided, cut wood flowered sided, and
that he really jerked and face-down threw;

its north-lying road, all beaded, all earringed, wing feather bowstring
 sided, down feather bowstring sided, cut wood flowered sided, and
 that he really uprooted and far threw;
and someplace sat the shaman man, and that there really far he threw;
then reached the talking tree;
approached it straight and circled and approached it straight, "Are you
 going to come in, being something blown by the wind and arrived
 here, what do you want to get and arrive here, being something
 blown by the wind and arrived here?" "Yes, because I tell you, ill will
 and plans, land I put down, people I set," he said;
there was its center-standing stalk, confidently he cut it and on his rump
 really hung it;
there was its chrysalis, that he plucked and with the morning red glow he
 wrapped it and on his rump it really hung;
there was its bark, and confidently owl hooks—so-called—he stuck on the
 back of his head, the remainder on his cheeks he fastened;
there was its south branch, that he broke off and confidently made into
 ceremonial sticks and them he really bundled and held.

Part 5

There was its center-lying road;
and he followed [it];
its south-lying road, all beaded, all earringed, wing feather bowstring
 sided, down feather bowstring sided, cut wood flowered sided and
 that he really jerked and face-down threw;
its north-lying road, all beaded, all earringed, wing feather bowstring
 sided, down feather bowstring sided, cut wood flowered sided and
 that he really uprooted and far threw;
and someplace sat the talker man, and that there really far he threw;
then reached the sun drinking water;
there was its kneeling place, all windy and all cloudy and it was not a thing
 to kneel in slowly;
he really knelt in it;
there was its grasping place, all windy and all cloudy and it was not a thing
 to grasp in slowly;
he really grasped in it, there he stooped and there drank, there he tried to
 look;
in it stood a blue smooth stone;

and under it there he thrust and left the enemy ceremonial sticks [brought
from the earth];
the talking tree ceremonial sticks remained and
those he held and.

Part 6

Continued;
there was its center-lying road;
and he followed [it];
its south-lying road, all beaded, all earringed, wing feather bowstring
sided, down feather bowstring sided, cut wood flowered sided and
that he really jerked and face-down threw;
its north-lying road, all beaded, all earringed, wing feather bowstring
sided, down feather bowstring sided, cut wood flowered sided and
that he really uprooted and far threw;
and someplace sat the warrior man, and that there really far he threw;
then reached the sun descending place;
quadruply smooth it lay.

Part 7

Continued and four times slid;
there beneath us [in the underworld] slowly he found the Elder Brother
Shaman;
approached him straight and circled and approached him straight, "Are
you going to come in, being something blown by the wind and
arrived here, what do you want to get and arrive here, what do you
want to get and arrive here, what to you want to get and arrive here,
what do you want to get and arrive here, being something blown by
the wind and arrived here?" "Yes, because I tell you, ill will and plans,
land I put down, people I set," he said;
then there from the west behind him it [a wind] arrived, there towards the
east it threw him and in front of the east it turned and back again him
it set;
there from the south behind him it arrived, towards the north it threw
him and in front of the north it turned and back again him it set;
there from the east behind him it arrived, towards the west it threw him
and in front of the west it turned and back again him it set;
here from above behind him it arrived, towards the sky it threw him and

in front of the sky it turned and back again him it set, thus it did, there
   around him it smoothed the land and
he [Elder Brother] was like a baby and
he [Earth Shaman] held him and there inside [the smoothed ground] him
   he set;
and there was his ghost root cigarette, *pawois* root cigarette;
and he breathed it on his front, deftly he [Elder Brother] greened;
and there was a grey gopher, his [Earth Shaman's] pet;
kinship to it he cried;
and there he sank and in the east popped out and there a kind of shining
   water found, a kind of eagle tail covering it there he found;
there next he sank and there popped out and there a kind of black water
   found, a kind of raven feathers covering it there he found;
there next he sank and there popped out and there a kind of blue water
   found, a kind of blue bird feathers covering it there he found;
there next he sank and there popped out and there a kind of yellow water
   found, a kind of hawk feathers covering it there he found;
there he sank and there popped out and there peeped out and there tried
   to look, "This lying road isn't a thing to be taken slowly, it is firmly
   placed and seated" thought the shaman [Gopher], and there around
   him lay various of his [the enemy's] possessions, very shortly he bit
   them off, he took them and
there sank homeward, four times popped out and reached the shaman's
   fire and beside it he released [the bitten off belongings];
the shaman man's mat was placed and
on it he sat;
then really stepped and stood my grown boys, like animals, like birds and
   they flew and poured against it [the enemy] and wrestled nothing and
   took it smoothly;
there around lay various of his possessions;
they gathered it and slowly bundled it and slowly around me turned;
thus you may wish and plan, it was a good life, and I took it and I brought
   it here.

NOTES

CHAPTER ONE. THE ATTRACTION OF ELOQUENCE

1. Raymond William Stedman suggests that the taciturn, inarticulate Indian, most familiarly represented to twentieth-century audiences by the Lone Ranger's Tonto, emerged in American popular culture in the mid-nineteenth century. Robert Montgomery Bird's infamous novel *Nick of the Woods* (1837) served as a kind of watershed in the depiction of Native American eloquence or lack thereof (Stedman 1982, 58–73). It should be noted also that most depictions that have drawn Indians lacking in communications skills have focused on their attempts to speak English, not their own languages.

2. For examinations of this speech that call into question the authenticity of the text that purports to represent Sealth's words, see Kaiser 1987 and especially Furtwangler 1997.

3. Bernard's reference to "the lack of abstract communication" in Native American discourse is, of course, incorrect. See chapter 3 for discussion of this idea.

4. The nonpublic circumstances of Tahgahjute's delivery of his eloquent message might disqualify it as "oratory," which seems by definition to be discourse delivered directly to its primary audience in a public situation. For further discussion of what became known as "Logan's Lament," see chapter 2 and especially McElwain 2001.

5. This idea is discussed more fully in chapter 3.

CHAPTER TWO. SOURCES AND RESOURCES FOR NATIVE AMERICAN ORATORY

1. See Saville-Troike 1982, 5–8, for relevant historical background.

2. For an outline of the particular concerns ethnographers of speaking should take into account, see Sherzer and Darnell 1972.

3. Bauman recognizes his work as a synthesis of ideas that had been circulating among folklorists and anthropological linguists during the late 1960s and early 1970s. Articulations of their ideas by some of the influential advocates of a

performance-oriented folkloristics appear in Paredes and Bauman 1972. For a recent critique of what was then a revolution in the study of folklore, see Shuman and Briggs 1993.

4. Primary materials that are not fully presented in this chapter appear in the appendix.

5. Though they circulated widely when they were issued, copies of Franklin's treaty chapbooks are, of course, now extremely rare. Although the Historical Society of Pennsylvania reissued several of them in 1938 (Van Doren and Boyd 1938), only about a thousand copies of that volume were printed. While some of the proceedings have been quoted from and cited by many historians, the full texts are hard to find, a situation ameliorated by the recent reprinting of one of them (the 1744 Lancaster Treaty), with a thorough introduction (Johansen 2001).

6. Julian Boyd provides some background for this negotiation in the modern edition of Franklin's treaties (Van Doren and Boyd 1938, xlvii–xlviii).

7. The spiritual milieu that contributed to the Flatheads' receptivity to Christianity is a prominent theme in the exhibit *Sacred Encounters,* mounted first at the Museum of the Rockies in Bozeman, Montana, in 1993. See Peterson 1993.

8. A brief survey of the ethnographic potentials of captivity narratives appears in Washburn 1983: xxxix–xlix.

9. Drinnon, though, makes a strong case for the authenticity of even this portion of Hunter's narrative (140–46). One might note also an earlier account that could provide support for the authenticity of Hunter's description of his journey to the Pacific. The third volume of Antoine Simon Le Page du Pratz's *Histoire de la Louisiane* (published originally in 1758) includes the narrative of Moncachtapé, a Yazoo who claimed to have made a trip to the West Coast a century before the purported experience of Hunter and his companions (Gaines 1999). Of course, Hunter's detractors might argue that Le Page du Pratz's *Histoire* could have provided a literary source for a spurious story.

10. The text of the speech as it appears in the *New York Times* for 17 June 1870 has been republished in Vanderwerth 1971: 187–90, where it contains several small errors in transcription from the newspaper source.

11. Other recently published examples include Foster 1974, Dauenhauer and Dauenhauer 1990, and Underhill et al. 1979.

CHAPTER THREE. THE PLAY OF TROPES IN
NATIVE AMERICAN ORATORY

1. The third and final edition Vico's *New Science* (1744) is available in a handy translation, revised and abridged by Thomas Goddard Bergin and Max Harold Fisch (1970). A good overview of Vico's thought appears in Berlin 1976: 3–142.

2. The text of this speech originally appeared in *Niles' Weekly Register* for 20 June 1829. I use the version that appears in Armstrong 1971, 56–57.

3. Basso, though, cautions us that the interpretation of metaphors often requires culture-specific methods. For example, in order to understand the metaphorical statements among the Western Apache known as "wise words," one must know that the metaphors always apply to behavior rather than appearance and always are to be taken as a negative evaluation of behavior (Basso 1976, 103–104).

CHAPTER FOUR. FROM PERFORMANCE THROUGH
DIALOGISM TO EFFICACY

1. An intercultural survey of the use of the pipe in contexts such as these appears in Paper 1988, 17–41.

2. Such a perspective is not absent from more recent assessments of Native American oratorical esthetics. Consider this from a generalized, romanticized volume that appeared under the aegis of Los Angeles's Southwest Museum: "The force and effectiveness of the Indian speech arts can scarcely be measured by European standards. To attempt to do so usually ruins their innate beauty and stultifies their inherent charm. The Indian communed with Nature, he was an expression of Nature, and consequently his eloquence was Nature's very own" (Jones 1965, 3).

EPILOGUE

1. Christopher Densmore, a recent biographer of Sagoyewatha, has noted earlier published versions of the speech in a response to Robie's original article (Densmore 1987), and Robie has responded to Densmore (Robie 1987) with some additional sources that he has located.

REFERENCES

Abrahams, Roger D. 1970. *Positively black*. Englewood Cliffs, N.J.: Prentice-Hall.

Adams, John Quincy. 1962. *Lectures on rhetoric and oratory*. New York: Russell and Russell.

Armstrong, Virginia Irving, ed. 1971. *I have spoken: American history through the voices of the Indians*. Chicago: Sage Books.

Asad, Talal. 1986. The concept of cultural translation in British social anthropology. In *Writing culture: the poetics and politics of ethnography,* edited by George E. Marcus and James Clifford, 141–64. Berkeley: University of California Press.

Asals, Heather. 1979. John Donne and the grammar of redemption. *English Studies in Canada* 5:125–39.

Attanasi, John, and Paul Friedrich. 1995. Dialogic breakthrough: catalyst and synthesis in life-changing dialogue. In Tedlock and Mannheim 1995, 33–53.

Aumann, F. R. 1965. Indian oratory. *Palimpsest* 46:251–56.

Austin, J. L. 1962. *How to do things with words*. Cambridge: Harvard University Press.

Bakhtin, Mikhail. 1981. *The dialogic imagination: four essays,* edited by Michael Holquist, translated by Caryl Emerson and Michael Holquist. Austin: University of Texas Press.

Bahr, Donald M. 1975. *Pima and Papago ritual oratory: a study of three texts*. San Francisco: Indian Historian Press.

——. 1994. Oratory. In *Dictionary of Native American literature,* edited by Andrew M. Wiget, 107–17. New York: Garland.

Bahr, Donald M., et al. 1994. *The short, swift time of gods on earth: the Hohokam chronicles*. Berkeley: University of California Press.

Bailey, F. G. 1981. Dimensions of rhetoric in conditions of uncertainty. In Paine 1981b, 25–38.

Baskerville, Barnet. 1979. *The people's voice: the orator in American society*. Lexington: University Press of Kentucky.

Basso, Keith H. 1976. "Wise words" of the Western Apache: metaphor and semantic theory. In *Meaning in anthropology,* edited by Keith H. Basso and Henry A. Selby, 93–121. Albuquerque: University of New Mexico Press.

Bauman, Richard. 1984. *Verbal art as performance.* Prospect Heights, Ill.: Waveland.

Bauman, Richard, and Charles L. Briggs. 1990. Poetics and performance as critical perspectives on language and social life. *Annual Review of Anthropology* 19:59–88.

Becker, Alton L., and Bruce Mannheim 1996. Culture troping: languages, codes, and texts. In Tedlock and Mannheim 1996, 237–52.

Bergin, Thomas Goddard, and Max Harold Fisch, eds. and trans. 1970. *The new science of Giambattista Vico.* Revised and enlarged. Ithaca: Cornell University Press.

Berkhofer, Robert F., Jr. 1978. *The white man's Indian: images of the American Indian from Columbus to the present.* New York: Random House.

Berlin, Isaiah. 1976. *Vico and Herder: two studies in the history of ideas.* New York: Viking.

Bernard, Jessie. 1928. Political leadership among North American Indians. *American Journal of Sociology* 34:296–315.

Bierhorst, John, ed. 1971. *In the trail of the wind: American Indian poems and ritual orations.* New York: Farrar, Straus, and Giroux.

Bloch, Maurice. 1975a. Introduction. In Bloch 1975b, 1–28.

———, ed. 1975b. *Political language and oratory in traditional society.* London: Academic Press.

Boas, Franz. 1901. *Kathlamet texts.* Bureau of American Ethnology Bulletin 26. Washington: GPO.

———. 1940. *Race, language, and culture.* Chicago: University of Chicago Press.

Bourke, John G. 1891. *On the border with Crook.* New York: Scribner's.

Brennais, Donald L. 1984. Straight talk and sweet talk: political discourse in an occasionally egalitarian community. In *Dangerous words: language and politics in the Pacific,* edited by Donald L. Brennais and Fred R. Myers, 69–84. New York: New York University Press.

Burns, Allan F. 1996. Video production as a dialogue: the story of Lynch Hammock. In Tedlock and Mannheim 1996, 75–96.

Buswell, Lois E. 1935. The oratory of the Dakota Indians. *Quarterly Journal of Speech* 21:323–27.

Camp, Charles. 1978. American Indian oratory in the white image: an analysis of stereotypes. *Journal of American Culture* 1:811–17.

Cartwright, Peter. 1956. *Autobiography of Peter Cartwright,* edited by Charles L. Wallis. New York: Abingdon.

Cass, Lewis. 1826. Review of *Manners and customs of several Indian tribes,* by John D. Heckewelder, and *Historical notes respecting the Indians of North America,* by John Halkett. *North American Review* 22:53–119.

Catlin, George. 1841. *Letters and notes on the manners, customs, and conditions of the North American Indians.* . . . 2 volumes. London: By the author.

Cazeneuve, Jean. 1972. *Lucien Lévy-Bruhl,* translated by Peter Rivière. New York: Harper and Row.

Channing, Walter. 1815. Essay on American language and literature. *North American Review* 1:307–14.

Chittenden, Hiram Martin, and Alfred Talbot Richardson. 1905. *Life, letters and travels of Father Pierre-Jean De Smet, S. J. 1801–1873.* . . . 4 volumes. New York: Francis P. Harper.

Clark, Gregory, and S. Michael Halloran. 1993a. Introduction: transformations of public discourse in nineteenth-century America. In Clark and Halloran 1993b, 1–26.

——, eds. 1993b. *Oratorical culture in nineteenth-century America: transformations in the theory and practice of rhetoric.* Carbondale: Southern Illinois University Press.

Clements, William M., ed. 1986. *Native American folklore in nineteenth-century periodicals.* Athens: Ohio University Press.

——. 1996. *Native American verbal art: texts and contexts.* Tucson: University of Arizona Press.

Clifford, James. 1988. *The predicament of culture: twentieth-century ethnography, literature, and art.* Cambridge: Harvard University Press.

Codere, Helen. 1966. Introduction. *Kwakiutl ethnography,* by Franz Boas, edited by Helen Codere, xi–xxxii. Chicago: University of Chicago Press.

Colden, Cadwallader. 1958. *The history of the Five Indian Nations depending on the province of New-York in America.* Ithaca: Cornell University Press.

Corkran, David H. 1962. *The Cherokee frontier: conflict and survival, 1740–62.* Norman: University of Oklahoma Press.

Cox, Ross. 1832. *Adventures on the Columbia River, including the narrative of a residence of six years on the western side of the Rocky Mountains, among various tribes of Indians hitherto unknown; together with a journey across the American continent.* New York: J. and J. Harper.

Cuming, Alexander. 1928. Journal of Sir Alexander Cuming. In *Early travels in the Tennessee country 1540–1800,* edited by Samuel Cole Williams. Johnson City, Tenn.: Watauga Press.

Cushing, Frank Hamilton. 1891–92. Outlines of Zuñi creation myths. *Annual Report of the Bureau of American Ethnology* 13:321–447.

D'Andrade, Roy. 1995. *The development of cognitive anthropology.* Cambridge: Cambridge University Press.

Dauenhauer, Nora Marks, and Richard Dauenhauer, eds. 1990. *Haa tuwunáagu yís, for healing our spirit: Tlingit oratory.* Seattle: University of Washington Press.

Davis, Gerald L. 1985. *I got the word in me and I can sing it, you know: a study of the performed African-American sermon.* Philadelphia: University of Pennsylvania Press.

Davis, Richard Beale. 1978. *Intellectual life in the colonial South, 1585–1763.* Knoxville: University of Tennessee Press.

Debo, Angie. 1941. *The road to disappearance.* Norman: University of Oklahoma Press.

Deloria, Philip J. 1998. *Playing Indian.* New Haven: Yale University Press.

Denig, Edward. 1930. Indian tribes of the upper Missouri, edited by J. N. B. Hewitt. *Annual Report of the Bureau of American Ethnology* 46:375–628.

Densmore, Christopher. 1987. More on Red Jacket's reply. *New York Folklore* 13, 3–4:121–22.

Densmore, Frances. 1929. *Papago music.* Bureau of American Ethnology Bulletin No. 90. Washington: GPO.

Derounian-Stodola, Kathryn Zabelle, and James Arthur Levernier. 1993. *The Indian captivity narrative, 1550–1900.* New York: Twayne.

Diket, A. L. 1966. The noble savage convention as epitomized in John Lawson's *A new voyage to Carolina. North Carolina Historical Review* 43:413–29.

Dippie, Brian W. 1982. *The vanishing American: white attitudes and U. S. Indian policy.* Middletown: Wesleyan University Press.

Dodge, Richard Irving. 1882. *Our wild Indians: thirty-three years' personal experience among the red men of the great west. . . .* Hartford, Conn.: A. D. Worthington.

Donne, John. 1953–62. *The sermons of John Donne,* edited by Evelyn M. Simpson and George R. Potter. 10 volumes. Berkeley: University of California Press.

Dorson, Richard M. 1958. The eclipse of solar mythology. In *Myth: a symposium,* edited by Thomas A. Sebeok, 25–63. Bloomington: Indiana University Press.

Drinnon, Richard. 1972. *White savage: The case of John Dunn Hunter.* New York: Schocken.

Dundes, Alan. 1964. Text, texture, and context. *Southern Folklore Quarterly* 28: 251–65.

Duranti, Alessandro. 1992. Oratory. In *International encyclopedia of communication,* edited by Erik Barnouw et al., 3:234–36. New York: Oxford University Press.

Dusenberry, Verne. 1959. Gabriel Nattau's soul speaks. *Journal of American Folklore* 72:155–60.

Eastman, Charles Alexander. 1902. *Indian boyhood.* Boston: Little, Brown.

———. 1936. *From the deep woods to civilization: chapters in the autobiography of an Indian.* Boston: Little, Brown.

Edmunds, R. David. 1984. *Tecumseh and the quest for Indian leadership.* Glenview, Ill.: Scott, Foresman.

Ek, Richard A. 1966. Red Cloud's Cooper Union address. *Central States Speech Journal* 17:257–62.

Eliade, Mircea. 1959. *The Sacred and the profane: the nature of religion,* translated by Willard R. Trask. New York: Harcourt Brace World.

Evans, E. Raymond. 1976. Notable persons in Cherokee history: Ostenaco. *Journal of Cherokee Studies* 1:41–54.

Evers, Lawrence J. 1983. Cycles of appreciation. In *Studies in American Indian literature: critical essays and course designs,* edited by Paula Gunn Allen, 23–32. New York: Modern Language Association.

Fahey, John. 1974. *The Flathead Indians.* Norman: University of Oklahoma Press.

Fernandez, James. 1986. *Persuasions and performances: the play of tropes in culture.* Bloomington: Indiana University Press.

Fewkes, J. Walter. 1890. On the use of the phonograph in the study of the languages of American Indians. *Science* 15:267–69.

Fine, Elizabeth C. 1984. *The folklore text from performance to print.* Bloomington: Indiana University Press.

Finnegan, Ruth. 1977. *Oral poetry: its nature, significance and social context.* New York: Cambridge University Press.

Foster, George E. 1889. *Literature of the Cherokees. Also bibliography and the story of their genesis.* Ithaca, N.Y.: Office of the Democrat.

Foster, Michael K. 1974. *From the earth to beyond the sky: an ethnographic approach to four Longhouse Iroquois speech events.* Ethnology Division, Mercury Series Paper No. 20. Ottawa: National Museum of Man.

———. 1985. Another look at the function of wampum in Iroquois-white councils. In Jennings et al. 1985, 99–114.

Friedman, Albert B. 1961. *The ballad revival: studies in the influence of popular on sophisticated poetry.* Chicago: University of Chicago Press.

Frisch, Jack A. 1978. Iroquois in the west. In *Handbook of North American Indians. Volume 15. Northeast,* edited by Bruce G. Trigger. Washington: Smithsonian Institution Press.

Furtwangler, Albert. 1997. *Answering Chief Seattle.* Seattle: University of Washington Press.

Gaines, James F. 1999. Moncachtapé's voyage: a precursor to Lewis and Clark. Unpublished ms.

Ganter, Granville. 2001. "You are a cunning people without sincerity": Sagoyewatha and the trials of community representation. In Mann 2001b, 165–95.

Gearing, Fred. 1962. *Priests and warriors: social structure for Cherokee politics in the 18th century.* Menasha, Wis.: American Anthropological Association.

Georges, Robert. 1969. Toward an understanding of storytelling events. *Journal of American Folklore* 82:313–28.

Goddard, Ives. 1977. Some early examples of American Indian Pidgin English from New England. *International Journal of American Linguistics* 43:37–41.

Goetsch, Paul, and Gerd Hurm, eds. 1992. *The Fourth of July: political oratory and literary reactions 1776–1876.* Tübingen: Narr.

Gossen, Gary H. 1974. *Chamulas in the world of the sun: time and space in a Maya oral tradition.* Cambridge: Harvard University Press.

Grant, Ludovick. 1909. Historical relation of facts delivered by Ludovick Grant, Indian trader, to his excellency the governor of South Carolina. *South Carolina Historical and Genealogical Magazine* 19:54–68.

Gray, Hannah H. 1963. Renaissance humanism: the pursuit of eloquence. *Journal of the History of Ideas* 24:497–514.

Gustafson, Sandra M. 2000. *Eloquence is power: oratory and performance in early America.* Chapel Hill: University of North Carolina Press.

Hale, Horatio. 1883. *The Iroquois book of rites.* Brinton's Library of Aboriginal American Literature II. Philadelphia: Daniel G. Brinton.

Hanks, William F. 1987. Discourse genres in a theory of practice. *American Ethnologist* 14:668–92.

Heckewelder, John. 1876. *History, manners, and customs of the Indian nations who once inhabited Pennsylvania and the neighbouring states.* Philadelphia: Historical Society of Pennylvania.

Henderson, Alice Corbin. 1917. Aboriginal poetry III. *Poetry* 9:256.

——. 1919. Poetry of the North-American Indians. *Poetry* 14:41–47.

Hendricks, Janet Wall. 1993. Creating meaning and evoking emotion through repetition: Shuar war stories. In *New voices in Native American literary criticism,* edited by Arnold Krupat, 77–119. Washington: Smithsonian Institution Press.

Hennepin, Louis. 1880. *A description of Louisiana,* translated by John Gilmary Shea. New York: John G. Shea.

Hinsley, Curtis J., Jr. 1981. *Savages and scientists: the Smithsonian Institution and the development of American anthropology 1846–1910.* Washington: Smithsonian Institution Press.

Hobart, Mark. 1975. Orators and patrons: two types of political leaders in Balinese village society. In Bloch 1975b, 75–92.

Hochbruck, Walter. 1992. "I ask for justice": Native American Fourth of July orations. In Goetsch and Hurm 1992, 155–67.

Howard, Oliver O. 1907. *My life and experiences among our hostile Indians. . . .* Hartford, Conn.: A. T. Worthington.

Hudson, Charles. 1976. *The southeastern Indians.* Knoxville: University of Tennessee Press.

Hulbert, Archer Butler, and William Nathaniel Schwarze, eds. 1910. *David Zeisberger's history of the northern American Indians.* NP: Ohio State Archaeological and Historical Society.

Hunter, John Dunn. 1823. *Manners and customs of several indian tribes located west of the Mississippi. . . .* Philadelphia: J. Maxwell.

——. 1973. *Memoirs of a captivity among the Indians of North America,* edited by Richard Drinnon. New York: Schocken Books.

Hyde, George E. 1937. *Red Cloud's Folk: a history of Oglala Sioux Indians.* Norman: University of Oklahoma Press.

Hymes, Dell. 1972. Toward ethnographies of communication: the analysis of communication events. In *Language and social context: selected readings,* edited by Pier Paolo Giglioli, 21–44. Hammondsworth: Penguin.

——. 1974. *Foundations in sociolinguistics: an ethnographic approach.* Philadelphia: University of Pennsylvania Press.

——. 1981. *"In vain I tried to tell you": essays in Native American ethnopoetics.* Philadelphia: University of Pennsylvania Press.

———. 1985. Language, memory, and selective performance: Cultee's "Salmon's Myth" as twice told to Boas. *Journal of American Folklore* 98:391–34.

Jacobs, Wilbur R. 1973. Cadwallader Colden's noble Iroquois savages. In *The colonial legacy, volume III: historians of nature and man's nature,* edited by Lawrence H. Leder, 34–58. New York: Harper and Row.

James, Thomas. 1953. *Three years among the Indians and Mexicans,* edited by Milo Milton Quaife. Chicago: Lakeside Press.

Jeffers, Susan. 1991. *Brother eagle, sister sky: a message from Chief Seattle.* New York: Dial.

Jefferson, Thomas. 1982. *Notes on the State of Virginia,* edited by William Peden. New York: Norton.

Jennings, Francis, et al., eds. 1985. *The history and culture of Iroquois diplomacy: an interdisciplinary guide to the treaties of the Six Nations and their league.* Syracuse: Syracuse University Press.

Johansen, Bruce E. 2001. "By your observing the methods our wise forefathers have taken, you will acquire fresh strength and power": closing speech of Canassatego, July 4, 1744, Lancaster Treaty. In Mann 2001b, 83–105.

Johnson, Nan. 1993. The popularization of nineteenth-century rhetoric: elocution and the private learner. In Clark and Halloran 1993b, 139–57.

Jones, Dorothy V. 1988. British colonial Indian treaties. In *Handbook of North American Indians, volume 4: history of Indian-white relations,* edited by Wilcomb E. Washburn, 185–94. Washington: Smithsonian Institution.

Jones, Louis Thomas. 1965. *Aboriginal American oratory: the tradition of eloquence among the Indians of the United States.* Los Angeles: Southwest Museum.

Kaiser, Rudolph. 1987. Chief Seattle's speech(es): American origins and European reception. In Swann and Krupat 1987, 497–536.

Kan, Sergei. 1983. Words that heal the soul: analysis of the Tlingit potlatch oratory. *Arctic Anthropology* 20:47–59.

Kennedy, George A. 1980. *Classical rhetoric and its Christian and secular tradition from ancient to modern times.* Chapel Hill: University of North Carolina Press.

Killoren, John J. 1994. *"Come, Blackrobe": De Smet and the Indian tragedy.* Norman: University of Oklahoma Press.

Klinck, Carl F., ed. 1961. *Tecumseh: fact and fiction in early records.* Englewood Cliffs, N.J.: Prentice Hall.

Krupat, Arnold. 1992. *Ethnocriticism: ethnography, history, literature.* Berkeley: University of California Press.

Lafitau, Joseph François. 1974–1977. *Customs of the American Indians compared with the customs of primitive times,* edited and translated by William N. Fenton and Elizabeth L. Moore. 2 volumes. Toronto: Champlain Society.

Lakoff, George. 1987. *Women, fire, and dangerous things: what categories reveal about the mind.* Chicago: University of Chicago Press.

Lakoff, George, and Mark Johnson. 1980. *Metaphors we live by.* Chicago: University of Chicago Press.

Lang, Andrew. 1900. The Red Indian imagination. *The Independent* 52:163–65.

Larson, Robert W. 1997. *Red Cloud: warrior-statesman of the Lakota Sioux.* Norman: University of Oklahoma Press.

Lawson, John. 1709. *A new voyage to Carolina;. . . .* London: NP.

Lawson, John. 1972. *Lectures concerning oratory,* edited by E. Neal Claussen and Karl R. Wallace. Carbondale: Southern Illinois University Press.

Long, Alexander. 1969. A small postscript on the ways and manners of the Indians called Cherokees . . . , edited by David H. Corkran. *Southern Indian Studies* 21:3–49.

Lowie, Robert H. 1967. Some aspects of political organization among the American aborigines. In *Comparative political systems: studies in the politics of pre-industrial societies,* edited by Ronald Cohen and John Middleton, 63–87. Garden City, N.Y.: Natural History Press.

Mallery, Garrick. 1881. Sign language among North American Indians compared with that among other peoples and deaf-mutes. *Annual Report of the Bureau of Ethnology for 1879–1880.* Washington: GPO. 263–552.

Mann, Barbara Alice. 2001a. "I hope you will not destroy *what* I have saved": Hopocan before the British tribunal in Detroit, 1781. In Mann 2001b, 145–64.

——, ed. 2001b. *Native American speakers of the eastern woodlands: selected speeches and analyses.* Westport, Conn.: Greenwood.

McElwain, Thomas. 2001. "Then I thought I must kill too": Logan's lament: a "Mingo" perspective. In Mann 2001b, 107–21.

Merrell, James H. 1989. *The Indians' new world: Catawbas and their neighbors from European contact through the era of removal.* Chapel Hill: University of North Carolina Press.

Miller, Wick R. 1996. The ethnography of speaking. In *Handbook of North American Indians. Volume 17: Languages,* edited by Ives Goddard, 222–43. Washington: Smithsonian Institution Press.

Möllhausen, Balduin. 1858. *Diary of a journey from the Mississippi to the coasts of the Pacific with a United States government expedition.* 2 volumes. London: Longmans.

Mooney, James. 1898. Calendar history of the Kiowa Indians. *Annual Report of the Bureau of American Ethnolology* 17:129–445.

Mulder, John R. 1969. *The temple of the mind: education and literary taste in seventeenth-century England.* New York: Pegasus.

Murray, David. 1991. *Forked tongues: speech, writing, and representation in North American Indian texts.* Bloomington: Indiana University Press.

Nammack, Georgiana C. 1969. *Fraud, politics, and the dispossession of the Indians: the Iroquois land frontier in the colonial period.* Norman: University of Oklahoma Press.

Ogden, Peter Skene. 1853. *Traits of American-Indian life and character by a fur trader.* London: Smith, Elder.

Olson, James C. 1965. *Red Cloud and the Sioux Indian problem.* Lincoln: University of Nebraska Press.

Paine, Robert. 1981a. When saying is doing. In Paine 1981b, 9–23.

——, ed. 1981b. *Politically speaking: cross-cultural studies of rhetoric.* Philadelphia: Institute for the Study of Human Issues.

Paper, Jordan. 1988. *Offering smoke: the sacred pipe and Native American religion.* Moscow: University of Idaho Press.

Paredes, Americo, and Richard Bauman, eds. 1972. *Toward new perspectives in folklore.* Austin: University of Texas Press.

Parker, Rev. Samuel. 1838. *Journal of an exploring tour beyond the Rocky Mountains, under the direction of the A.B.C.F.M. performed in the years 1835, '36, and '37. . . .* Ithaca: by the author.

Peterson, Jacquelyn, and Laura Peers. 1993. *Sacred encounters: Father De Smet and the Indians of the Rocky Mountain west.* Norman: University of Oklahoma Press.

Poole, D. C. 1988. *Among the Sioux of the Dakota: eighteen months' experience as an Indian agent 1869–70.* St. Paul: Minnesota Historical Society Press.

Powell, John Wesley. 1881a. Introductory. *Annual Report of the Bureau of Ethnology for 1879–1880,* xi–xxxiii. Washington: GPO.

——. 1881b. On limitations to the use of some anthropologic data. *Annual Report of the Bureau of Ethnology for 1879–1880,* 73–86. Washington: GPO.

Ramsey, Jarold. 1983. *Reading the fire: essays in the traditional Indian literatures of the far west.* Lincoln: University of Nebraska Press.

Randolph, J. Ralph. 1973. *British travelers among the southern Indians, 1660–1763.* Norman: University of Oklahoma Press.

Review of *History of the Indian tribes of North America . . . ,* by Thomas L. McKenney and James Hall. 1838. *North American Review* 47:134–48.

Robie, Harry. 1982. Kiotsaeton's Three Rivers address: an example of "effective" Iroquois oratory. *American Indian Quarterly* 6:238–53.

———. 1986. Red Jacket's reply: problems in the verification of a Native American speech text. *New York Folklore* 12, 3–4:99–117.

———. 1987. [Reply to Densmore.] *New York Folklore* 13, 3–4:123.

Rosaldo, Michelle. 1973. "I have nothing to hide": the language of Ilongot oratory. *Language in society* 2:193–223.

Rosenberg, Bruce E. 1988. *Can these bones live? The art of the American folk preacher.* Urbana: University of Illinois Press.

Ross, Alexander. 1849. *Adventures of the first settlers on the Oregon or Columbia River: being a narrative of the expedition fitted out by John Jacob Astor, to establish the "Pacific Fur Company"; with an account of some Indian tribes on the coast of the Pacific.* London: Smith, Elder.

Rothenberg, Jerome. 1992. "We explain nothing, we believe nothing": American Indian poetry and the problematics of translation. In *On the translation of Native American literatures,* edited by Brian Swann, 64–94. Washington: Smithsonian Institution Press.

Russell, Frank. 1908. The Pima Indians. *Annual Report of the Bureau of American Ethnology 1904–05* 26:3–389.

Sage, Rufus P. 1846. *Scenes in the Rocky Mountains, and in Oregon, California, New Mexico, Texas, and the Grand Prairies. . . .* Philadelphia: Carey and Hart.

Salmond, Anne. 1975. Mana makes the man: a look at Maori oratory and politics. In Bloch 1975b, 45–63.

Savage, Henry, Jr. 1979. *Discovering America 1700–1875.* New York: Harper and Row.

Saville-Troike, Muriel. 1982. *The Ethnography of communication: an introduction.* Baltimore: University Park Press.

Schoolcraft, Henry Rowe. 1851. *Historical and statistical information, respecting the history, condition and prospects of the Indian tribes of the United States: collected and prepared under the direction of the Bureau of Indian Affairs per act of Congress of March 3d, 1847, part I.* Philadelphia: Lippincott, Grambo.

———. 1853. *Information respecting the history, condition and prospects of the Indian tribes of the United States . . . , part III.* Philadelphia: Lippincott, Grambo.

——. 1953. *Narrative journal of travels through the northwestern regions of the United States extending from Detroit through the great chain of American lakes to the sources of the Mississippi River in the year 1820,* edited by Mentor L. Williams. East Lansing: Michigan State University Press.

Sears, Lorenzo. 1896. *The History of oratory from the age of Pericles to the present time.* Chicago: Griggs.

Seeger, Anthony. 1986. Oratory is spoken, myth is told, and song is sung, but they are all music to my ears. In Sherzer and Urban 1986, 59–82.

Sherry, Beverley. 1975. Speech in *Paradise Lost. Milton Studies* 8:247–66.

Sherzer, Joel. 1983. *Kuna Ways of Speaking: An Ethnographic Perspective.* Austin: University of Texas Press.

——. 1990. *Verbal art in San Blas: Kuna culture through its discourse.* Cambridge: Cambridge University Press.

Sherzer, Joel, and Regna Darnell. 1972. Outline guide for the ethnographic study of speech use. In *Directions in sociolinguistics: the ethnography of communication,* edited by John J. Gumperz and Dell Hymes, 548–54. New York: Holt, Rinehart, and Winston.

Sherzer, Joel, and Greg Urban, eds. 1986. *Native South American discourse.* Berlin: Mouton.

Shuman, Amy, and Charles L. Briggs, eds. 1993. Theorizing folklore: toward new perspectives on the politics of culture. *Western Folklore* 52:109–400.

Slotkin, Richard. 1973. *Regeneration through violence: the mythology of the American frontier, 1600–1860.* Middletown, Conn.: Wesleyan University Press.

Smith, Erminnie A. 1883. Myths of the Iroquois. *Annual Report of the Bureau of Ethnology for 1880–1881* 2:47–116.

Soskice, Janet Martin. 1985. *Metaphor and religious language.* Oxford: Clarendon Press.

Speck, Frank G. 1915. The eastern Algonkian Wabanaki confederacy. *American Anthropologist* 17:492–508.

Stedman, Raymond William. 1982. *Shadows of the Indian: stereotypes in American culture.* Norman: University of Oklahoma Press.

Stegner, Wallace. 1992. *Beyond the hundredth meridian: John Wesley Powell and the second opening of the West.* Hammondswoth: Penguin.

Strathern, Andrew. 1975. Veiled speech in Mount Hagen. In Bloch 1975b, 185–203.

Sugden, John. 1998. *Tecumseh: a life.* New York: Henry Holt.

Sutton, Roberta Briggs. 1966. *Speech index: an index to 259 collections of world famous orations and speeches for various occasions.* 4th edition. New York: Scarecrow.

Sutton, Roberta Briggs, and Charity Mitchell. 1972. *Speech index: an index to 259 collections of world famous orations and speeches for various occasions.* 4th edition. Supplement, 1966–1970. Metuchen, N.J.: Scarecrow.

Swann, Brian, ed. 1994. *Coming to light: contemporary translations of the Native literatures of North America.* New York: Random House.

Swann, Brian, and Arnold Krupat, eds. 1987. *Recovering the word: essays on Native American literature.* Berkeley: University of California Press.

Swanton, John R. 1946. *The Indians of the southeastern United States.* Bureau of American Ethnology Bulletin No. 137. Washington: GPO.

Tannen, Deborah. 1996. Writing for the mouse: constructed dialogue in conversation. In Tedlock and Mannheim 1996, 198–217.

Tate, Thad W. 1983. The discovery and development of the southern colonial landscape: six commentators. *Proceedings of the American Antiquarian Society* 93:289–311.

Tedlock, Dennis. 1972. *Finding the center: narrative poetry of the Zuni Indians.* New York: Dial.

Tedlock, Dennis, and Bruce Mannheim, eds. 1996. *The Dialogic emergence of culture.* Urbana: University of Illinois Press.

Teit, James. 1930. The Salishan tribes of the western plateaus. Edited by Franz Boas. *Annual Report of the Bureau of American Ethnology for 1927–1928* 45:23–396.

Thompson, Stith. 1929. *Tales of the North American Indians.* Cambridge: Harvard University Press.

Thwaites, Reuben Gold, ed. 1959a. *The Jesuit relations and allied documents: travels and explorations of the Jesuit missionaries in New France 1610–1791.* 79 volumes. New York: Pageant.

——, ed. 1959b. *Original journals of the Lewis and Clark Expedition, 1804–1806.* New York: Antiquarian Press.

——, ed. 1966. *Early western travels 1748–1846: a series of annotated reprints of some of the best and rarest contemporary volumes of travel, descriptive of the aborigines and social and economic conditions in the middle and far west, during the period of early American settlement.* 32 volumes. New York: AMS Press.

Timberlake, Henry. 1765. *The memoirs of Lieut. Henry Timberlake, (who accompanied the three Cherokee Indians to England in the year 1762) containing whatever he observed remarkable or worthy of public notice.* London: for the author.

Turner, Frederick W., III, ed. 1974. *The portable North American Indian reader.* New York: Viking.

Turney-High, Harry Holbert. 1937. *The Flathead Indians of Montana.* Menasha, Wis.: American Anthropological Association.

Turton, David. 1975. The relationship between oratory and the exercise of influence among the Mursi. In Bloch 1975b, 163–83.

Underhill, Ruth M. 1938. *Singing for power: the song magic of the Papago Indians of southern Arizona.* Berkeley: University of California Press.

———. 1946. *Papago Indian Religion.* New York: Columbia University Press.

Underhill, Ruth M, et al. 1979. *Rainhouse and ocean: speeches for the Papago year.* Flagstaff: Museum of Northern Arizona Press.

Urban, Greg. 1991. *A discourse-centered approach to culture: native South American myths and rituals.* Austin: University of Texas Press.

VanDerBeets, Richard, ed. 1973. *Held captive by Indians: selected narratives 1642–1836.* Knoxville: University of Tennessee Press.

Vanderwerth, W. C., ed. 1971. *Indian oratory: famous speeches by noted Indian chiefs.* Norman: University of Oklahoma Press.

Van Doren, Carl, and Julian P. Boyd. 1938. *Indian treaties printed by Benjamin Franklin, 1736–1762.* Philadelphia: Historical Society of Pennsylvania.

Velie, Alan R., ed. 1991. *American Indian literature: an anthology.* Revised edition. Norman: University of Oklahoma Press.

Walker, Deward, Jr., and Roderick Sprague. 1998. History until 1846. In *Handbook of North American Indians, volume 12: Plateau,* edited by Deward Walker Jr., 138–48. Washington: Smithsonian Institution.

Wallace, Paul A. W. 1945. *Conrad Weiser, 1696–1760: friend of colonist and Mohawk.* Philadelphia: University of Pennsylvania Press.

Washburn, Wilcomb E. 1983. Introduction. In *Narratives of North American Indian captivity: a selective bibliography,* edited by Alden T. Vaughan, xi–lviii. New York: Garland.

White, Peter, ed. 1980. *Benjamin Tompson, colonial bard: a critical edition.* University Park: Pennsylvania State University Press.

Whitman, Willson. n.d. *Jefferson's letters.* Eau Claire, Wis.: E. M. Hale.

Williams, Samuel Cole, ed. 1930. *Adair's history of the American Indians.* Johnson City, Tenn.: Watauga Press.

Witherspoon, Gary. 1977. *Language and art in the Navajo universe.* Ann Arbor: University of Michigan Press.

Woodard, Charles L. 1989. *Ancestral voice: conversations with N. Scott Momaday.* Lincoln: University of Nebraska Press.

Wroth, Lawrence C. 1975. The Indian treaty as literature. In *Literature of the American Indians: views and interpretations,* edited by Abraham Chapman, 324–37. New York: New American Library.

Yankah, Kwesi. 1995. *Speaking for the chief: Okyeame and the politics of Akan royal oratory.* Bloomington: Indiana University Press.

Zolbrod, Paul. 1995. *Reading the voice: Native American oral poetry on the written page.* Salt Lake City: University of Utah Press.

INDEX

Abnaki, 109

abstract language: primitive mind incapable of, 82–83; versus figurative language, 80–85. *See also* metaphor in oratory

Adair, James, 11, 107, 120–21

Adams, John, 63

Adams, John Quincy, 13

Alchise, 60

Algonquians, 44, 83, 109, 123

American Indian Literature (Velie), 128

Ames, Fisher, 14

Anahootz, 59

Anishinaabe, 6, 69

Annual Reports (of the BAE), 69

Apache, 59–60, 72, 73, 74, 92

Arapahos, 111

Arikaras, 6

Aristotle. *See* rhetoric, Aristotelian view of

Armstrong, Virginia Irving, 127

Assiniboine, 105

Attaculaculla, 115

Aubrey, Josephus, 114

Austin, J. L., 119

BAE. *See* Bureau of American Ethnology

Bahr, Donald M., xiii, 74–75, 77, 104, 129

Bakhtin, Mikhail, 112

Basso, Keith, 92, 98

Bauman, Richard, 24, 26–27

Bear Looking Up. *See* Big Face

Bemis, J. D., 125

Biard, Pierre, 4, 83

Bierhorst, John, 127

Big Elk, 110

Big Face, 46–47, 49

Blackfeet, 50, 99, 112

Blackrobe. *See* Jesuits

Boas, Franz, 26, 70, 76, 105

Bourke, John Gregory, 21, 60

Brackenridge, H. M., 42, 44

Bradbury, John, 6

Brant, Joseph. *See* Thayendanégea

Brebeuf, Jean de, 117

Brennan, José Lewis, 72, 73, 76, 77

Brenneis, Donald, 89

Bressani, Francesco, 83–84, 87

Briggs, Charles, 24

Brinton, Daniel Garrison, 83

Broken Arm, 119–20

Brown, Charles Brockden, 57

Brulés, 67, 107

Buffon, Comte de, 12, 27, 64

Bureau of American Ethnology (BAE), ix, xi, 69–74

Burnet, William, 36

Burns, Allan F., 112

Burton, Richard, 111

Buzzard, 75

calumet, 106, 109

Canassatego, 126

Captain Pipe. *See* Hopocan

captivity narratives. *See* sources of oratory, captivity narratives

Carlyle, Thomas, 15

Cartwright, Peter, 17–18

Cass, Lewis, 3, 54–56, 58, 87–88, 113, 122

Catawbas, 41–42, 97

Catholicism. *See* Jesuits

Catlin, George, xi, 43–44, 117

certum, 80–82

Chamula, 104

Channing, Walter, 18

Chapin, Israel, 125

Cheda, 37–38

Cherokees, 61–64, 115, 120–21

Chief Joseph. *See* Hin-mah-too-yah-laht-ket

chiefs: oratorical skills of, 5, 6, 118; roles of, 5. *See also* oratory, leadership qualities and

Choctaw, 118

Chonpunnish, 117, 119

Christianity, 6, 7, 10, 14, 87, 94, 124. *See also* Jesuits, Methodists, Moravians, Presbyterians, Puritans

Clark, William. *See* Lewis and Clark

Clifford, James, 23–24

Clinton, George, 36

Cochise, 59, 60

Colden, Cadwallader, 36–38, 95

Coleridge, Samuel Taylor, 17

Comanches, 99–102

Coming to Light (Swann), 128

Condolence Ceremony, 32

Connetarke, 61

Cooper, James Fenimore, 57

Cooper, Peter, 65

Cordaro, 100–102, 106

Corkran, David H., 62

Corps of Discovery. *See* Lewis and Clark

Cox, Ross, 49

Crook, George, 60

Crosby, Howard, 65, 67

Cuming, Alexander, 61–62

Cushing, Frank Hamilton, 70

Dakota, 5, 59

Dauenhauer, Nora Marks and Richard, 130

Davis, Gerald L., 103

Dekanisora, 36

Denig, Edwin T., 105

Densmore, Frances, 73

Descartes. *See* rhetoric, Cartesian view of

De Smet, Pierre, 21, 45–50

Dictionary of Native American Literature (Wiget), xiii

Dodge, Richard Irving, 8, 60, 104, 120

Donne, John, 9

Dorson, Richard M., 125

Dougherty, John, 105–106

Drinnon, Richard, 54, 56, 58

Drips, Andrew, 46

Dundes, Alan, 30

Duponceau, P. S., 54

Duranti, Allessandro, xiv

Dusenberry, Verne, 50

Duwamish, 125

Eastman, Charles Alexander, 115–16

Edgar Huntly (Brown), 57

Edmunds, R. David, 56–57

Elder Brother Shaman, 74–75

Eliade, Mircea, 42

entextualization, 24, 30

ethnographic surveys. *See* sources of oratory, ethnographic surveys

ethnography of speaking, 24–26

ethnopoetics, 24, 28–29

Evers, Larry, 130

"fakelore," 125

Fernandez, James, 87, 90

Fewkes, J. Walter, 76

figurative language. *See* metaphor in oratory

Five Nations. *See* Iroquois

Flatheads, 45–50, 112

Foster, George E., 115

Foster, Michael, 104, 129

Franklin, Benjamin, 32–33, 118, 126

Furtwangler, Albert, 125

Ganter, Granville, 128

Geronimo, 60

Gibson, John, 27

Gossen, Gary H., 104

Grant, Ludovick, 62

Grant, Ulysses S., 65–67

Gros Ventres, 6

Gustafson, Susan, 14

Haa Tuwunáagu Yís, for Healing Our Spirit (Dauenhauer), 130

Hale, Horatio, 83

Hanks, William F., 116

Harrison, William Henry, 58

Haudenosaunee, 126. *See also* Iroquois

Hayes, Rutherford B., 59

Hebrew-Indian hypothesis. *See* Ten Lost Tribes of Israel

Heckewelder, John, 86, 126

Henderson, Alice Corbin, 19

Hennepin, Louis, 7–8

Herochshe, 105–8

Herzog, George, 76

Hin-mah-too-yah-laht-ket, 59, 86

History, Manners, and Customs of the Indian Nations (Heckewelder), 126

History and Culture of Iroquois Diplomacy, The (Jennings), 129

History of the Five Indian Nations (Colden), 36–37

Hochbruck, Wolfgang, 20

Hohokam, 75

Hopocan, 126

Howard, Oliver O., 59–60

Hunter, John Dunn, 21, 53–59, 110–11

Huron, 79, 83–84, 87, 108, 110, 116, 123

Hymes, Dell, 10, 24, 28, 29, 76, 104

I Have Spoken (Armstrong), 127

I'itoi. *See* Elder Brother Shaman

Ilongot (Philippines), 90, 121

Indian Boyhood (Alexander), 115–16

Indian Oratory (Vanderwerth), 127–28

Indians. *See* Native Americans; *and names of specific tribes*

Ingoldesby, Richard, 37–38

International Encyclopedia of Communications (Barnouw), xiv

International Journal of American Linguistics, 71, 76

In the Trail of the Wind: American Indian Poems and Ritual Orations (Bierhorst), 127

Iowa (Indians), 105–6, 108

irony. *See* oratory, irony in

Iroquois, 28, 35–38, 47, 50, 70, 85, 89–90, 93–98, 107, 108, 110, 114, 124, 125, 126, 129

Jackson, Andrew, 3, 90, 101

James, Edwin, 105–8, 110, 117

James, Thomas, 98–102, 106, 108

Jefferson, Thomas, 12, 20, 27–28, 57, 63, 64, 122

Jesuit Relations, 44, 108

Jesuits, 6, 10, 11, 21, 44–50, 79, 83, 87, 107–8, 110, 112, 114, 116–17

Jeune, Paul le, 6, 110, 116–17, 123

Johansen, Bruce E., 126, 129

Johnson, William, 109

Johnston, Charles, 51

Jonson, Ben, 9

Jouvency, Joseph, 10

Kaiser, Rudolph, 125

Kalispel, 48

Ka'maltkak, 71–72, 74–76

Kansas (Indians), 105–7

Kaw. *See* Kansas

Keokuk, 108

Kickapoos, 57

Kiowa, ix–x

Klink, Carl F., 55–56

Klock, George, 110

Knickerbocker, 4, 58

Kotsoteka, 100

Krupat, Arnold, 17, 124

Kuna (Panama), 113, 121–22

Lafitau, Joseph François, 11

Lakoff, George, 85, 87

Lang, Andrew, 70

Lawson, John, 6–7, 21, 40–44

Lechat, 99–100

Lenapés, 51, 126

Lévy-Bruhl, Lucien, 83, 85

Lewis, Meriwether. *See* Lewis and Clark

Lewis and Clark, 39, 108, 117, 119

Lion Bear, 59

Littel's Living Age, 12

Locke, John, 13

Logan, James. *See* Tahgahjute

Logan, James (Pennsylvania official), 35

"Logan's Lament," 122–23, 125

Long, Alexander, 61

Long, John, 109

Long, Stephen H., 105, 107, 108

Lord Dunmore's War, 12, 27

Lowie, Robert H., 5

Macpherson, James, 16

Mallery, Garrick, 111

Mandans, 6, 99

Mangas Coloradas, 60

Manibozho, 83

Mann, Barbara Alice, 126

Maori (New Zealand), 113

McCormack, John, 61, 64
McElwain, Thomas, 27–28
Melpa (Papua New Guinea), 121
Memoirs of a Captivity Among the Indians of North America from Childhood to the Age of Nineteen (Hunter), 53–58
Mercier, François le, 108
metaphor in oratory, 79–80, 85; audience manipulated by, 98–102; authority of, 89–90; diplomacy and, 89; persuasiveness of, 90–91; "poverty of language" and, 15–16, 80, 82, 85; purpose of, 86; strategy and, 92–98; transcendence of, 92; verbal artistry of, 88–89. *See also* abstract language
Methodists, 17–18
Miller, Wick R., 114
Millet, Pierre, 107, 110
Milton, John, 10, 13
Mingo, 12, 27, 93
missionaries. *See* Christianity; Jesuits; sources of oratory, missionaries' reports
Missouri (Indians), 105–6
Moeurs des sauvages ameriquains comparées aux moeurs des premiers temps (Lafitau), 11
Mohawk, 33, 93, 95
Möllhausen, Balduin, 118
Momaday, N. Scott, ix–x, xii
Montagnais, 4, 110, 117
Mooney, James, ix–x
Moravians, 86, 110, 115, 126
Müller, Max, 82–83
Murray, David, 80
Muskogee, 91–92, 94, 101

myths. *See* Native Americans, myths of; sacred time

Narragansetts, 51
Native Americans: myths of, 7–8, 73–74; negative views of, 3; songs of, 6, 7, 25, 61, 62; stereotypes regarding oratory of, 3; storytelling of, 6–7
Native American tribes. *See names of specific tribes*
Native Eloquence (Bemis), 125
Navajo, 84–85
Neal, John, 54
New England Crisis (Thompson), 14–15
New Science (Vico), 80–82
New Voyage to Carolina, A (Lawson), 40–42
New York Daily Tribune, 65, 67–69
New York Herald, 65, 66–69
New York Times, x, 65–66
newspapers. See *New York Daily Tribune*; *New York Times*; *Niles Weekly Register*; *Seattle Sunday Star*; sources of oratory, newspaper accounts; *Virginia Gazette*
Nez Perce, 48, 50, 59
Niles Weekly Register, 91
North American Review, 10, 18
Notes on the State of Virginia (Jefferson), 12, 28, 122

Oconostota, 115
Ogden, Peter Skene, 112
Oglala Lakota, 64–69, 107
Ohio (Indians), 93
Okanagas, 118

Omaha, 109, 110, 117

Oneida, 33–35, 37–38

Onkiswathetami. *See* Skikellamy

oratory: accessibility of, 8; American literary culture and, 18–20; anthologies of, 127–28; definition of, xii–xiv; documentation of, ix; irony in, 91–92; leadership qualities and, 5, 6, 88; mortuary customs and, 41–42; negative view of, 8–9, 13–15; positive views of, 9–12; rhetoric and, 8–9; ritual and, 42–44; scholarly treatment of, 129–30; spontaneity of, 16–18; textual authenticity of, 124–26; translation of, 27–30; "vanishing American" stereotype and, 20–21. *See also* ethnography of speaking; ethnopoetics; metaphor in oratory; performance folkloristics; performance of oratory; rhetoric; sources of oratory

Osage, 53–57, 100–101

Ostenaco, 61–64

Otos, 105–6, 108

Ouray, 111

Overhills, 61–62

Palmer, Anthony, 33, 35

Papago, 72–73, 74

Papago Indian Religion (Underhill), 129

Parrish, Jasper, 125

Parry-Lord hypothesis, 103

Pascal, 13

Passamaquoddy, 76

"Pedro," 60

Pend d'Oreiles, 46

Percy, Thomas, 16

performance folkloristics, 24, 26–28

performance of oratory: body language in, 107–8; dialogism and, 112–14, 116, 118, 123; formality of, 103–4; influencing audience with, 113–14, 116–22; paralinguistic features of, 110; "poverty of language" and, 110–11; public nature of, 104–5, 113; training for, 115–16. *See also* calumet; performance folkloristics; wampum

Peters, Richard, 33, 35–36

Pima and Papago Ritual Oratory (Bahr), 74

Pima Ethnography (Russell), 73

Pimans, 21, 71–76, 129, 130

Poole, D. C., 107

Portable North American Indian Reader (Turner), 128

Potawatomis, 57

"poverty of language." *See* metaphor in oratory, "poverty of language" and

Powell, John Wesley, xi, 69–70, 105

prayers, xiii, 42–43

Presbyterians, 17–18

Puritans, 14–15, 17, 52

Ramsey, Jarold, 48

Red Cloud, 21, 64–69

Red Iron, 59

Red Jacket. *See* Sagoyewatha

Renaissance humanism, 9, 11

rhetoric: Aristotelian view of, 8–12, 80–81; Cartesian view of, 8–9, 13–15, 80–81

Ridge, John, 91–92, 94, 101
Rivet, François, 47
Robie, Harry, 31–32, 124–25, 129
Romanticism, 16–17, 57
Rosaldo, Michelle, 89
Rosenberg, Bruce E., 103
Ross, Alexander, 49, 118
Rothenberg, Jerome, 28
Rowlandson, Mary, 51, 52
Russell, Frank, 21, 71–76, 77

sacred time, 42–44, 73
Sage, Rufus P., 39–40
Sagoyewatha, 19, 31, 113, 125–26, 128, 129
Santanta. See Satethieday
Santee, 116
Satethieday, ix–x, xii
Scaiohady. See Skikellamy
Scarouady, 33
Schoolcraft, Henry Rowe, 6, 69
Sealth, 4, 21, 64, 65, 125
Sears, Lorenzo, 19
Seattle. See Sealth
Seattle Sunday Star, 64
Second Awakening, 17
Seeger, Anthony, xii
Senecas, 93, 95, 124–25, 128
sermons, xiii
Shawnees, 51, 54–57
Sherzer, Joel, xii, 28
Shining Shirt, 48
Shokleng (Brazil), 113
Shoshone, 108
Shuar (Ecuador), 122
Singing for Power (Underhill), 129
Sioux, 43, 117
Six Nations. See Iroquois

Skikellamy, 35
Sloughter, Henry, 37
Smith, Erminnie A., 70
Smith, Jedediah, 47
Smith, John E., 66
Society of Jesus. See Jesuits
soldiers' memoirs. See sources of oratory, soldiers' memoirs
songs. See Native Americans, songs of
sources of oratory: captivity narratives, 21, 50–59; ethnographic surveys, 21, 69–77; missionaries' reports, 21, 44–50; newspaper accounts, 21, 64–69; soldiers' memoirs, 21, 59–64; travel accounts, 21, 39–44; treaties, 21, 32–38
Speck, Frank G., 109
Speckled Snake. See Ridge, John
Spokane Gary, 48
Spotted Tail, 67
Standing Grizzly Bear. See Big Face
Standing Turkey. See Connetarke
Stephen, Adam, 61
Stevens, Isaac, 64, 125
Stoddard, Solomon, 17
storytelling. See Native Americans, storytelling of
Sumpter, Thomas, 61
Suyá (Brazil), xii
Swann, Brian, 128

Tahgahjute, 12, 20, 21, 27–28, 63, 64, 65, 122–23. See also "Logan's Lament"
Tales of the North American Indians (Thompson), 71

Tanaghrisson. *See* Thanayieson
Tannen, Deborah, 112
Tare-heem, 58
Tecumseh, 3, 54–58, 113
Tedlock, Dennis, 29
Ten Lost Tribes of Israel, 11
Tenskatwa, 54
Te-o-kun-kho, 43
textualization, 24. *See also* oratory,
    translation of
Thanayieson, 93–98, 101
Thayendanégea, 19
Thin Leather. *See* Ka'maltkak
Thompson, Benjamin, 14–15
Thompson, David, 47
Thompson, Stith, 71
*Three Years Among Indians and Mexi-
    cans* (James), 99–101
Timberlake, Henry, 21, 28, 61–64
Tlingit, xii, 59, 129, 130
Tohono O'odham, 72, 74, 76, 129
travel accounts. *See* sources of ora-
    tory, travel accounts
treaties. *See* sources of oratory,
    treaties
Tschut-che-nau, 58
Turner, Frederick W., 128
Turney-High, Harry Holbert, 48
Tuscaroras, 40

Underhill, Ruth M., 73, 76, 77,
    129–30
Urban, Greg, 28
Ute, 99, 111

Vanderwith, W. C., 127–28
Van Doren, Carl, 32–33
Vanyiko, Thomas, 76
Velie, Alan R., 128
verum, 80–82
Vico, Giambattista, 80–82, 85
Victorio, 60
Vimont, Barthelmy, 108, 112, 115
Virginia Gazette, 27–28, 64

wampum, 32, 34, 35; oratorical role
    of, 108–10
Wasacaruja, 106
Weiser, Conrad, 33, 35–36, 93, 98,
    101, 126
Wied, Maximilian zu, 108
Williams, Roger, 14, 69
Williamson, Jesse P., 5
Williamson, Peter, 51
Woodard, Charles L., ix
Wordsworth, William, 17

Zeisberger, David, 110, 115
Zuni, 70, 76

ABOUT THE AUTHOR

WILLIAM M. CLEMENTS is on the faculty at Arkansas State University, where he teaches English, folklore, and cultural anthropology. His previous publications on American Indian subjects include *Native American Verbal Art: Texts and Contexts* (University of Arizona Press, 1996).